Home-Based Business FOR DUMMIES®

3RD EDITION

Home-Based Business FOR DUMMIES®

3RD EDITION

by Paul and Sarah Edwards
and Peter Economy

WILEY
Wiley Publishing, Inc.

Home-Based Business For Dummies®, 3rd Edition

Published by
Wiley Publishing, Inc.
111 River St.
Hoboken, NJ 07030-5774
www.wiley.com

Published by Wiley Publishing, Inc., Indianapolis, Indiana

Published simultaneously in Canada

For general information on our other products and services, please contact our Customer Care Department within the U.S. at 877-762-2974, outside the U.S. at 317-572-3993, or fax 317-572-4002.

For technical support, please visit www.wiley.com/techsupport.

Wiley also publishes its books in a variety of electronic formats. Some content that appears in print may not be available in electronic books.

Library of Congress Control Number: 2009940874

ISBN: 978-0-470-53805-0

Manufactured in the United States of America

10 9 8 7 6 5 4 3 2 1

WILEY

About the Authors

Paul and Sarah Edwards are award-winning authors of 17 books with over two million books in print. Sarah, a licensed clinical social worker with a PhD in ecopsychology, and Paul, a licensed attorney, are recognized as pioneers in the working-from-home field. With the emergence of a global economy that challenges the environment and everyone's personal, family, and community well-being, they are focusing their efforts on finding pathways to transition to a sustainable Elm Street economy in which home business plays a vital role. Paul and Sarah write a quarterly column for *The Costco Connection.* They hosted *The Working From Home Show* on HGTV and have been regular commentators on CNBC.

Paul and Sarah provide a wealth of ongoing information, resources, and support, at `www.pathwaystotransition.com`.

Peter Economy, who lives in La Jolla, California, is a home-based business author, ghostwriter, and publishing consultant, and the author or coauthor of more than 50 books, including *Why Aren't You Your Own Boss?* with Paul and Sarah Edwards (Three Rivers Press), *Managing For Dummies,* 2nd Edition, and *Consulting For Dummies,* 2nd Edition, with Bob Nelson (Wiley), and *Writing Children's Books For Dummies* with Lisa Rojany Buccieri (Wiley). Peter is also associate editor for the Apex Award-winning magazine *Leader to Leader.*

Peter combines his writing experience with more than 15 years of hands-on management experience. He received his bachelor's degree in economics from Stanford University and a postgraduate certificate in business administration from the Edinburgh Business School. Peter invites you to visit his Web site at `www.petereconomy.com`.

Dedication

To the millions of home-based businesspeople whose entrepreneurial spirit shines as a beacon, inspiring those around you and lighting a path to the success you so richly deserve.

Authors' Acknowledgments

We give our sincere thanks and appreciation to our Wiley publishing team: Stacy Kennedy, Natalie Harris, Amanda Langferman, and Erin Mooney. We would also like to thank our technical editor Beverley Williams for her hard work, and Jim Schneider and Russell Ingledew for their contributions to this book.

Paul and Sarah also extend their thanks to Peter Economy for his dedication to this project.

Peter thanks Paul and Sarah Edwards for the opportunity to work with them on this dynamic topic and for sharing their extensive experience and wisdom with him. Together, we rediscovered the joy of doing the work that we truly love and the power of teamwork.

Publisher's Acknowledgments

We're proud of this book; please send us your comments at http://dummies.custhelp.com. For other comments, please contact our Customer Care Department within the U.S. at 877-762-2974, outside the U.S. at 317-572-3993, or fax 317-572-4002.

Some of the people who helped bring this book to market include the following:

Acquisitions, Editorial, and Media Development

Project Editor: Natalie Faye Harris

(Previous Editions: Mark Butler, Corbin Collins)

Acquisitions Editor: Stacy Kennedy

(First Edition: Kathy Welton)

Copy Editor: Amanda M. Langferman

Assistant Editor: Erin Calligan Mooney

Editorial Program Coordinator: Joe Niesen

Technical Editor: Beverley Williams

Editorial Manager: Christine Meloy Beck

Editorial Assistants: Jennette ElNaggar, David Lutton

Art Coordinator: Alicia B. South

Cover Photos: Creatas Images

Cartoons: Rich Tennant (www.the5thwave.com)

Composition Services

Project Coordinator: Lynsey Stanford

Layout and Graphics: Ashley Chamberlain, Samantha Cherolis, Timothy Detrick, Melissa K. Jester

Proofreaders: Melissa Cossell, Toni Settle

Indexer: Ty Koontz

Publishing and Editorial for Consumer Dummies

Diane Graves Steele, Vice President and Publisher, Consumer Dummies

Kristin Ferguson-Wagstaffe, Product Development Director, Consumer Dummies

Ensley Eikenburg, Associate Publisher, Travel

Kelly Regan, Editorial Director, Travel

Publishing for Technology Dummies

Andy Cummings, Vice President and Publisher, Dummies Technology/General User

Composition Services

Debbie Stailey, Director of Composition Services

Contents at a Glance

Table of Contents

Introduction

Who doesn't dream of starting one's own business and being one's own boss? Increasingly, this dream is becoming more relevant to the challenges of the economy that's emerging today. And it's not just a pie-in-the-sky dream anymore; starting a home-based business is a reality that has created opportunity and satisfaction for many people who decided to take the plunge — just as it can for you.

Home-Based Business For Dummies, 3rd Edition, presents and explains an incredibly wide variety of information — aimed at ensuring your home-business success. Whether you need information on choosing the right business opportunity, avoiding scams, marketing your business, pricing your products and services, keeping accounts and books, understanding legal do's and don'ts, or growing your business, you find the help you need here.

This book provides you with the very best ideas, concepts, and tools for starting and successfully operating your home business. We've updated the information presented in the previous edition to ensure that you have the latest and most accurate information at your fingertips. Apply this information and we're convinced that you can create exactly the kind of business you've always dreamed of and find exactly the level of success you've always wanted.

About This Book

Home-Based Business For Dummies, 3rd Edition, is full of useful information, tips, and checklists for everyone who aspires to start a successful home-based business. Your current level of business experience (or lack thereof) doesn't matter. Don't worry about not having years of it under your belt or about not knowing the difference between *direct selling* and *franchising.* For a fraction of the amount you'd pay to get an MBA, this book provides you with an easily understandable road map to today's most innovative and effective home-based business techniques and strategies.

The information you find here is firmly grounded in the real world. This book isn't an abstract collection of theoretical mumbo-jumbo that sounds good but doesn't work when you put it to the test. Instead, we've included only the best information, the best strategies, and the best techniques — the exact same ones that top business schools teach today. This book is a toolbox full of solutions to your every question and problem.

This book is also fun — it reflects our strong belief and experience that running a business doesn't have to be a bore. We even help you maintain a sense of humor in the face of the challenges that all home-based businesspeople face from time to time — after all, we've been there and done that!

And one more thing: The Internet has forever changed the world of business, which includes home-based businesses. This book contains the latest information on using e-commerce, starting and operating a successful business on the Internet, and using blogs and Web sites to your advantage. It's also chock-full of our own personal Internet bookmarks for the best home-business resources the Web has to offer.

Conventions Used in This Book

When writing this book, we included some general conventions that all *For Dummies* books use. We use the following:

- *Italics* to point out any words you may not be familiar with — and remind you that definitions are somewhere nearby
- **Boldface** to point out all keywords in bulleted lists and the actual steps in numbered lists
- `Monofont` to point out all Web sites and e-mail addresses

When this book was printed, some Web addresses may have needed to break across two lines of text. If you come across a two-line Web address, rest assured that we haven't put in any extra characters (such as hyphens) to indicate the break. So when you're using one of these Web addresses, just type in exactly what you see in this book, pretending that the line break doesn't exist.

What You're Not to Read

Although we think every word in this book is worth your time, we know you probably don't have time to read them all. With that understanding in mind, we make it easy for you to identify material that you can skip by placing it into sidebars. So feel free to skip the sidebars, or the gray boxes in each chapter, which contain information that's interesting and related to the topic at hand, but not absolutely essential for the success of your home-based business.

Foolish Assumptions

While we were writing this book, we made a few assumptions about you. For example, we assume that you have at least a passing interest in starting your own business. Maybe you've already started a home-based business, or perhaps it's something you may want to try. We also assume that you can produce and deliver products or services that people will be willing to pay you for. These products and services can be most anything — you're limited only by your imagination (and your bank account). Finally, we assume that you don't already know everything there is to know about starting your own home-based business and that you're eager to acquire some new perspectives on the topic.

How This Book Is Organized

We've organized this book into five parts. The chapters within each part cover specific topic areas in detail. As a result, you can easily find the topic you're looking for. Look in the index or table of contents for your general area of interest and then find the chapter that concerns your particular needs. Whatever the topic, odds are it's covered somewhere in this book.

Each part addresses a major area of the hows, whats, and whys of starting your own home-based business. The following is a summary of what you find in each part.

Part I: Beginning at the Beginning

For most people, starting a home-based business is a big undertaking. But every great journey begins with some small first steps. In this part, we take a look at what you need to know about starting a home-based business and take you on a tour of the very best home-based business opportunities for both today and tomorrow. We consider the basics of starting your own home-based business and the ins and outs of effective marketing. Finally, we discuss how to create a sustainable income in challenging times.

Part II: Managing Your Money

Money is the blood that keeps any business running: It allows you to pay for your supplies, your computer, and other equipment and makes it possible for you to put something aside for a rainy day. In this part, we take a close look at keeping track of your money and deciding what prices to charge your customers. We examine how to get health insurance and plan for your retirement. We also take a look at how to use the tax laws to your advantage.

Part III: Avoiding Problems

Starting a business takes a lot more work than simply announcing to your neighborhood that you're "in business." You have to choose and register a business name, consider zoning regulations, and set up and equip your home office. In this part, we present the most common legal considerations for home-based businesspeople and discuss which kinds of business relationships are most important to establish and how you can establish them. Finally, we give you our best advice on avoiding scams and rip-offs.

Part IV: Making It Work: Moving Ahead

Creating a successful home-based business requires more than a good idea; you need the ability to separate your business from your personal life and to know when it's okay to mix the two. In this part, you find out about how to make the Web work for you. And you discover tips for establishing a serious business attitude while ensuring that your business coexists peacefully with the people you share your home with. You also find out how to successfully grow your business, if you so choose.

Part V: The Part of Tens

In this concise and lively set of condensed chapters, you can find tips to help start and maintain your home-based business. We show you how to succeed in your home-based business, which home-business opportunities we project will be good well into the future despite fluctuations in the economy, and what to do when times are tough.

Icons Used in This Book

Icons are handy little graphic images that are meant to point out particularly important information about starting your own home-based business. Throughout this book, you find the following icons, conveniently located along the left margins:

This icon directs you to tips and shortcuts you can follow to make your home-based business a success.

We've seen some pretty interesting things while working with home-based businesses, including our own. This icon points out some of our stories.

Sometimes you need advice that goes beyond what we can provide in this book. When that's the case, we use this icon to show you it's time to see a professional.

Remember the important points of information that follow this icon, and your home-based business will be all the better for it.

Danger! Ignore the advice next to this icon at your own risk!

Paul and Sarah Edwards, two of the authors, provide insightful answers to a variety of home-business questions. This icon points out these tough questions and their answers.

Where to Go from Here

If you're new to business, you may want to start at the beginning of this book and work your way through to the end. A wealth of information and practical advice awaits you. Simply turn the page and you're on your way! If you already own and operate a home-based business and are short of time (and who isn't short of time?), turn to a particular topic to address a specific need or question you have. Regardless of how you find your way around this book, we're sure you'll enjoy the journey.

Part I

Beginning at the Beginning

"Oh, we're doing just great. Philip and I are selling decorative jelly jars on the Web. I run the Web site and Philip sort of controls the inventory."

In this part . . .

Starting your own home-based business can be a very exciting time for you and for those around you. Before you can start on your journey, however, you need to take your first step. In this part, we tell you what you need to know about home-based businesses and delve into the questions of which business is best for you and what opportunities offer the greatest rewards. We explore the basics of starting your own business and then move on to the essentials of marketing and the most effective ways to create a sustainable income in challenging times.

Chapter 1

What You Need to Know about Home-Based Businesses

In This Chapter

- Understanding the basics of home-based businesses
- Taking a look at the pros and cons of having a home-based business

Congratulations! You've decided to start a home-based business. We welcome you as you join with millions of others who have already made the decision to start a home-based business. According to the Small Business Administration (SBA), there are more than 27 million businesses in the United States today. Of these businesses, 99.7 percent (or about 26.9 million) are *small businesses* (which the government defines as businesses with fewer than 500 employees). Of these, just more than half — 52 percent, or about 13.5 million — are home-based businesses. Now that's a *lot* of home-based businesses!

Take it from us: Owning your own home-based business may be the most rewarding experience of your entire life — and not just in a financial sense (although many home-based businesspeople find the financial rewards to be significant). Having your own home-based business is also rewarding in the sense of doing the work you love and having control over your own life.

Of course, every great journey begins with the first step. In this chapter, we provide you with an overview of this book, taking a look at the basics of home-based business — including getting started, managing your money, avoiding problems, and moving ahead. Finally, we consider some of the good news — and the bad — about starting your own home-based business and explain how to know when it's time to make the move.

TRUE STORIES

Paul and Sarah's journey home

Paul and Sarah began working from home before it was fashionable for anyone other than people in the construction trades, writers, artists, and craftspeople to do so. In fact, the neighbors wondered whether Paul was unemployed.

Sarah actually led the way home to set up a psychotherapy practice as a way of reducing the stress she felt in her prior government positions and to actively raise Paul and Sarah's young son. Sarah said, "I didn't feel I had many choices as a working mother. Juggling a successful career and motherhood meant being exhausted most of the time and not being able to do either job with the dedication I wanted. I was determined, however, to have both a career and a family, so I did my best in a difficult situation." Doing her best meant a trip to the hospital with a stress-related illness, during which the doctor told her she would die if she didn't change her lifestyle — that was her wake-up call. She left her secure government job and opened a private psychotherapy practice in her home. In the 25 years since, Sarah hasn't regretted her decision for even one day.

For Paul, the decision wasn't an easy one, and it took some time for him to get used to the idea of having a home-based business. "Initially, I was hesitant about working from home," said Paul. "I had concerns about the image it might create and worried that I wouldn't get my work done. So when I started my own consulting firm, I opened a downtown office and hired a secretary." As time went on, Paul spent less time at his downtown office and more time working at home. Eventually, he decided to close the downtown office altogether and invited his secretary to join him in his home office.

In 1980, Paul and Sarah decided to write a book about working at home. They wished such a book had existed for them when they got started. That book, *Working from Home,* is now in its fifth edition, and they've written 16 others. For excerpts from those books, as well as daily messages, tips, and support, visit their Web site at `www.pathwaystotransition.com`.

Looking at the Basics of Home-Based Business

Not surprisingly, a *home-based business* is a business based in your home. Whether you do all the work in your home or you do some of it on customers' or third-party premises, whether you run a franchise, a direct-sales operation, or a business opportunity, if the center of your operations is based in your home, it's a home-based business.

Each part of this book is dedicated to a specific aspect of starting and running your home-based business. In the following sections, we take a closer look at the topics we cover in the rest of this book.

Determining the kind of business you want to have

After you decide you're going to start your own home-based business, you have to answer two questions: Exactly what kind of home-based business do you want to start, and what's the best way to market your products or services?

You basically have two types of home-based businesses to choose from: businesses you start from scratch and businesses you buy. The latter category is further split into three types: franchises, direct-selling opportunities, and business opportunities. Whether you prefer to march to your own drummer and start your business from the ground up or get a business-in-a-box depends on your personal preferences.

The advantage of a business you start from scratch is that you can mold it to fit your preferences and the existing and emerging markets, which provides you with a boundless variety of possibilities. Businesses started from scratch account for the majority of viable, full-time businesses — in other words, they tend to be more successful over the long run than businesses you can buy. In their book *Finding Your Perfect Work* (Tarcher), Paul and Sarah provide characteristics of more than 1,500 self-employment careers, along with hundreds of examples of unique businesses that people have carved out for themselves. If you have a business idea that doesn't fit an existing category, you can get feedback on your business concept at `www.conceptfeedback.com`.

Each type of home business that you can buy, on the other hand, has its own spin. The following sections illustrate how the three types are different from one another.

Franchise

A *franchise* is an agreement in which one business grants another business the right to distribute its products or services. Some common home-based franchises include the following:

- Aussie Pet Mobile (mobile pet grooming)
- Jani-King (commercial cleaning service)
- Jazzercise (dance/exercise classes)
- ServiceMaster Clean (cleaning service)
- Snap-On Tools (professional tools and equipment)

Direct selling

Direct selling involves selling consumer products or services in a person-to-person manner, away from a fixed retail location. The two main types of direct-selling opportunities are

- **Single-level marketing:** Making money by buying products from a parent company and then selling those products directly to customers
- **Multi-level marketing:** Making money through single-level marketing and by sponsoring new direct sellers

Some common home-based direct-selling opportunities include the following:

- Shaklee (household cleaning products)
- The Pampered Chef (kitchen tools)
- Green Irene (green products and consulting)
- Longaberger Company (baskets)
- Mary Kay, Inc. (cosmetics)
- Fuller Brush Company (household and personal-care products)

Business opportunity

A *business opportunity* is an idea, product, system, or service that someone develops and offers to sell to others to help them start their own, similar businesses. With a business opportunity, your customers and clients pay you directly when you deliver a product or service to them. (Another way to think of a business opportunity is that it's any business concept you can buy from someone else that isn't direct selling or franchising.) Here are several examples of business opportunities that you can easily run out of your home:

- Astro Events of America (inflatable party rentals)
- Debt Zero LLC (debt settlement)
- ClosetMaid (storage and organizational products)
- Vendstar (bulk-candy vending machines)

Interested in how to find more companies and how to get in touch with them? Entrepreneur Media (`www.entrepreneur.com`) and `www.gosmallbiz.com` have extensive information on business opportunities you can buy. You can also do a search on Google (`www.google.com`), using the keywords *business opportunity*.

After you decide on a business, you have to find the money to get it started. Then you have to market your products or services and persuade people to buy them. You can choose conventional methods of promotion, such as advertising and public relations, or you can leverage new selling opportunities, such as the Internet, to your advantage. Or you can (and probably should) do both. It's your choice — you're the boss! Check out the rest of Part I for more information on choosing and marketing your business and on creating a sustainable income in challenging times.

Managing your money

Money makes the world go 'round, and because we're talking about your financial well-being here, it's very important that you have a handle on your business finances. To get the handle you need, do the following:

- **Find the money you need to start your business.** The good news is that many home-based businesses require little or no money to start up. If you decide to buy a franchise or business opportunity from someone else, however, you definitely need some amount of startup funding. To find this funding, consider all your options, including friends and family, savings, credit cards, bank loans, and more.
- **Keep track of your money.** In most cases, keeping track of your money means using a simple accounting or bookkeeping software package, such as QuickBooks, Quicken, or Microsoft Office Accounting, to organize and monitor your business finances.
- **Set the right price for your products and services.** If you set your prices too high, you'll scare customers away; if you set them too low, you'll be swamped with customers, but you won't make enough money to stay afloat. Be sure to charge enough to cover your costs while generating a healthy profit.
- **Obtain health insurance, and plan for your retirement.** When you have your own business, you're the one who needs to arrange for health insurance and set up IRAs, 401(k)s, or other retirement plans for the day when you're ready to hang up your business and fade away into the sunset.
- **Pay taxes.** As someone famous once said, "The only things you can count on in life are death and taxes." Well, taxes are a definite, so make sure you pay all the taxes you owe for your home-based business.

Check out Part II of this book for a lot more information on managing your money.

Avoiding problems

Eventually, every business — home based or not — runs into problems. Whether the problems are being late on a delivery or hitting a snag with the Internal Revenue Service, as the owner of your own business, you need to avoid problems whenever possible and deal with them quickly and decisively when you can't avoid them. Some of the problems you may deal with include the following:

- **Legal issues:** After a good accountant, the next best friend of any business owner is a good attorney. Keep one handy to help you deal with legal issues when they inevitably arise.
- **Issues with support services:** Finding skilled and reliable outside support services — lawyers, accountants, bankers, business consultants, and insurance brokers — isn't necessarily an easy task, especially if your business is in a small town where you're pretty much stuck with what's down the road.
- **Scams and rip-offs:** More and more home-based business scams seem to appear every day, so don't rush into any business opportunity. Take your time and fully explore every opportunity before you sign on the dotted line. And remember, if it looks too good to be true, it probably is!

Move on to Part III to find out more about how to avoid problems in your home-based business.

Moving ahead

One of the best things about owning your own business is watching it develop, mature, and grow. After all, a growing business is the gift that keeps on giving — all year 'round, year after year. To keep your business moving ahead, consider doing the following:

- **Make the Web work for you.** Doing business and generating sales and interest in your business via the Internet is practically a given for any home-based business today. You can make the Web work for you in any number of ways, from starting a blog or Web site to networking with others through online forums or social networking sites, such as Twitter, Facebook, and LinkedIn.
- **Maintain a serious business attitude.** Just because your business is located at home instead of in a big office building downtown doesn't mean you shouldn't treat it like the business it is. While you can have

fun and work all kinds of creative schedules, don't forget that the business part of your business is important, too; you have to treat your business like a business if you hope to be successful.

- **Look for ways to grow.** For many businesses, growth can turn an operation that is doing well financially into an operation that is doing *great!* Growth allows you to take advantage of economies of scale that may be available only to larger businesses, to serve more customers, and to increase profits. For these reasons and more, growing your business should always be on your agenda.

To discover in-depth information on these particular topics and more, check out Part IV sooner rather than later.

TRUE STORIES

Making the journey to independence

When Peter graduated from Stanford University with majors in human biology and economics, he had no idea what he wanted to do for work, aside from some vague notion that he should "get into business." He worked a number of jobs, starting in the federal government as a contract negotiator and then moving into the private sector for many years as an administrative manager before ending up back in local government. As time wore on, working for others became less and less palatable to him, and becoming his own boss became a seductive proposition. In 1990, Peter was fortunate to be approached by his good friend Bob Nelson to write a book on the topic of negotiation. Although Peter had no real desire to write a book, a bit of gentle persuasion (and the promise of a $2,500 advance) helped bring him around. This first book, *Negotiating to Win* (Scott Foresman), started him on a new career as a business writer.

In time, Peter was able to seriously consider devoting himself fully to starting a home-based business as a professional writer. In 1997, he got the kick in the pants he needed to make the move when he was told that, thanks to funding cuts, he would be laid off from his local government job. And although a week later his employer found additional funds and asked him to stay, he already had one foot out the door, and there was no turning back.

Today Peter runs his own home-based writing business. He works harder than he ever has before but has the satisfaction of knowing that every bit of work he does has a direct payoff for him and his family — not some distant company owners or shareholders. But although he works harder than ever, he also gets to spend far more time with his wife and kids than he ever did before, and the commute to his office has been reduced from half an hour each way to about 30 seconds. Is he happy? Yes. Would he go back to working a regular 9-to-5 job? Not on your life!

Do you have specific questions or comments for Peter? He'd love to hear from you. Visit his Web site at `www.petereconomy.com` and drop him a line.

Leaving your full-time job for your part-time business

An important, basic consideration that many home-based business owners face is whether or not to leave a full-time job in favor of a home-based business. Before you give up your full-time job, ask yourself these questions:

- Has there been a steadily growing flow of new customers in your home-based business?
- Has your business, even though it's only been part-time, produced a steady flow of income through seasonal or other cycles typical of the business?
- Are you turning away business because of limits on your time? If not, do you think business would increase if you had the time to market or take on more customers?

Being able to answer at least two of these questions in the affirmative is a good sign that it would be safe to leave your full-time job. Of course, you should also be aware of any developments that could worsen the outlook for your business to grow, such as pending legislation, new technology, the movement of the kind of work you do outside the United States (*outsourcing* or *cloud computing*), or the decline of an industry your business depends on.

If your day job has been providing you the contacts you've needed to build your part-time business, you need to find ways to replace them before you leave your job.

Breaking the umbilical cord of a paycheck is an uncomfortable step for most people. So the closer the current income from your business is to the amount of money you need to pay your basic business and living expenses, the more confident you can be.

Examining the Good News and the Bad

Anyone can start a home-based business. You can be 10 years old or 100, male or female, rich or poor or somewhere in between, experienced in business — or not. According to a recent study by the Ewing Marion Kauffman Foundation, the median age of company founders is 40 years old, the majority (69.9 percent) were married when they started their first business, and more than half (51.9 percent) were the first in their families to start a business.

So how do you know if starting a home-based business is right for you? Like most things in life, starting your own home-based business has both advantages and disadvantages, but the good news is that the advantages probably outweigh the disadvantages for most prospective home-business owners. So in the spirit of putting your best foot forward, we start with the good news.

Good reasons to start a home-based business

When you start a home-based business, you may be leaving behind the relative comfort and security of a regular career or 9-to-5 job and venturing out on your own. Or you may be entering the world of work again after devoting many years of your life to raising a family. How far out you venture on your own depends on the kind of home-based business you get involved in. For example, many franchises provide extensive support and training, and *franchisees* (the people buying the franchise opportunities — you, for example) are able to seek advice from experienced franchisees or from the *franchisor* (the party selling a franchise opportunity) when they need it. This support can be invaluable if you're new to the world of home-based business.

At the other end of the spectrum, some business opportunities offer little or no support whatsoever. If you're a dealer in synthetic motor oil, for example, you may have trouble getting the huge, multinational conglomerate that manufactures the oil to return your calls, much less send you some product brochures. And you won't find any training or extensive, hands-on support if you run into the inevitable snags, either.

This wide variety of home-based opportunities brings us to the good news about starting and running your own home-based business:

- **You're the boss.** For many owners of home-based businesses, just being their own boss is reason enough to justify making the move out of the 9-to-5 work world.
- **You get all the benefits of your hard work.** When you make a profit, it's all yours. No one else is going to try to take it away from you (except, perhaps, the tax man — see Chapter 9).
- **You have the flexibility to work when and where you want.** Are you a night owl (like Peter, who wrote these words at 4:58 a.m.)? Perhaps your most productive times don't coincide with the standard 9-to-5 work schedule that most regular businesses require their employees to adhere to. And you may find that — because interruptions from co-workers are no longer an issue and the days of endless meetings are left far behind — you're much more productive working in your own workshop than in a

regular office. With your own home-based business, you get to decide when and where you work.

- **You get to choose your clients and customers.** The customers may always be right, but that doesn't mean you have to put up with the ones who mistreat you or give you more headaches than they're worth. When you own your own business, you can fire the clients you don't want to work with. Sounds like fun, doesn't it? (Believe us, it is!)
- **You can put as much or as little time into your business as you want to.** Do you want to work for only a few hours a day or week? No problem. Ready for a full-time schedule or even more? Great! The more effort you put into your business, the more money you can make. As a home-based business owner, you get to decide how much money you want to make and then pick out the kind of schedule that will help you meet your goal.

These reasons to start your own home business are just the tip of the iceberg. But when you add up everything, you're left with one fundamental reason for owning your own home-based business: freedom.

REMEMBER

Admittedly, starting a home-based business isn't for everyone. In fact, for some individuals, it can be a big mistake. If, however, you have an entrepreneurial spirit, and you thrive on being independent and in charge of your life, a home-based business may be just the thing for you.

You have only one life to live. If you're tired of working for someone else, being second-guessed by your boss, or having your creativity stifled, if you're full of great ideas (ideas you know will lead you to success if you have the opportunity to put them into practice), or if you long for something better, we have a message for you: There is something better. It's called a home-based business. When you find the business that's right for you, it can change your life and the lives of those around you.

The pitfalls of owning your own home-based businesses

Starting a home-based business isn't the solution to every problem for every person. Although many home-based businesses are successful and the people who started them are happy with the results, more than a few home-based businesses end up causing far more headaches than their owners anticipated. Some home-based business owners even go bankrupt as a direct result of the failure of their businesses. Starting your own business is hard work, and there are no guarantees for its success.

So the next time you're lying on your sofa, dreaming of starting your own home-based business, don't forget to consider some of the potential pitfalls:

- **The business is in your home.** Depending on your domestic situation, working in your own home — a home filled with any number of distractions, including busy children, whining spouses or significant others, televisions, loaded refrigerators, and more — can be a difficult proposition at best.
- **You're the boss.** Yes, being the boss has its drawbacks, too. When you're the boss, you're the one who has to motivate yourself to work hard every day — no one's standing over your shoulder (except maybe your cat) watching your every move. For some people, focusing on work is very difficult when *they* are put in the position of being the boss.
- **Health insurance may be unavailable or unaffordable.** If you've ever been without health insurance for a period of time, or if you've been underinsured and had to make large medical or dental payments, you know just how important affordable health insurance is to your health and financial well-being. According to a recent study, 62.1 percent of all bankruptcies are medical related, and 92 percent of these debtors had medical debts of more than $5,000. Unfortunately, when you work for yourself, finding good health insurance isn't a given. In fact, it can sometimes be downright difficult, depending on where you live and work. (Find out about the different health insurance options available to home-based business owners in Chapter 8.)
- **A home-based business is (usually) a very small business.** As a small business, you're likely more exposed to the ups and downs of fickle customers than larger businesses are. And a customer's decision not to pay could be devastating to you and your business.
- **You may fail or not like it.** No one can guarantee that your business is going to be a success or that you're going to like the business you start. Failure may cost you dearly, including financial ruin (no small number of business owners have had to declare bankruptcy when their businesses failed), destruction of personal relationships, and worse. However, not all small businesses close because of financial problems. The Small Business Administration has found that at the time of closing, one out of three businesses is financially sound.

Regardless of these potential pitfalls, starting a home-based business remains the avenue of choice for an increasing number of people. Are you ready to join them?

Taking the Home-Based Business Quiz

Many people talk about starting home-based businesses, and many dream about becoming their own bosses. Making the transition from a full-time career to self-employment, however, is a big change in anyone's life. Are you really ready to make the move, or should you put the idea of having your own home-based business on the back burner for a while longer?

TIP

To help you decide, take the following home-based business quiz. Circle your answer to each of these questions, add up the results, and find out if you're ready to take the plunge!

1. How strong is your drive to succeed in your own home-based business?

   A. I can and will be a success. Period.

   B. I'm fairly confident that if I put my mind to it, I will succeed.

   C. I'm not sure. Let me think about it for a while.

   D. Did I say that I wanted to start my own business? Are you sure that was me?

2. Are you ready to work as hard as or harder than you have ever worked before?

   A. You bet — I'm ready to do whatever it takes to succeed!

   B. Sure, I don't mind working hard as long as I get something out of it.

   C. Okay, as long as I still get weekends and evenings off.

   D. What? You mean I'll still have to work after I start my own business? Isn't that why I hire employees?

3. Do you like the idea of controlling your own work instead of having someone else control it for you?

   A. I don't want anyone controlling my work but me!

   B. That's certainly my first choice.

   C. It sounds like an interesting idea — can I?

   D. Do I have to control my own work? Can't someone control it for me?

4. Have you developed a strong network of potential customers?

   A. Yes, here are their names and numbers.

   B. Yes, I have some pretty strong leads.

C. Not yet, but I've started kicking around some ideas with potential customers.

D. I'm sure that as soon as I let people know that I'm starting my own business, customers will line up.

5. Do you have a plan for making the transition into your home-based business?

A. Here it is — would you like to read the executive summary or the full plan?

B. Yes, I've spent a lot of time considering my options and making plans.

C. I'm just getting started.

D. I don't believe in plans — they crimp my style.

6. Do you have enough money saved to tide you over while you get your business off the ground?

A. Will the year's salary that I have saved be enough?

B. I have six months' expenses hidden away for a rainy day.

C. I have three months' worth.

D. I'm still trying to pay off my college student loans.

7. How strong is your self-image?

A. I am self-esteem!

B. I strongly believe in my own self-worth and in my ability to create my own opportunities.

C. I feel fairly secure with myself; just don't push too hard.

D. I don't know — what do you think?

8. Do you have the support of your significant other and/or family?

A. They're all on board, are an integral part of my plan, and have been assigned responsibilities.

B. They're in favor of whatever makes me happy.

C. I'm pretty sure they'll support me.

D. I'm going to tell them about it later.

9. If it's a necessary part of your plan, will you be able to start up your home-based business while you remain in your current job?

   A. Sure — in fact, my boss wants in!

   B. If I make a few adjustments in my schedule, I can't see any other reason why I can't.

   C. Would you please repeat the question?

   D. Maybe I'll be able to work on it for a couple of hours a month.

10. What will you tell friends when they ask why you quit that great job?

    A. I'm free at last!

    B. That the benefits clearly outweigh the potential costs.

    C. I don't know; maybe they won't ask.

    D. I'll pretend that I'm still working for my old organization.

Give yourself 5 points for every A answer, 3 points for every B, –3 for every C, and –5 for every D. Now tally up the numbers, and compare your results with the ranges of numbers below.

By comparing your total points with the points contained in each of the six following categories, you can find out whether you're ready to jump into your own home-based business:

25 to 50 points: Assuming you were honest with yourself as you answered the preceding questions (you were, weren't you?), you're ready! What are you waiting for? There's no time like the present to take the first step on your journey to success with your own home-based business. Whether you decide to drop your day job or work into your new business gradually, you're ready to give it your all. Read the rest of this book for tips on making your endeavor a raging success.

1 to 24 points: You're definitely warming up to the idea of starting your own home-based business. Consider starting your own business in the near future, but make sure to keep your day job until you have your venture well under way. Read this book to get a better idea of how to make a relatively painless and successful transition from your present career to your own home-based business.

0 points: You can go either way on this one. Why don't you try taking this test again in another month or two? Our advice? Read this book before you begin your own home-based business.

–1 to –24 points: Unfortunately, you don't appear to be quite ready to make the move from career to home-based business. We strongly recommend that you read this book and then take this test again in a few months. Maybe working for someone else isn't the worst thing that can happen to you.

–25 to –50: Forget it. You were clearly born to work for someone else. Take this book and sell it to a co-worker.

Are you ready to make the move to starting a home-based business? If the quiz indicates otherwise, don't worry — you'll have plenty of opportunities in the future. When you're ready for them, they'll be ready for you. If you're ready now, congratulations! The rest of this book shows you what you need to do to make owning a successful home-based business a reality.

Keeping up with the scuttlebutt

Q: I've never regretted starting my own business, but the one thing I do miss is being in the middle of the corporate buzz. How can I stay connected with what's going on downtown?

A: You may be able to get connected without leaving your home by joining and participating in groups on social networking sites like LinkedIn, Facebook, and Twitter. If social networking isn't for you, the first step is to figure out just what you're missing from being in the buzz of corporate life. Being part of the daily routine of an organization provides people with a whole array of experiences. Some, like office politics and dreadfully dull meetings, are a joy to get away from. But others, like the following, leave a void that you must find ways to fill:

- **Feeling like you're part of the downtown business community:** Even when you're working from home, it's important to get out of the house and participate in the business world. Join the chamber of commerce, and go to luncheons, after-work mixers, or evening meetings. Get active in various civic and charitable activities in your community. After all, they can lead to valuable business relationships while keeping you up with what's going on in town.
- **Getting in on the inside information and latest scuttlebutt in your field:** You can replace this need by becoming active in a local chapter of your professional or trade association or by participating in its online forum. To find professional and trade associations in your field, do a Google search using the keyword *association* and the name of your field.

  Though the Web isn't a substitute for face-to-face contact, beyond the social networking sites, you can use it to locate other individuals, networks, and organizations in your own community through, for example, the message board operated by a trade or professional group you belong to.
- **Establishing the esprit de corps from being part of a group that's working together toward a common goal:** If you crave group experiences, affiliate with others and work on joint projects instead of working strictly solo.

(continued)

(continued)

- **Finding moral support and positive peer pressure to stay focused — someone with whom to bounce ideas around, celebrate victories, and commiserate disappointments:** To fulfill this need, form a group of colleagues with whom you can meet weekly over lunch and call regularly to spur one another on toward your goals.
- **Seeking out the expertise of superiors you can turn to for advice, getting honest feedback, or talking over strategies and crucial decisions:** If you're missing this type of interaction, seek out a mentor, form an advisory board for your business, or hire a consultant whose experience you respect. Some professional associations have formal mentor programs that offer this kind of contact. If yours doesn't, suggest that it consider adding such a service — or even volunteer to help organize it.

Chapter 2

Mirror, Mirror on the Wall, What's the Best Business of All?

In This Chapter

- Starting a new business from the ground up
- Buying an established business
- Considering your options
- Specializing to find where you fit best

So what do you do after you decide that starting a home-based business is right for you? First, you have to choose which kind of home-based business to start. Although on the surface making this decision may seem like a fairly easy proposition, for many people it isn't. With thousands and thousands of businesses to choose from, each with its own set of pros and cons, you may feel a little bit like a kid in a candy store. Not to mention, an opportunity that's hot today can be as cold as a Minnesota winter tomorrow.

Before picking your business, research your options thoroughly. And above all, listen to your heart. Be sure that the opportunity is right for *you* — that it's first and foremost something you will truly love doing — but at the same time that it's going to provide the potential for long-term success. After all, we're talking about your future here (and, perhaps, the well-being of you and your family), and what you do today to prepare for it will pay off in a big way down the road.

In this chapter, we take a closer look at the many different home-based business options available to you. Be sure to turn to Chapter 17 for a look at ten particularly hot home-business opportunities.

Starting Something from Scratch

You probably find a certain amount of pleasure in making something out of nothing with your own two hands. It's the same pleasure a sculptor gets from creating a beautiful piece of art or a violinist gets from mastering a difficult piece of music. You may not get it right the first time — after all, it took Thomas Edison thousands of tries before he hit on the right material for a successful light bulb filament — but when you do find the right formula for success, the feeling of satisfaction you experience is hard to beat.

Perhaps the quickest and least expensive way to start your own home-based business is to do so from scratch. No need to fill out a bunch of applications, save up money to buy into a franchise, or take weeks or months to learn some complex, proprietary way of doing business. If you really want to, there's no reason why you can't start your own business from scratch — right now. Your friends, relatives, neighbors, and co-workers are doing it, and you can, too.

A number of years ago, Peter's wife, Jan, started a successful medical-billing business out of their home. She built it from scratch. After deciding to start her business, the first thing she did was create a simple flyer on the family computer, print 100 copies, and distribute them throughout the neighborhood. Although her original idea — and the offer in Jan's flyer — was to do typing and desktop publishing, when her next-door neighbor, a psychologist, suggested that she take on the billing for his thriving practice, a new business was born! She soon took on the billing for several psychologists, and her little enterprise grew.

If you decide to start a home business from scratch, you're in good company. Did you know that some of today's largest, most successful companies were originally home-based businesses? Here are a few notable examples:

- **Hewlett-Packard:** With $538 in working capital, Bill Hewlett and David Packard started their fledgling company in Packard's garage in Palo Alto, California. Today Hewlett-Packard is a multinational corporation with sales in excess of $118 billion a year.
- **Apple Computer:** In 1976, two members of Palo Alto, California's Homebrew Computer Club — Steven Jobs and Stephen Wozniak — raised $1,300 by selling Jobs's Volkswagen van and Wozniak's Hewlett-Packard programmable calculator to launch Apple Computer. The company — which began life in the garage of Steven Jobs's parents' home — today has annual revenues of more than $32 billion.
- **Amazon.com:** Jeff Bezos, founder and CEO of Amazon.com, started his business in his rented, two-bedroom house in Bellevue, Washington. To make room for his new home-based business, Bezos converted his garage into a workspace. And to save money — of which he had precious little in those early days — he converted three wooden doors into desks, using some 2 x 4s, and a handful of metal brackets. The cost? Sixty dollars per desk. Today Amazon.com rakes in more than $19 billion a year — enough to pay for all the desks that Jeff Bezos would ever want to buy.

Of course, these home-based business success stories are exceptional, but many home-based business owners find exactly the level of success they're seeking — while paying the bills, doing exactly the work they want to do, spending more time with loved ones, and serving the customers they want to serve. The real beauty of owning your own home-based business is that it's first and foremost *your* business. When you start a business from scratch, you write the rules, and you decide what's important. You may grow your business into the next Apple Computer, or you may simply enjoy a bit of extra income to supplement your earnings from a full-time career or other sources.

Here are a few examples of people who found exactly the level of success they were looking for by starting their own home-based businesses:

- Dan Dorotik of Lubbock, Texas, started his own successful business — Career Documents, a résumé-writing service — when he left his job to move to a different city with his fiancée and found himself out of work. "When I saw the money coming in, I realized that if you're really good at something — and if you're smart at the business and marketing side of it while maintaining the quality of the work — you can make a very good living for yourself," said Dan.
- In 1998, former door-to-door fax machine salesperson Sara Blakely cut the feet off a pair of pantyhose to "look smashing" in a pair of slacks. A year later, she was awarded a patent for her footless body-shaping pantyhose, and, by 2000, she had created her own business — Spanx — with $5,000 in personal savings in the back of her apartment in Atlanta, Georgia. After earning scads of celebrity endorsements, including Oprah Winfrey, Drew Barrymore, Valerie Bertinelli, Marsha Cross, and others, Spanx now sells more than $350 million worth of its products a year.
- In high school and pregnant, Alexis Demko knew that she'd have to find some way to support herself and her child. So she started her El Cajon, California–based business — Demko Demolition Warehouse — which specializes in recycling and selling items such as light fixtures and cabinets salvaged from building demolition projects. She has done so well with her business that at just age 20, she was named entrepreneur of the month by *CosmoGIRL!* magazine.

When starting a business from scratch, you can use one of two main approaches: Choose to do the same kind of work you've been doing in your regular job or career, or choose to do something totally different. In the following sections, we take a closer look at each approach and the advantages each one offers you.

Ten home-based business opportunities

Entrepreneur magazine (online at www.entrepreneur.com) keeps track of the hottest ideas for new businesses (all of which, coincidentally, can be home based). Here are some ideas from its most recent list (in alphabetical order):

- College planning consultants
- Crafts and handmade goods
- Green apparel
- Green business services
- In-home nonmedical care
- Senior services
- Solar energy products
- Specialty lingerie
- Tech training and enrichment courses
- Upscale cupcakes

Doing what you've been doing in a job

As you consider the different options available to you in starting your own business, one of your first thoughts will undoubtedly be to do what you've already been doing in your full-time job.

And why not? You know the job, you're already experienced in the business, and you know exactly what to expect. You also know what your customers want and how to give it to them. You may even have a network of potential customers waiting to sign up for your products and services. Not surprisingly, doing what you've been doing has several advantages, including the following:

- You can start up your business more quickly (like right *now*) and more easily than if you choose to do something you've never done before.
- You don't have to spend your time or money on training courses or workshops, and you don't have to worry much about a learning curve.
- You'll be much more efficient and effective because you've already discovered the best ways to do your job, along with time-saving tricks of the trade.
- You can capitalize on your good reputation, which may be your most important asset.
- You can tap in to your network of business contacts, clients, and customers (when ethically appropriate) and generate business more quickly than when you start something new and different (see Chapter 3 for more tips on turning your current business contacts into customers).

Some facts about women-owned businesses

Here are some interesting facts from the National Association of Women Business Owners about the impact women-owned businesses are having in the United States today:

- Just more than 10 million firms are 50 percent or more owned by women, employing more than 13 million people and generating $1.9 trillion in sales as of 2008.
- Seventy-five percent of all women-owned businesses are majority (51 percent or more) owned by women for a total of 7.2 million firms, employing 7.3 million people and generating $1.1 trillion in sales.
- Women-owned firms account for 40 percent of all privately held firms.
- One in five firms with revenue of $1 million or more is woman owned.
- Three percent of all women-owned firms have revenues of $1 million or more compared with 6 percent of men-owned firms.

Many women — and men — find that by starting their own businesses, they become the bosses, and they get to decide how to run their businesses. Doesn't everyone dream about one day being the boss and calling the shots?

For many people, doing something they've been doing is the best choice. So because doing what you've been doing is often the quickest and least expensive avenue for starting your own home-based business, be sure to take a close look at this option before you consider any others. And as you build your home-based business, check out SoloGig (`www.sologig.com`), a good source of temporary, contract, and freelance work opportunities in a wide variety of categories, to help you get started.

Doing something new and different

Although doing what you've been doing in a job offers many advantages, doing something new and different has its own set of high points. If you're burned out on your current job and you dream of making radical changes in your career or lifestyle — for example, trading your high-pressure career as an attorney for a much more relaxing home-based massage business — doing something new and different may well be exactly what the doctor ordered.

The following are some key advantages of doing something new and different:

- Getting a fresh start in your career can be an extremely energizing experience with positive repercussions for every aspect of your life, opening up exciting new possibilities and opportunities for you along the way.
- Tapping in to new career options allows you to find work that may not have even existed when you first started your career — for example, designing Web sites or computer-network consulting.

Many successful home-based business owners have created businesses that have nothing to do whatsoever with what they'd been doing in their full-time jobs. If you're sufficiently motivated, nothing can stand between you and success, no matter which business you choose. If you're looking to shake up the status quo or to make a break from the past, doing something completely new may well be the best option for you.

Buying a Business

For many people, buying a ready-made home-based business is the way to go. Instead of figuring out how to run a business the hard way — through trial and error — when you buy a business, you buy a proven product, system, and support organization. Of course, you have to pay for these benefits from the get-go, but the investment — if you make it wisely — can easily be eclipsed by the financial rewards of your new business.

As you consider the different home-based business opportunities available to you, keep the following tips in mind:

- **Be sure you fit the business.** Some franchises and network marketing opportunities require that you adhere to strict company rules and procedures, including the clothes you wear and the way you present yourself and your business. If you're not comfortable with these kinds of restrictions, avoid such businesses.
- **Be sure a market exists for the product or service you plan to offer.** Talk to others who have bought the business you're interested in, and ask them for their honest and candid feedback on the attractiveness of the opportunity. Don't just rely on a list of happy people provided by the company — do some research, contact or visit owners at their places of business, and find people who may be more willing to tell you the real story.
- **Be sure the company you select is credible and viable.** This consideration may very well be the most important one you make. Upward of 90 percent of businesses that offer franchises, direct-selling opportunities, and business opportunities (all three of which we describe in the following sections) go bust within five years, leaving their owners high and dry (and sometimes bankrupt and out of work). Be sure that any company you're considering has been in business for five years or more.

The major categories of home-based businesses that you can buy are franchises, direct-selling opportunities, and business opportunities, which we cover in the following three sections.

Four options for finding a new opportunity

Over the past two decades, Paul and Sarah have interviewed thousands of self-employed individuals to discover exactly how they found the paths that ultimately led them to their chosen destinations. As a result of these interviews, Paul and Sarah found that the roots for new businesses come from the following four sources and that successful home-based business owners invariably tap in to one or more of them:

- **Talent:** Each person has one or more innate talents or skills at which he or she excels. When you're able to tap in to this talent or gift and when others value it and are willing to pay for it, developing a business around it can be rewarding, both financially and emotionally. About one in six home-based business owners become successful by taking advantage of their special talents or skills.
- **Mission:** Those who follow a higher purpose — to make a positive difference in the lives of the people and the world around them — are following a mission. Although fewer than one in six people take this route in creating their home-based businesses, for those who do, the personal rewards of seeing the impact of their work on others can be profound.
- **Passion:** For some home-based business owners, the passion they feel to be their own bosses or to pursue the work they truly love is so strong that it creates success in and of itself. For the person with a fire in his belly, no obstacle stands between him and the successful achievement of his goals. About one in four home-based business owners has chosen this path to success.
- **Assets:** Everyone brings assets when starting a home-based business. In some cases, these assets may take the form of previous work experiences; in other cases, they may take the form of a network of friends or business contacts. Although almost half of people who start home-based businesses tap in to their assets to do so — making it the most popular route by far — these businesses typically don't fare as well as those based on talent, mission, or passion. Why? Assets by themselves don't create excitement, intensity of purpose, or motivation, and absent these kinds of emotions, the business owners don't feel much drive to succeed.

As you review potential business opportunities, be aware of your own talents, mission, or passion, and keep them foremost in your mind because your success will be directly proportional to the motivation you bring to your work.

Home-based franchises

If you've ever eaten at a McDonald's restaurant, you know what a franchise is. No matter which McDonald's restaurant you visit, whether it's in Iowa, England, or Hong Kong, you can be fairly certain that your cheeseburger and French fries are going to look, feel, and taste the same. In a place attracted to corporate icons such as the golden arches, franchising has taken the world of business by storm. According to a recent report published by the International Franchise Association (`www.franchise.org`), franchises employ more than 11 million people and produce more than $880 billion of economic output a year, just within the United States.

Ten ways to do what you love

Can you honestly say that you love your job? If not, have you ever thought about what you'd do for a living if you had the opportunity to do anything? Guess what? You do have the opportunity to do what you love! Millions of home-based business owners are doing just that and creating incredible success for themselves in the process. Here are ten ways you can do what you love:

- Provide a service to others who do what you love
- Focus on doing just the things you love
- Teach others to do what you love
- Write about what you love
- Speak about what you love
- Create a product related to what you love
- Sell or broker what you love
- Promote what you love
- Organize what you love
- Set up, repair, restore, fix, or maintain what you love

Although popular franchises such as Subway, Liberty Tax Service, Ace Hardware, and Pizza Hut are easy to recognize, you probably can't think of a popular home-based franchise. Although many home-based franchises are out there, you may not be aware that they're available in an incredible array of sizes, shapes, and styles. From cleaning services to babysitting to photography studios, home-based franchising opportunities cover a wide variety of businesses and can fit most anyone's needs.

Defining a franchise

A *franchise* is an agreement in which one business grants another business the right to distribute its products or services. Typically, the company that grants the franchise has developed a successful and proven business model that others can easily replicate. According to franchising expert Gregory Matusky, three elements define a franchise company:

- Use of a trademark or a trade name
- Payment of fees or royalties
- Significant assistance provided by the franchisor

As the old saying goes, "It takes two to tango." Similarly, every franchise agreement involves the following two key parties:

- **Franchisor:** The company that owns the franchise trademarks, trade secrets, and successful business model
- **Franchisee:** The individual or other entity who pays the franchisor for use of the trademarks, trade secrets, and successful business model

Of course, all the trademarks, successful business models, and assistance come at a price. The franchisee pays fees to the franchisor in the form of one or more of the following:

- A one-time payment
- An ongoing flat-fee payment
- Ongoing sliding-scale payments
- Ongoing royalties
- Advertising fees

The fees that the franchisee pays to the franchisor vary considerably from opportunity to opportunity. For example, the initial fee to buy into a McDonald's franchise is around $45,000. However, actual startup costs for a location (leases, building, equipment, labor, supplies, and so on) run from about $950,000 to $1.8 million. On top of those costs, franchisees are required to pay a royalty rate of 12.5 percent or more on every dollar they bring in. Despite all these fees, McDonald's franchises — though certainly unsuitable for a home-based business — are considered to be among the most desirable of all franchises.

On the other hand, Jani-King, a popular home-based business franchise that specializes in commercial cleaning services, has an upfront franchise fee of between $8,600 and $16,300, startup costs of $11,000 to $35,000, and an ongoing royalty rate of 10 percent. This investment is substantially more affordable than the bricks-and-mortar opportunity presented by a McDonald's franchise, *and* you can run the business out of your own home. Of course, each franchise has its pluses and minuses — you have to decide which is best for you.

For an extensive listing of franchising opportunities, both home based and not, check out *Entrepreneur* magazine's Franchise 500 list at `www.entrepreneur.com`. If you're the slightest bit interested in buying a franchise, chances are you'll find this list to be interesting reading!

Tackling legal issues in franchising

As with many areas of business, franchising is chock-full of laws and regulations. In addition to the usual bevy of federal laws, many states have their own stringent rules and regulations that supersede federal laws. Keep in mind that most franchising laws and regulations actually protect the franchisor, not the franchisee! Here's a look at the two main franchising documents you need to examine closely before you even think about buying a franchise:

- **Franchise disclosure document:** In states that don't have their own specific franchising laws, the Federal Trade Commission (FTC) has established a comprehensive code of regulations that are often referred to as the *franchise rule.* As a part of the franchise rule, franchisors are required to provide prospective franchisees with a detailed disclosure statement, called the *franchise disclosure document* (FDD). Prior to 2007, this document was known as the *uniform franchise offering circular* (UFOC).

Before you consider buying a franchise, be sure you get a copy of the company's FDD and study it carefully. It contains valuable information that can have a dramatic impact on your decision to buy into a particular franchise opportunity. If you have any questions, ask the franchisor for clarification.

An FDD contains the following valuable information, among other things:

- The franchisor's name and address and a listing of any parent companies or affiliates
- A complete and accurate description of the business
- A listing of executives and directors affiliated with the franchisor
- Background information on the franchisor and principals in the company, including business experience and track records
- Detailed information on the number of franchises, their failure rate, and their termination rate (Failure is a matter of closing a company's doors, usually for financial reasons. Some franchise operators prevent failure from happening by reacquiring the franchise from the franchise holder. The franchise is therefore terminated but technically not a failure, which helps keep the statistics about success in franchising looking good.)
- Bankruptcy and litigation histories of the franchisor and principal officers
- Initial fees (including the franchise fee)
- Other fees (including royalties and other payments to be paid to the franchisor after the business is underway)
- Estimated initial investment
- An itemized list of goods and services that must be purchased, rented, or leased directly from the franchisor
- Availability and terms of franchisor-provided financing (if applicable)
- Restrictions on what you can sell and how you have to operate the business
- Assistance, advertising, computer systems, and training provided by the franchisor

- Information on the renewal, cancellation, and termination of the franchise
- The franchisor's financial performance representations and financial statements
- Copies of contracts the franchisee has to sign

For further information on franchising laws and regulations, consult your state attorney general's office, or visit the FTC's Web site at `www.ftc.gov`.

- **Franchising agreement:** Franchises depend on *franchise agreements* — contracts setting forth the rights and obligations of the franchisor and the franchisee — to define the legal relationship among all involved parties. A franchise agreement is negotiable. Be sure to read and understand it thoroughly before you sign it. Even better, have a competent lawyer who specializes in franchise law take a look at it. Believe us: A few hundred bucks invested in a legal review upfront may save you many thousands of dollars (and countless headaches) down the road.

  Here are the most common elements of a franchising agreement:

  - **Grant of franchise:** Defines the nature of the franchising agreement
  - **Use of trademarks, patents, and copyrights:** Spells out exactly how you can use the franchisor's trademarks, patents, and copyrights
  - **Definition of the parties:** Lists the parties to the agreement and sets forth the independent relationship between the parties
  - **Payments:** Spells out the franchise fee and any other required royalties or payments
  - **Term of agreement:** Enumerates the length of time that the agreement will be in effect (About half of all franchise agreements run for ten years, although a large percentage have five-year agreements.)
  - **Renewal of franchise agreement:** Details the mechanism for renewing the agreement
  - **Development and opening:** Details the length of time you have to open your business after signing the agreement, usually 90 to 120 days
  - **Territory:** Spells out any restrictions on the areas in which you may operate (Generally, the larger the territory, the larger the franchise fee payable.)

- **Advertising:** Sets forth requirements for using the franchisor's logos, advertising designs, trademarks, and so on in advertising
- **Equipment and supplies:** Spells out what supplies and services the franchisee must purchase directly from the franchisor
- **Franchisor-provided training and assistance:** Details the training that the franchisor offers, as well as any ongoing support and assistance
- **Assignment of franchise:** Describes any special rules for transferring ownership to another person or entity if the franchisee decides to sell the business
- **Termination of franchise agreement:** Sets forth the legal requirements for terminating the agreement

Be absolutely sure that you understand every part of your franchising agreement — and agree with its terms and conditions — before you sign it. We don't mean that you should just read it over and be generally familiar with the opportunity; we mean understand *exactly* what every sentence means and how it will impact the way you do business, as well as your rights and obligations now and in the future. You have your greatest leverage as you consider a variety of franchising opportunities — not after you sign your agreement.

The pros and cons of franchising

Buying a franchise brings potential positives and negatives. When deciding whether buying a franchise is the best way to start your own home-based business, weigh the pros and cons we discuss here, and discover the best path for you. Here are some of the elements that franchises often have in their favor:

- Buying into a franchise that has a proven track record and ongoing training and support can translate into a quick startup phase and almost immediate cash flow. And don't forget: Happiness is a positive cash flow (see Chapter 6 for more about this idea).
- Established, successful franchises are proven systems that are almost guaranteed to meet your financial expectations. As long as you play the game by the franchisor's rules, it's hard to lose.
- A good franchisor provides extensive training in how to operate and market the business, which is a definite plus for those people who have never actually owned or run a business before.
- You have access to a network of other people who are in a business just like yours. Many franchisors sponsor special Web sites, conferences, or

conventions that get franchisees together to talk shop and share their experiences.

- Many franchisors provide opportunities for regional and national cooperative advertising — saving you money while giving your business more exposure than you'd probably get on your own.

Of course, you also need to think about the downsides to buying a franchise. Before you sign on the dotted line of that franchise agreement, be sure you're comfortable with these potential negatives:

- You have to follow the franchise's policies and procedures whether you agree with them or not (which ultimately means the franchisor is the boss). If you don't, you may be in violation of your franchise agreement — potentially resulting in nasty lawsuits, loss of income, and the termination of your business. For some prospective home-based business owners, the whole point of starting a business is to get away from following someone else's rules.
- You work without a great deal of supervision and direction. No one's going to get on the phone to wake you up if you're late to work; no one's going to constantly urge you to work harder or sell more. If you're not a self-starter, or if you lack the confidence to sell yourself and your products or services, you may jeopardize your prospects for success by franchising.
- You may be required to pay an ongoing fee or royalty to the franchisor for the life of your business. Of course, if you're making lots of money, these fees likely won't be a problem. But if your business is marginal, franchise fees and royalties can quickly become an anchor that drags you and your business down with it.
- Franchises aren't guarantees. Your business may or may not be a success, despite all your hard work, all the money you invest, and all the time you devote to it. Any business is a risk, and a home-based business that you own makes that risk a very personal one.
- The franchise agreement may not protect you against competition from other distributors, particularly those using the Internet. Long story short, you may make less money than you thought or were led to believe you would.

What kind of people do best with franchises? Research indicates that a number of personality traits come into play, including a person's influence with others, his willingness to comply with company rules, and his ability to think on his own two feet. To take a detailed test to see whether your personality traits match those of the people who have been most successful in franchises, check out Paul and Sarah's book *Home Businesses You Can Buy* (Tarcher).

If you decide that franchising is something you'd like to explore further, thoroughly research all the possible opportunities to find the best fit for you. After you identify an opportunity that you want to pursue, talk to current owners of the franchise, and get their candid opinions of the opportunity — both the good and the bad. And be sure to see what kinds of information you can find about your prospective franchise on the Internet. Disgruntled franchisees often aren't shy about telling others about their bad experiences, and some post their stories on the Web. Some even set up their own Web sites specifically to warn others. Just be sure that you take such stories with a grain of salt until you can verify that they're indeed true.

REMEMBER

Buying and operating a franchise will likely require a lot of money and a lot of your time and effort over a long period of time. It's in your best interest to be absolutely sure — before you sign the franchise agreement — that it's the best one for you.

Direct-selling opportunities

Direct selling means selling a consumer product or service in a face-to-face manner away from a fixed retail location. According to the Direct Selling Association (`www.dsa.org`), this kind of business has taken the world by storm. In a recent year, 15 million American men and women sold more than $30 billion worth of products through direct-selling opportunities. The kinds of products sold included home and family care products, such as cleaning supplies, cookware, and cutlery; personal care products, such as cosmetics, jewelry, and skin care products; wellness products, such as weight-loss products and vitamins; and leisure and educational products, such as encyclopedias, toys, and games.

The companies that offer direct-selling opportunities are household names: Nu Skin, Pampered Chef, Amway, The Fuller Brush Company, Tupperware, Nikken, Primerica, and many others.

I explain the two main types of direct-selling opportunities — single-level and multi-level marketing — along with their pros and cons in the following sections.

Single-level marketing

Single-level marketing is simple: A direct seller makes money by buying products from a parent organization and selling them directly to his or her customers. Home-based businesspeople have been pursuing single-level marketing for years, and you probably recognize the names of some of the most successful organizations:

- Avon
- Electrolux
- Tupperware
- Kirby

Although much of the media spotlight that shines so brightly on the direct-selling industry tends to focus on multi-level marketing organizations, single-level marketing produces about 20 percent of direct-selling revenues, or just under $6 billion according to recent statistics.

Multi-level marketing

Multi-level marketing (also known as *network marketing* or *person-to-person marketing*) gives you two ways to make money — by buying products from the parent company and selling them to customers and by sponsoring new direct sellers and earning a commission from their efforts. From its humble beginnings in California in 1945, when Lee Mytinger and William Casselberry formed California Vitamins to sell their vitamin supplement (called Nutrilite), multi-level marketing has grown to an incredible $24 billion in sales a year in the United States alone, employing more than 10 million people.

What makes multi-level marketing special is its unique system of selling, in which salespeople take on the following two key roles:

- **Distributor:** As a distributor of a product, your job is to buy a product from the parent company and sell it directly to the public — usually to friends, relatives, and work associates. Every time you sell an item, you make a profit.
- **Recruiter:** As a recruiter, you sign up other distributors to work for you. Every time your distributor buys an item from the parent company, you receive a percentage of the profit.

As you sign up new distributors, you create what's known as a *downline:* all the people you sponsor into the program, as well as the people they sponsor, and so on. In multi-level marketing, an *upline* is a distributor's sponsor, as well as the other sponsors above him or her in the organization.

The most highly successful multi-level marketers make far more money through their downlines than they do actually selling products themselves. For this reason, many multi-level marketers focus most of their efforts on recruiting new distributors to join their downlines and motivating the individuals in their downlines to recruit new distributors.

Finding a home-based business that's compatible with a military career

Q: I'm currently an active Navy member looking for a business to take me out of the Navy. I need something with low startup costs and overhead — a business that could start as a part-time venture and bloom into something full time. I've been searching for a while. I appreciate any suggestions.

A: Many full-time businesses can be started from home, on the side. In fact, part time is the preferable way to start out on your own. You can test the viability of your idea and go through the learning curve while you still have income from your full-time job coming in. The best sideline businesses don't require a lot of marketing or administrative tasks, leaving you free to devote your limited time to income-producing work. In other words, you want to choose a service or product that's in high demand and easy to sell. Also, your business has to have flexible hours so you can run the business after or around your current working hours.

Whatever business you choose needs to be something you truly enjoy doing, something you know enough about to do well (or are willing to invest time learning while you still have a job), and something for which you can identify a specific market that you can easily reach.

Often the best solutions are quite unique to the business owner. For example:

- A woman who wanted to be at home with her children had an inspiration: Because her husband collects bow ties, she decided to become a Web merchant selling handmade bow ties through the Internet.
- An aerospace engineer had been an avid amateur photographer for years before starting a sideline photography business. By the time his full-time job was downsized, he already had a growing clientele in his side business.

These businesses certainly won't work for everyone, but they were ideal matches for their owners. Look closely at your interests, skills, and assets, and think of how you can use them to meet the needs of specific individuals or companies who'd gladly pay for your help. You also need to pay attention to some factors that are particular to starting a business while on active duty. For one, if you live in military housing, you need to get permission to use your home for your business from your local command, although this permission is usually granted.

Also be sure you're clear on the ethical limits of doing business with other members of the military. Many military personnel go into business with their spouses so that their businesses get developed without conflicting with their military duties. Keep in mind that soliciting to other members of the military of a junior ranking — including their spouses and dependents — is a no-no. Primarily, then, you may be building in the nonmilitary population. After you're consistently earning enough income from a part-time business to cover your bare-minimum living and business expenses, you're ready to make the jump to full time. Find a detailed listing of military-spouse business advice and do's and don'ts at `www.military.com/spouse`.

A multi-level marketing organization *cannot* only recruit distributors — and collect fees from them — without also selling products. Such an arrangement is called a *pyramid scheme,* and it's against U.S. law. A pyramid scheme is set up specifically to make its creators rich while relieving everyone else of their hard-earned money. Be particularly careful about so-called opportunities in which you sell something that has little or no intrinsic value, such as a "special" report on how to make money on the Internet. Such thinly veiled pyramid schemes will land you in very hot water if you're caught.

The pros and cons of direct selling

According to the enthusiastic sales pitches of recruiters for many direct-selling opportunities, signing up to sell their products will put you squarely on the road to riches. Although you may very well turn out to be highly successful (every direct-selling opportunity has its successes, often people who get into the business early and establish a large multi-level marketing downline), you also may not. Of course, no kind of business can guarantee profits — direct selling included — but direct selling does have its advantages.

Direct-selling opportunities are geared to the home-based businessperson, and the right opportunity may be just what you're looking for. Here are some of the positive attributes of direct selling:

- Because startup costs are generally low, you have little financial risk if the business fails — certainly lower than most franchises and business opportunities. (Beware of direct-selling opportunities with high startup costs — they're often scams! Check out Chapter 12 for tips on how to elude these scams.)
- High earning potential is possible (although relatively few people actually make six-figure incomes). Mary Kay, Inc., really does give out pink Cadillacs to its top salespeople, for example. If you're the right person in the right place at the right time, the sky really is the limit.
- Most direct-selling programs are designed specifically to be home-based businesses and are often geared to women (89 percent of U.S. direct sales businesses are one-person distributorships, and 88 percent of all direct sellers in the country are women).
- Your direct-selling parent company generally provides you with sales and promotional materials, as well as bookkeeping, sales tracking, and commission data.
- You can work as many or as few hours as you like. All kinds of work arrangements — part time and full time — abound in direct selling. In fact, the clear majority of people who have chosen direct-selling opportunities work part time, some while working other, full-time jobs.

Is that direct-selling opportunity real or not?

As with any other business you may be considering, check out a direct-selling opportunity before making a commitment. Unfortunately, direct selling has a bit of a reputation for being fraught with less-than-reputable opportunities and — in some cases — outright fraud. The Direct Selling Association (DSA) at `www.dsa.org` offers the following advice for checking out any direct-selling opportunity before buying into it:

- **Identify a company and a product that appeal to you.** Check the DSA list of member companies, or look in your local phone book.
- **Take your time deciding.** A legitimate opportunity won't disappear overnight. Think long-term.
- **Ask questions.** Ask about the company and its leadership, products or services, startup fees, realistic costs of doing business, average earnings of distributors, return policies, and anything else you're concerned about. Get a copy of all company literature — and read it!
- **Consult others who have had experiences with the company and its products.** Check to see whether the products or services are actually being sold to consumers.
- **Investigate and verify all information.** Don't assume that official-looking documents are accurate or complete or even produced by the company, as opposed to the person trying to recruit you. Have an attorney take a look at the documents to verify them.
- **Get help evaluating the company.** Check the list of Direct Selling Association members at `www.dsa.org`, or call your local better business bureau, state attorney general, or consumer-protection offices.

Because of the need to continuously recruit a downline of new distributors in multi-level marketing — to replace those who fall by the wayside, as well as to grow organizations — competition for recruits can be quite lively. This intense competition tends to put a lot of pressure on the people being recruited. Aside from these kinds of minor indignities, you may experience a number of other negatives with direct selling. Here are just a few:

- Many direct-selling businesses are here today, gone tomorrow. Although a number of companies have been around for years and will likely be around for years to come (including such companies as Amway, which celebrated its 50th anniversary in 2009, and Mary Kay, Inc., which has been in business since 1963), far too many direct-selling firms have life spans you can measure in months.
- Direct selling has a poor reputation with many people, often making recruiting new distributors (and selling products) a difficult proposition.
- Motivating your downline to sell more products and sign up new distributors can require more of your time and attention than you may imagine. Plus, the more distributors you sign up, the bigger the job.

- Few people in direct selling make enough money to make it a full-time profession. According to industry figures, about 90 percent of the individuals working in direct sales do so on a part-time basis. Of this number, about half make $500 or less a year in direct sales; the other half make *up to* $5,000 a year. Rarely do direct salespeople make enough money in their own businesses to support themselves and their families.
- Friends, relatives, and co-workers may quickly tire of your constant attempts to sell them products or recruit them into your downline. If they cross the street or duck behind a tree when they see you coming, you're pushing too hard.

Business opportunities

If the ready-made company you're thinking of buying into isn't a franchise and isn't direct selling, chances are it's a business opportunity. While franchises and direct-selling opportunities have well-defined, unique structures, business opportunities come in all flavors, shapes, and sizes. In general, however, a *business opportunity* is an idea, product, system, or service that someone has developed and offered to sell to others to help them start their own, similar businesses.

Business opportunities can take many forms, but they all fall into one or more of the following eight categories:

- **Broker:** A broker is someone who buys or sells products or services for a parent company, often acting as an agent. Common examples include real estate and insurance brokers. Although brokers are independent contractors, the parent company generally pays them commissions for their efforts.
- **Dealer:** Dealers represent lines of products, which are purchased from a parent company and sold directly to consumers. An example of a dealer is someone who sells windows or wooden doors that are produced by several different companies to local home builders and who uses his or her home as a base of operations.
- **Distributor:** Distributors buy products from wholesalers (and sometimes from manufacturers) and resell them to direct-sales organizations, brokers, and dealers. Distributors generally don't sell directly to consumers or end users.
- **Licensee:** Licensees buy the right to sell, market, produce, or use established product brand names, technologies, or systems. A bit like a franchise, licensees have much greater freedom to run their businesses as they see fit.

- **Mail-order business:** Mail-order businesses take orders for products (and, in rare cases, services) over the phone or via e-mail or the Internet and send those products to end users. In some cases, mail-order businesses can have products shipped directly (sometimes called *drop shipped*) from their manufacturers, removing the need to maintain a product inventory and dramatically improving cash flow.
- **Vendor:** Vendors sell materials and supplies to other companies for their own consumption (office supplies, for example), for use in their own production processes (titanium ingots, for example), or for resale to consumers or other companies.
- **Manufacturer:** Manufacturers build and produce products that are eventually sold to consumers. Manufacturers can sell directly to consumers in a variety of ways (direct sales, mail order, or the Internet) or to brokers, dealers, wholesalers, and others.
- **Wholesaler:** Wholesalers buy products directly from manufacturers, mark up the price, and sell them to *retailers* — the people who deal directly with the end consumer. In most cases, wholesalers don't sell directly to the public.

Although some of these categories overlap to some degree, each represents a unique facet of the total universe of business opportunities available to you. As you can imagine, the kind of business opportunity you select has a significant influence on how you do business, to whom you sell, and the way you market your products and service your customers.

For many people, business opportunities are exactly the right choice for a home-based business. But is a business opportunity the right choice for you? Take a look at the pros and cons of business opportunities, and decide for yourself. The following advantages make business opportunities attractive propositions:

- Business opportunities aren't as strictly managed by parent companies as are franchises or multi-level marketing businesses. This relaxed management gives you substantial independence and freedom to run the business as you see fit.
- Many business opportunities offer good, steady income. The upside may not be as dazzling as some multi-level marketing opportunities, but the chances of your succeeding on a full-time basis are much greater.
- Many business opportunities are suitable as home-based businesses.
- Startup costs are generally far less than most franchising opportunities.
- You can work whatever hours you want to — part time or full time. Many people pursue a home-based business opportunity while maintaining a full-time job.

WARNING!

Of course, business opportunities also have their potential problems. Consider the following cons before you sign on the dotted line:

- The independence of most business opportunities can be a disadvantage if you don't already have some experience in sales or in running your own business. Few business opportunities provide the level of support that good franchises or direct-selling opportunities do.
- The federal government offers little regulation of business opportunities, and state and local regulations vary. Beware of scams — you can find plenty! If something sounds too good to be true (getting rich stuffing envelopes or clicking Web sites), it probably is.
- Most owners of legitimate business opportunities work far harder than they ever did in their regular 9-to-5 jobs. Chances are, you will, too.
- Your business opportunity may fail. Be sure to have the financial resources available (in other words, sufficient savings in the bank) to weather a serious business setback or misfortune.

TIP

As with any other business, thoroughly explore all your options before you invest your hard-earned money in a particular business opportunity. Most business opportunities require little in the way of an upfront payment — so even if things don't work out how you planned, you can change course and give a different one a try.

Identifying Which Option Is Best for You

Between creating your own business from scratch and buying a business, you can find an amazing array of options and opportunities. In fact, all your choices may be a little overwhelming. How do you decide which option is the best one for you and make sure you don't make the wrong choice?

Although you can't be 100-percent sure how a particular path will turn out until you embark on it, you can use the following indicators to help you gain a better sense of which option is the best one for you to pursue:

- **How strong your desire to sell is:** Some people naturally love to sell. Do you? Most direct-sales and business opportunities require a lot of selling — no sale, no income. Does the opportunity you're considering (and the style of selling you have to adopt to be successful) fit with your natural selling ability and desire? If not, this option may not be the best one for you.

- **What ideas you already have:** You may already have some ideas about the business you want to start and how you want to run it. You have more freedom to pursue your own unique ideas if you start it from scratch or if you pursue a business opportunity. Franchises and-direct selling opportunities generally require that you closely follow the parent company's established system.
- **How independent you are:** Do you relish the idea of being your own boss and calling your own shots, or do you want to have the comfort that comes from following someone else's direction? Either approach is fine, so long as it matches your personality. When you start a business from scratch or buy into a business opportunity, you really are your own boss, which means you're pretty much on your own when it comes to running your business. Most franchises require that you follow strict policies and procedures and take direction from the parent company. Direct-selling organizations are usually somewhere in between. You won't find a right or wrong answer here — you have to assess which situation you're most comfortable with.
- **How much money you want to make:** Do you just want a little extra money for a rainy day, perhaps on a part-time basis? Or do you want to make enough money to pursue your business full time? Your answers to these questions point you toward certain businesses and away from others (for example, about half of the people in direct-selling opportunities, such as Avon or Mary Kay, Inc., make $500 or less a year).
- **How unique you want to be:** Do you want to stand out from the crowd, or would you be happier blending into a well-established corporate identity? Starting a business from scratch allows you to be as unique as you want to be. Franchises, direct-selling opportunities, and business opportunities allow you to closely affiliate with an established corporate identity.
- **How much control you want:** Different business options have dramatically different levels of control. Starting a business from scratch may put you in full control, while buying a franchise may give you little control over how the business is marketed and run. Be sure that you're aware of the level of control you want and that the business you choose provides it.
- **What your long-term goals are:** Is your goal to make lots of money? Meet interesting people? Work as little as you possibly can? Retire early? Whatever your long-term goals are, make sure the opportunity you select is compatible with and helps you achieve them. Check with

other people who have invested in your prospective opportunity, and see where they are in their lives. Were they able to leave their careers behind? Are they now independent and able to have that little cabin on the lake that they always dreamed of? Were they able to retire early? Make sure you find out the reality behind the sizzling sales pitch for your particular opportunity before you jump head first into it.

Finding Your Niche by Specializing

People need to know exactly what business you're in. If you try to be everything to everybody, you'll end up pleasing precious few customers. The best way to avoid this situation is to find a business niche and specialize in it. An expert is worth a lot more to clients than someone without specific experience. Would you rather have your silk shirt cleaned by someone who has years of experience working with silk or by the local laundromat? Chances are you're willing to pay more for someone who specializes in cleaning your delicate (and expensive) silk shirt.

In business, people want to work with people who know what they're doing. So you need to be one in a million, not one of a million, which often means you need to specialize.

Follow these eight steps to find your business niche by specializing:

1. **Assess and outline your current expertise.**
2. **Identify your strengths and weaknesses.**
3. **Build on your strengths, and fill in the gaps in your experience.**
4. **Articulate a point of view (in writing) for how you work.**
5. **Collect evidence to support your point of view.**
6. **Review and begin documenting your experience.**
7. **Identify the patterns suggested by your experience.**
8. **Explain (in writing to yourself) what you've discovered.**

As your expertise increases, you make yourself easier to market and, thus, are able to make more money. The specialist pyramid, which appears in Figure 2-1, shows the relationship between expertise and money.

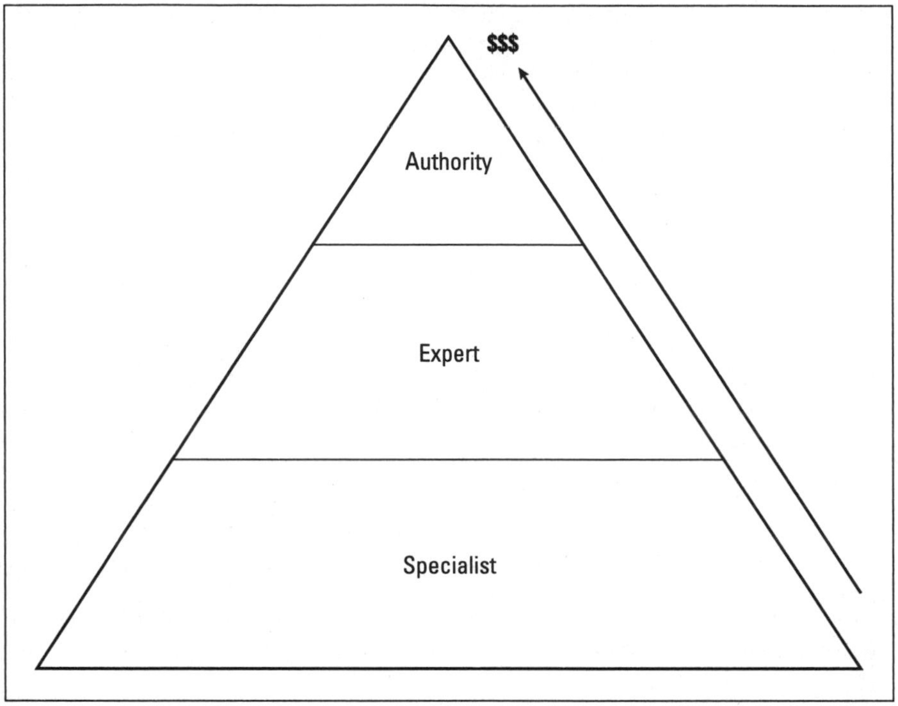

Figure 2-1: The specialist pyramid.

Chapter 3

The ABCs of Starting Your Own Business

In This Chapter

- Reviewing career transition strategies
- Starting a home-based business that will last
- Discovering six financial entry plans
- Identifying 21 sources of startup funds
- Developing an effective business plan

One of the biggest obstacles lying in the way of many prospective home-based business owners is a very simple but very important question: What are you going to live on while you get your new business off the ground? Money doesn't grow on trees (at least not yet), and, to ensure the long-term success of your business, you have to start with sufficient income — from whatever source — to pay your bills.

Seven out of every ten Americans at some time in their lives decide they want to start and own their own businesses. Yet, most of them don't. Why not? In many cases, they're afraid they don't have enough money to do it. The fact is, although certain home businesses require a significant investment in equipment and inventory, many home-based businesses require little or no money to start. But aside from startup costs, you have to put in a lot of work and careful planning to build a business that will pay the bills over the long run, which is why understanding the right ways (and the wrong ways) to transition into your own business is so very important.

In this chapter, we review the steps for transitioning to a home-based business — specifically, what you need to do before you leave your day job behind (or before you're laid off or retired). We cover how to secure financing and where to find the money you need. And, finally, we show you how to develop an effective business plan.

Transitioning into Your Home-Based Business

Starting your own business is exciting. For those people who have spent all their working lives employed by someone else, it's often the culmination of a dream that's lasted for years or even decades. Imagine the power and personal satisfaction you'll feel when you realize you're the boss and you call the shots — from setting your own work schedule, to deciding how to approach your work, to choosing your computer and office furniture. Believe us, it's a feeling you won't soon forget.

But there's a right way and a wrong way to make the move. Your goal is to make sure you maintain a sufficient supply of cash to pay the startup costs of your business while paying for the rest of your life — the mortgage or rent, the car loans, the health insurance, the gas and electric, your daughter's piano lessons, and the list goes on and on.

The fact is, few businesses — home based or otherwise — within the first six months of operation bring in all the money necessary to get them off the ground and keep them going for a prolonged period of time. In other words, you need *a lot of cash* — from a job, your spouse or partner's job, your savings, or loans from friends, family, or a bank — to keep both your business and your personal life going until the business generates enough revenue to take over.

Although you have to decide for yourself exactly what schedule to follow while transitioning into a home-based business, unless you're unemployed or retired, we generally recommend that you start your business on a part-time basis while you continue to hold down your regular full-time job. Why? For a number of reasons, including the following:

- You can develop and test your new business with virtually no risk — you still have your regular job to fall back on if your new business doesn't work out (and remember, no matter how great your business idea is, there's a chance it won't work out).
- You aren't under the intense pressure to perform and show the results that you'd have to show if your new business were your only source of income.
- You can keep your established health insurance, retirement plan, time off, and other benefits. Given the difficulty and expense of securing a decent healthcare plan when you're on your own and not under the umbrella of your employer, healthcare alone may be reason enough to keep your day job while you start your own business.

- You have a steady source of income you can use to pay your bills while you establish your new business.
- You may be able to take advantage of tax benefits, like the ability to write off early losses against income (see Chapter 9 for more on taxes and deductions).
- You have a stronger basis for obtaining bank loans and other financing for your new business.

Of course, the decision is ultimately up to you. When starting a home-based business, follow your heart and make sure the transition fits into your schedule and your life.

In the following sections, we take a close look at six steps you need to take before you leave your regular job to devote all your time and energy to being your own boss. We also walk through the different steps involved in the process of establishing your home-based business.

Knowing what to do before leaving your day job

After you're consistently earning enough income from your part-time, home-based business to cover your bare-minimum living and business expenses, you're ready to make the jump to a full-time commitment of your time and attention. Before you turn in your resignation, however, take the following six steps:

1. **Find out when any company benefit plans you have will vest or increase in value.** If you have a 401(k) or other retirement plan to which your employer has been contributing, it may not be fully available to you until you've served a particular number of years of service. Finding out this information may help you determine the best time to resign. It'd be a shame, for example, if you quit two weeks before the value of your retirement benefits was set to jump from 80 to 100 percent of your current salary.
2. **Find out when you can expect to receive any bonus money or profit sharing.** You may, for example, be slated to receive an annual performance bonus or profit sharing a month after the end of the company fiscal year. This information can help with the financial planning for your home-based business because it lets you know when you'll have the money available to help you get your business off the ground.

3. **Get all annual health exams, have all routine procedures done, and fill all prescriptions while you and your family are still covered by your medical/dental/vision insurance.** Check to see whether you can convert your group coverage to an individual policy at favorable rates or what other health coverage options are open to you. (Some group plans can be converted, but be very careful about changes in coverage, co-pays, and deductibles that may actually end up costing you much more money in the long run.) See Chapter 8 for more on healthcare options for the self-employed.

   Don't forget that if you work in the United States, you're likely covered by COBRA (the Consolidated Omnibus Budget Reconciliation Act of 1985), which requires your employer to allow you to continue your identical group health coverage for a period of 18 months or more. However, qualified individuals may be required to pay the entire premium for coverage up to 102 percent of the cost to the plan.

   The American Recovery and Reinvestment Act of 2009 (ARRA) provides for premium reductions and additional election opportunities for health benefits under COBRA. Eligible individuals pay only 35 percent of their COBRA premiums and the remaining 65 percent is reimbursed to the coverage provider through a tax credit. The premium reduction applies to periods of health coverage beginning on or after February 17, 2009, and lasts for up to nine months for those eligible for COBRA during the period beginning September 1, 2008, and ending December 31, 2009, as a result of an involuntary termination of employment that occurred during that period.

4. **If you own a house and you need some extra cash to help you through the transition, consider taking out a home equity line of credit or other loan before leaving your current job.** Having a line of credit or loan to draw upon can be invaluable during the first two years of your new business, and your chances of getting approved for it are much greater while you're employed in a regular job. That's right — after you leave your job, you probably won't qualify for a line of credit or other loans for your business until your business has been successful for two or more years.

5. **Pay off or pay down the balance on your credit cards while you still have a steady job.** Doing so helps your credit rating (always a good thing) and provides you with another source of potential funds to help you finance various startup costs (and depending on the nature of your business, you may have plenty of those!).

6. **Take advantage of training and educational opportunities, conferences, and meetings that can result in preparation or contacts that will prepare you for your own business.** Doing so enables you to hit the ground running when you decide it's time to start your own business.

Your odds of success are better than you think

A lot of bad information about how long businesses (including home-based businesses) can be expected to survive after founding has circulated throughout the business community. Almost everyone has heard this particular stat: 95 percent of the businesses started in any given year will be gone within five years.

Guess what? It's not true. In reality, most home-based businesses survive for five years or more after their founding. According to surveys conducted by IDC/LINK, an average of only 5 percent of home-based businesses drop out each year. So after five years have gone by, only 25 percent of home-based businesses have dropped out — far less than the average for all businesses, which can be over 50 percent! How, then, can you ensure that your home-based business thrives and doesn't become an unfortunate statistic?

The Small Business Administration (SBA) has uncovered four key indicators of business success. They are

- **Sound management practices:** Including an ability to manage projects, handle finances, and communicate effectively with customers
- **Industry experience:** Including the number of years you've worked in the same kind of business you intend to start and your familiarity with suppliers and potential customers
- **Technical support:** Including your ability to seek and find help in the technical aspects of your business
- **Planning ability:** Including an ability to set appropriate business goals and targets and then create plans and strategies for achieving them

If you, or the combination of you and a partner, possess all four traits, the probability of your business succeeding is much higher than if you're missing one or more of these traits. If you're missing any of these traits, find people who can help you fill in the gaps.

WARNING!

Don't make your announcement or submit your resignation until you're really ready to go. Some companies are (sometimes justifiably) paranoid about soon-to-be former employees stealing ideas, proprietary data, or clients, which can make for a very hasty exit, with a personal escort, when you do resign.

After completing these steps, you're ready to take what may well be one of the most significant steps forward you'll ever take in your life: starting your own home-based business. For those about to embark on this path, we salute you!

Understanding what you have to do to start your own home-based business

In the sections that follow, we go through exactly what you need to do to start up your own home-based business. We cover these topics in much greater detail in Chapters 4, 6, 10, and 11.

Develop a business plan

Despite what you may read on many small business Web sites or blogs, many home-based business owners can get by without drafting a business plan. Indeed, just the thought of having to draft a 50-page tabbed and annotated, multipart business plan is enough to scare many potential home-based business owners away from their dreams. Truth be told, most business owners today use their business plans to obtain financing from third parties, such as banks or investors, and many successful businesses — home based or not — have been started without one. That said, the process of drafting a business plan can be very beneficial — both to you as a business owner and to your business. Taking the time to draft a plan helps you do the right things at the right time to get your business off the ground; plus, it forces you to think through what the challenges will be and what you can do about them before they overwhelm you.

In essence, a good business plan

- Clearly establishes your goals for the business
- Analyzes the feasibility of a new business and its likelihood of being profitable over the long haul
- Explores the expansion of an existing business
- Defines your customers and competitors (very important people to know!) and points out your strengths and weaknesses
- Details your plans for the future

REMEMBER

Even if you think your business is too small to have a business plan, it's really worth your time to see what it's all about — the process of developing the plan for your business will produce a clarity of thought that you can't find any other way. See the "Putting Together a Business Plan" section later in this chapter for details on developing an effective business plan.

Consult outside professionals

As a new home-based businessperson, you need to consider establishing relationships with a number of *outside professionals* — trained and experienced people who can help you with the aspects of your business in which you may have little or no experience. By no means do you have to hire someone from each category I describe in this section. But if you run into questions that you can't easily answer yourself, don't hesitate to call on outside professionals for help as you go through the business startup process (and be sure to check out Chapter 11 for detailed information on this topic).

REMEMBER

Any professional advice you get at the beginning of your business may well save you heartache and potentially expensive extra work down the road.

Here are just some of the outside professionals you may choose to consult as you start your home-based business:

- **Lawyer:** An attorney's services are an asset not only in the planning stages of your business, but also throughout its life. An attorney can help you choose your legal structure, draw up incorporation or partnership paperwork, draft and review agreements and contracts, and provide information on your legal rights and obligations. Look for an attorney who specializes in working with small businesses and startups.
- **Accountant:** Consult an accountant to set up a good bookkeeping system for your business. Inadequate recordkeeping is a principal contributor to the failure of small businesses. Regardless of how boring or intimidating it may seem, make sure you understand basic accounting and the bookkeeping system or software you're using, and don't forget to closely review all the regularly produced financial reports related to your business (and make sure you actually receive them!).
- **Banker:** The capital requirements of a small business make establishing a good working relationship with a local banker absolutely essential. For example, bankers can approve immediate deposit of checks that would normally be held for ten days. They're also good sources of financial information — and for obtaining cash to tide you over when times are tough or financing expansion of your business when times are good.

  We recommend establishing a relationship with your banker *before* applying for a loan, not after you decide to initiate the loan process. This relationship may make the difference between getting approved for the loan you need and being turned down.
- **Business consultant:** Every person has talents in many areas, but no one can be a master of everything. Consultants are available to assist in the areas where you need expert help. You can use business, management, and marketing consultants; promotion experts; financial planners; and a host of other specialists to help make your business more successful. Don't hesitate to draw on their expertise when you need it.
- **Insurance agent/broker:** Many kinds of insurance options are available for business owners, and some are more necessary than others. An insurance agent or broker can advise you about the type and amount of coverage that's best for you and your business. The agent may also be able to tailor a package that meets your specific needs at reasonable rates. Check out Chapter 8 for more information on health insurance.

The relationships you establish with outside professionals during the startup phase of your business can last for years and can be of tremendous benefit to your firm. Be sure to choose your relationships wisely. In the case of outside professionals, you often get what you pay for, so be penny-wise but don't suffer a poor-quality outside professional simply to save a dollar or two.

Choose the best legal structure for your business

Most home-based businesses begin as either sole proprietorships or partnerships because they're the easiest business structures to run and the least expensive. But as these businesses grow, many explore the transition to another kind of legal entity. Before you decide what kind of business you want yours to be, consider the pros and cons of the following legal structures:

- **Sole proprietorship:** A *sole proprietorship* is the simplest and least regulated form of organization. It also has minimal legal startup costs, making it the most popular choice for new home-based businesses. In a sole proprietorship, one person owns and operates the business and is responsible for seeking and obtaining financing. The sole proprietor (likely you) has total control and receives all profits, which are taxed as personal income. The major disadvantages include unlimited personal liability for the owner (if the business is sued for some reason, the owner is personally liable to pay any judgments against the company) and potential dissolution of the business upon the owner's death.

- **Partnership:** A *partnership* is relatively easy to form and can provide additional financial resources. Each partner is an *agent* for the partnership and can borrow money, hire employees, and operate the business. Profits are taxed as personal income, and the partners are still personally liable for debts and taxes. Personal assets can be attached if the partnership can't satisfy creditors' claims. A special arrangement called a *limited partnership* allows partners to avoid unlimited personal liability. Limited partnerships must be registered and must also pay a tax to the appropriate authorities in their jurisdiction. On the plus side, partnerships allow people to combine their unique talents and assets to create a whole greater than the sum of its parts. On the other hand, though, partnerships can become sheer living hell when partners fail to see eye to eye or when relationships turn sour.

  When entering into any partnership, consult a lawyer, and insist on a written agreement that clearly describes a process for dissolving the partnership as cleanly and fairly as possible.

- **Limited liability company:** A *limited liability company* (LLC) is often the preferred choice for new operations and joint ventures because LLCs have the advantage of being treated as partnerships for U.S. income tax purposes while also providing the limited liability of corporations. However, LLCs have the disadvantage of generally being more expensive to set up than sole proprietorships or partnerships. Owners of limited liability companies, called *members,* are comparable to stockholders in a corporation or limited partners in a limited partnership. To create a limited liability company, articles of organization are filed with the secretary of state. The members must also execute an operating agreement that defines the relationship between the company and its members. Note that not all states have this option available.

- **Corporation:** As the most complex of business organizations, the *corporation* (also known as a *C corporation*) acts as a legal entity that exists separately from its owners. Although this separation limits the owners from personal liability, it also creates a double taxation on earnings (corporate tax and personal tax). A corporate structure may be advantageous because it allows the business to raise capital more easily through the sale of stocks or bonds; plus, the business can continue to function even without key individuals. The corporation also enables future employees to participate in various types of insurance and profit-sharing plans. Costs to incorporate vary from state to state — contact your secretary of state for more information.

  A special type of corporation, an *S corporation,* allows owners to overcome the double tax and shareholders to offset business losses with personal income; however, if you offset losses for an S corporation against regular income, you basically guarantee that you'll be audited.

  With C corporations, you need to be careful you aren't erroneously classified by the government as a *professional service corporation,* which is treated much less advantageously than other C corporations. Professional service corporations are corporations in which the owners (who are licensed professionals) substantially perform certain personal services, including accounting, actuarial science, architecture, consulting, engineering, health, veterinary services, law, and performing arts.

As you set up your new home-based business, take time to carefully think through the ramifications of your business's legal structure. Each option has many potential advantages and disadvantages for your firm, and each can make a big difference in how you run your business. If you have any questions about which kind of legal structure is right for your business, talk to an accountant or seek advice from an attorney who specializes in small businesses. Chapters 9 and 10 can also help you sort through the options.

Decide on a name

Naming your business may well be one of the most enjoyable steps in the process of starting up your own home-based business. Everyone can get in on the action: your friends, your family, and especially your clients-to-be.

Consider your business name carefully — you have to live with it for a long time. Your business name should give people some idea of the nature of your business, it should project the image you want to have, and it should be easy to visualize. Names can be simple, sophisticated, or even silly. Try to pick one that can grow with your business and not limit you in the future.

Along with a name, many businesses develop a logo, which provides a graphic symbol for the business (see Chapter 14 for more ideas). As with your name, your logo needs to project the image you want, so develop it carefully. Spend a few extra dollars to have a professional graphic artist design your logo for you.

After you come up with a name, register it with your local government to make sure it isn't already in use. (See Chapter 10 for more details.) If you don't check first, you may have to throw out your stationery and business cards and redesign your logo and Web site when you eventually find out that another company has your name — and registered it 15 years before you did!

Take care of the red tape (and it will take care of you)

Taking care of all the local, state, and federal government legal requirements of starting up a business is something that too many budding home-based entrepreneurs put off or ignore. Unfortunately, ignoring the many legal requirements of going into business may put you and your business at risk.

Getting through the maze of government regulations can certainly be one of the most confusing aspects of starting up and running a business. But even though this process can be intimidating, you have to do it — and do it correctly — because noncompliance can result in costly penalties and perhaps even the loss of your business. Consider this step as one that fortifies the professionalism of your business at the same time that it helps you rest easy at night, knowing that you're following the rules. Do you want people to take you seriously? Then you need to establish your business in a professional way.

WARNING! Even very small or part-time businesses have certain requirements. It's your responsibility to adhere to any and all regulations that apply to your business. Fortunately, a lot of people and organizations — government small business development centers, chambers of commerce, and sometimes lawyers and certified public accountants — are willing and eager to answer questions and help you with this task. For your sake — and the sake of your business — don't hesitate to ask someone for help when you need it.

Get the insurance you need

In today's expensive, litigious world of business, insurance isn't really an option — it's essential. Without it, all your years of hard work can be lost in a minute because of a catastrophic loss.

TIP So what kinds of insurance do you need for your business? We recommend that you talk to an insurance agent and discuss your business and its needs with him or her. Some of the most common kinds of business insurance include the following:

- **Health insurance:** Includes medical, dental, vision, and other coverage designed to maintain and promote employee health and wellness and to protect employees against catastrophic loss in case of injury or illness
- **Basic fire insurance:** Covers property losses due to fire and sometimes covers loss of business, as well

- **Extended coverage:** Protects against conditions not covered by fire insurance, including storms, explosions, smoke damage, and various other disasters
- **Liability insurance:** Covers claims against your business for bodily injury incurred on the business's premises
- **Product liability coverage:** Covers liability for products manufactured or sold
- **Professional liability and/or errors-and-omissions insurance:** Protects the business against claims for damages incurred by customers as a result of your professional advice or recommendations
- **Vandalism and malicious mischief coverage:** Covers against property losses resulting from vandalism and related activities
- **Theft coverage:** Protects your business from burglary and robbery
- **Vehicle insurance:** Covers collision, liability, and property damage for vehicles used for business
- **Business interruption insurance:** Covers payment of business earnings if the business is closed for an insurable cause, such as fire, flood, or other natural disaster
- **Workers' compensation:** Provides disability and death benefits to employees and others who work for you, as defined by your state law, who are injured on the job

A homeowner's policy isn't usually enough insurance for a home-based business for a couple of reasons. First, your typical homeowner's policy provides only limited coverage for business equipment and doesn't insure you against risks of liability or lost income. Second, your homeowner's policy may not cover your business activities at all.

Insurance is the kind of thing you don't think about until you need it. And in the case of insurance, when you need it, chances are you *really* need it! Take time to set up proper coverage now — before it's too late.

Decide on an accounting system

Accounting is one of those topics that makes people nervous (with visions of IRS audits dancing in their heads), but keeping books doesn't have to be complicated. In fact, simplicity is the key to a good system for home-based businesses. Keep in mind that your records need to be complete and up-to-date so that you have the information you need for business decisions and taxes.

When you establish an accounting system, we recommend that you pick up one of the excellent computer software programs dedicated to this purpose. Programs such as Quicken, QuickBooks, and Peachtree do everything your home-based business will ever need — and more.

The two basic bookkeeping methods are *single entry* and *double entry.* Single entry is simpler, with only one entry required per transaction. We prefer this method for most home-based businesses, and the vast majority can operate very well with the single-entry system. If you go this route, we recommend that you use Quicken. Double entry requires two entries per transaction and provides cross-checks and decreases errors. Consider going with a double-entry system if someone else manages your books, if you use your accounting system for inventory management, or if you want more sophisticated reporting for analyzing your business. If you decide that double entry is for you, we recommend QuickBooks, Microsoft Office Accounting Professional, or Peachtree Complete Accounting.

You can also choose between two methods to keep track of the money coming in and going out of your business: *cash* or *accrual.* Most small businesses use the cash method, in which income is reported in the year it's received and expenses are deducted in the year they're paid. Under the accrual method, income is reported when it's earned, and expenses are deducted when they're incurred, whether money has changed hands yet or not.

The accounting methods you use depend on your business. You may want to talk to an accountant for help in setting up your system. Even with the support of a professional, however, you need to understand your own system thoroughly.

Many home-based businesses can get by without detailed financial reporting or analysis — after all, if you can keep up with your bills and perhaps have a little bit of money to sock away in your savings account, you must be making money, right? If you really want to understand your business's financial situation, however, you need some basic financial reports.

The following financial statements are the minimum necessary to understand where your business stands financially. With them in hand, you can review your business's financial strengths and weaknesses and make accurate plans for the future.

- **Balance sheets:** *Balance sheets* show the worth of your business — the difference between its assets and its liabilities. Your balance sheet can tell you whether or not you'd have any cash left over if you shut down your business today and paid off all your bills and loans and liquidated your assets.
- **Profit-and-loss statements:** *Profit-and-loss (P&L) statements* show you the difference between how much money your business is bringing in *(revenue)* and how much money it's spending *(expenses).* If you're bringing in

more money than you spend, you have a profit. If you're spending more money than you bring in, you have a loss.

- **Cash-flow projections:** Cash-flow projections tell you where your money is going and whether or not you're likely to have sufficient money each month to pay your bills and operate the business. For many startup companies — especially those with employees, rent, and other significant recurring expenses — a cash-flow projection is the most important financial statement of all.

TRUE STORIES

Years after starting his home-based business, Peter still keeps a detailed cash-flow projection that shows expected revenues — by client — on a monthly basis for an entire year. By doing so, Peter can see any shortfalls that may be dangerous to his personal financial health far in advance, and he can address them before they become major problems.

For many more details about these and other financial matters, including the use of financial ratios to gauge the financial health of your business and a much more in-depth look at accounting software packages, be sure to check out Chapter 6.

Develop a marketing plan

If you want to be successful, you can't just start a business and then patiently wait for customers to walk in your door. You have to let potential customers know about your new business, get them in to have a look, and then encourage them to buy your product or service. Marketing is all of this and more. Your specific approach to marketing depends on your business, your finances, your potential client or customer base, and your goals.

Marketing sells your products and services, which brings in the cash you need to run your business. Marketing is so important to the survival (and success) of your business that it deserves a plan of its own. A *marketing plan* helps evaluate where your business currently is, where you want it to go, and how you can get there. Your marketing plan should also spell out the specific strategies and costs involved in reaching your goals. You can integrate it into your business plan as one comprehensive section. As with the business plan, you should refer to it regularly and update it as necessary.

Successful marketing for a small or home-based business doesn't happen all by itself. It requires a lot of work and careful analysis and is a terrific opportunity to use your creativity and hone your business sense. For a lot more information on marketing your home-based business, be sure to check out Chapter 4.

Seek assistance when you need it

An almost unlimited number of organizations and agencies — private, public, and not-for-profit — are ready, willing, and able to help you work through the process of starting up your home-based business. Check out the Web sites of each of the following organizations for an incredible amount of free information and help, and know that this list is only the beginning:

- **Small Business Development Centers:** `www.sbaonline.sba.gov/sbdc`
- **Service Corps of Retired Executives (SCORE):** `www.score.org`
- **U.S. Chamber of Commerce:** `www.uschamber.com`
- **Minority Business Development Agency:** `www.mbda.gov`
- **Federal Business Opportunities:** `www.fbo.gov`
- **National Business Incubation Association:** `www.nbia.org`
- **Small Business Administration (SBA) Small Business Planner:** `www.sba.gov/smallbusinessplanner`
- **U.S. Patent and Trademark Office:** `www.uspto.gov`

Six Ways to Get the Cash Flowing

Every new business starts at the beginning. No matter how much experience you have in your current job or how many other businesses you may have started in the past, when you create a new home-based business, you're starting from scratch. In the beginning, every sale counts, and your primary goal quickly becomes building financial momentum. The faster you get the cash flowing into your new business, the sooner you can leave your 9-to-5 job behind and dedicate yourself fully to your home-based business. Consider these six approaches to getting the cash flowing as you start your business:

- **Begin part-time with your new business.** When you start your own business, you usually have a choice to make: Keep your day job or quit. As we mention earlier in this chapter, we recommend that you keep your regular job for as long as you can while building your own business part-time. That way you still have your regular job to fall back on if your own business fails for whatever reason in its early stages. At some point — after your own business has built up a sufficient clientele — you can leave your regular job and devote yourself fully to your home-based business.

- **Work part-time at your old job.** If you have enough work in your home-based business to keep you fairly busy, but not enough to make it your full-time vocation, consider working part-time in your regular job. Depending on your particular situation, your current employer may be willing to be flexible with your schedule. For many employers, keeping a good employee part-time is better than losing her or him altogether.
- **Turn your employer into your first client.** If you're really good at what you do, what better way to get your business off the ground than to do work for your current employer on a contract basis? Not only do you give your employer the benefit of your expertise while contracting with a known entity, but you also develop your business while working with people you already know, using systems and procedures you're already familiar with.

Take care, however, to clearly separate yourself from your former employer as an independent contractor rather than continuing to work in the role of an employee. If you don't make this distinction clear, the IRS may disallow any tax deductions you take for your home-based business. See Chapter 9 for a discussion on how to ensure you're on the right side of this fine line.

- **Take business with you (ethically, of course!).** Although stealing clients away from a previous employer is unethical (and may very well land you in court, forcing you to pay an attorney a lot of money to get you out of trouble), you may be able to get your employer's blessing if you let him or her know exactly what you want to do. The advantage of taking clients with you to your new business is that you maintain the strong working relationship you already have in place — which greatly benefits both your new business and your new clients.
- **Finance your business with startup funds.** You need money to start a business — any business. By lining up sources of startup funds, you can ease the financial entry into owning your own home-based business. Although the list of potential sources of startup funds is practically endless, we let you in on the best ones in the "Figuring Out Where to Get Your Startup Funds" section later in this chapter.
- **Piggyback with your spouse or significant other.** If you're married or living with a significant other, he or she can continue to work his or her regular job, providing a steady paycheck, benefits, and more, while you start your own home-based business. Although your overall income will be reduced until you're able to crank up your sales, you have the shelter of a secure job and benefits. Such a shelter can save you a lot of sleepless nights, allowing you to focus your attention where it's most needed — on building your business.

Bringing a partner into your business

Q: I'm looking for a business partner for my company. Do you have any suggestions on how to find one?

A: The best business partner is someone with whom you have a long track record of working well — someone with whom you share common goals and philosophies and compatible work styles. The more experience you've had working together, the better. But don't despair if you can't find anyone from your existing pool of contacts to team up with. You can find partners by networking through professional and trade organizations or by getting referrals from others whose judgment you value and respect. Here's what we suggest:

- Don't go directly from stranger to business partner. That's like getting married on the first date. Instead of telling people you're looking for a business partner, put the word out that you're looking for an associate to run a joint venture with. This initial joint venture should be a short-term or discreet project that gives you a chance to get to know a prospective partner and see whether you have the chemistry to work well together.
- Ask for referrals from those in a position to know people who will meet your criteria: the officers of a trade association, the president of the chamber of commerce, the editor of the trade journal, or a valued supplier or client. You can network with such individuals online as well as in person. These days, you need not limit yourself to teaming only with colleagues in your locale. Many people successfully use e-mail, collaboration software, land lines, and Skype, to team up with associates anywhere in the country or even internationally.

As you talk with people about the possibility of collaborating on an initial venture, look for compatibility in the following areas:

- Strengths that complement yours
- Honesty
- Fairness
- Aesthetics and etiquette
- Personal integrity
- Positive attitudes about family/work priorities
- Money and financial smarts
- Timeliness and punctuality
- High quality and educational levels
- Good manners and treatment of others
- Positive attitudes about your profession or business

Take note of any red flags. If anything like the following comes up in initial conversations, watch out!

- A history of financial problems
- A history of combative relationships or lawsuits
- Soap opera tales of woe with previous partners or joint ventures
- Bad here-and-now behavior, such as being late to meetings or frequently putting down others
- Unwillingness to put plans and agreements in writing

When you find someone you click with, do several short-term projects or joint ventures together before committing to a formal, legal partnership. Make sure that your initial assessment is accurate and that you can, in fact, trust your partner and work well together.

Figuring Out Where to Get Your Startup Funds

The number-one concern of most people who plan to start their own home-based businesses isn't what kind of business to start, where to start it, or how to market their products and services. It's not who their customers will be, who their competition is, or whether or not they should involve a spouse in the business. Their number-one concern is money. More specifically, it's where to get the money they need to start up their home-based businesses.

It takes money to make money — especially when starting a new home-based business. With cash, you can buy the things your business needs to operate and stock up on the inventory of products you plan to sell to your customers and clients.

But where does this initial money come from, and what are the best ways to pull together the cash you need to start up your home-based business? Here are 21 of our best suggestions:

- **Bartering:** Although not strictly a source of cash, *bartering* with others — trading your products or services for theirs — can be a terrific way of getting the things you need to get your business off the ground. Need a computer? Well, if you're starting a massage business in your home, you may be able to find someone who'd love to trade some massages for a computer he or she's no longer using. Craigslist (`www.craigslist.org`) is a great place to give bartering a try.
- **Business idea competitions:** Some organizations sponsor business idea competitions with the prizes for best idea (or ideas) being startup funding. Technology organizations, such as the recent $80,000 Entrepreneur Challenge held at University of California, San Diego (`challenge.ucsd.edu`), often sponsor these competitions.
- **Credit cards:** Home-based business owners often turn to credit cards as a source of cash for business startup. A word of caution: Beware of extremely high interest rates and extra fees for cash advances. If you do decide to use a credit card for your business, try to dedicate one solely to your business expenses. Doing so makes figuring out your taxes for the year a much easier task.
- **Credit unions:** Because credit unions are owned by their members, they often offer better interest rates than regular banks or other financial institutions do. If you belong to a credit union, be sure to try there for a loan first. Keep in mind, however, that credit unions are generally even more adverse to risk than regular banks, so your credit has to be very strong for you to have a chance of getting the money you need.

- **Disability grants:** If you've been granted a disability payment because of an on-the-job injury that prevents you from pursuing your former vocation, the cash you receive may be useful as you begin a new career — a career at home.
- **Donations:** You can appeal to the world to contribute money to help you get your new business off the ground. With the huge growth in popularity of social media, such as Facebook, Twitter, and MySpace, it's possible to reach a very large crowd of like-minded individuals, some of whom may be willing to contribute to your venture.
- **Funds from investors:** Many new companies rely on cash from investors to fund their startup and initial operations. Be aware, however, that when you accept money from investors, you probably have to give them something in exchange. That something is usually equity in the company. And with equity comes the power to have a say in how the business is run. If you don't want anyone telling you how to run your business, you may not want to use investor funds to help you start your business.
- **Government grants:** A variety of federal, state, and local government programs provide small business startup funding. Unfortunately, however, you have to beat the bushes to find it, and the categories of people eligible to receive it may be highly restrictive.
- **Home equity line of credit:** If you have a home and have built up equity in it (the value of the home over and above what you owe for it), you may be eligible for an equity line of credit. These lines of credit have several great advantages: You don't pay any interest or payments unless you actually borrow against your line of credit (you may have to pay some sort of loan origination fee to set up the line of credit); home equity loan terms are often much longer than standard loans — up to 15 years or more; and the interest you pay is tax deductible. On the downside, you have to put your home up as collateral — if you default on your loan, you may lose your house. All in all, however, home equity loans can be a smart way to finance your new business.
- **Inheritances:** Although inheritances may be subject to taxation depending on exactly how much you inherit and in what way (check with a tax adviser for all the details), you may still be left with a substantial amount of funds that you can use to start your new business.
- **Intrapreneurship programs:** Some businesses encourage their employees who have a good idea to start their own companies — providing startup funding to assist them in the process. In exchange for the startup funding, the business may or may not require an ownership stake in the business. Check with your current supervisor or employer to see whether this option is available to you.

- **Life insurance policies:** Depending on the kind of life insurance policy you have (term, cash value, and so on), you may be able to cash it in or take out a loan against it. Read the fine print of your policy or consult your insurance agent to see whether you have this option. If you've had a cash-value policy for a long time, you may be pleasantly surprised at how much money is available to you for your new business.
- **Loans from friends and family:** When aspiring home-based entrepreneurs don't personally have the resources to finance their new business, friends and family are often the first potential sources of funding they turn to. As long as your request for a loan doesn't cause your relationships to sour, loans from friends and family can be a great way to put together the financing you need. Be sure to treat relatives and friends as you would any business relationship, using signed, written loan documents with clear terms and conditions.
- **Loans from suppliers or colleagues:** You believe in yourself, right? If your idea's a good one, chances are others will believe in you, too. Drop the hint to your colleagues or suppliers that you're looking for money to finance your new business, and you may well find yourself with the cash you need to get started.
- **Local seed-money funds, such as funds sponsored by the Amarillo Economic Development Center:** Many local governments offer seed money to help finance new businesses in their communities. Check with your local small business office to see what's available in your community.
- **Microloan programs:** The government and a number of foundations offer a variety of microloan programs, particularly targeted to women and minorities. Check with your local Small Business Administration office to find out what's available and whether you qualify.
- **Personal assets, such as a boat, extra vehicle, camper, and so on:** You may be able to find the startup funds you need by selling some of your superfluous personal assets. Think big yard sale, eBay, `www.craigslist.org`, or your local classified ads.
- **Personal savings:** Savings accounts are probably the first place most soon-to-be home-based business owners turn to when looking for cash to start up their new businesses. And why not? You get instant loan approval — no matter how good or bad your credit report may be — and you can't beat the interest rate of 0 percent!
- **Reduced tax withholdings:** If you aren't taking any exemptions on your income tax withholding at work, you can unlock an instant stream of cash by increasing your exemptions in line with the deductions you expect to have available when you file your annual income taxes. Simply follow the instructions on the IRS form or consult your accountant for more information.

How to patent your ideas

Q: I'd like to sell patented ideas to companies that manufacture similar products. But because I don't have a lot of disposable income or collateral, how do I finance my patent searches and applications? Also, when I write to companies about my ideas, I get rejection letters or no response. How do I get my foot in the door to sell companies my ideas?

A: Patent attorney and author David Pressman recommends waiting to send letters to manufacturers until after you've completed a thorough patent search and submitted your patent application. You can hire a professional searcher for under $1,000, but if you're a conscientious worker and have the time, you can do your own search. Pressman outlines how to do so in his book *Patent It Yourself* (Nolo). You can also check out David Hitchcock's *Patent Searching Made Easy* (Nolo) for more information on patent searching. Or you can begin your search on the Internet at `patft.uspto.gov` or at a Patent and Trademark Depository Library in your state. You can find a list of Patent and Trademark Depository Library sites at the Patent and Trademark Depository Library Program (PTDLP) page on the U.S. Patent and Trademark Office Web site at `www.uspto.gov`. For patents issued before 1971, you have to go to a depository library.

Even if you choose to do the patent search yourself, however, you still have some expense because, after you've completed your search, you have to pay a fee for each patent application, currently under $200 for a small entity. Pressman recommends that you find and write to suitable companies after you file an application. Most companies, he says, respond with a form letter requesting that you sign an enclosed waiver form. Some people do offer to sell their patented ideas for a lump sum, but he finds that most seek to license their ideas instead, usually for around 5 percent of sales.

Pressman urges you not to get involved with an invention development company. These companies offer to review your ideas and then charge an inflated price to complete a search for you. If you'd rather be just the idea man and leave the financing, model building, searching, and filing to others, we suggest putting together your own development team. Ideally, you have contacts to draw upon for such a team from your experience in the fields related to whatever ideas you're developing. If not, you can begin making such contacts by networking through professional organizations either face-to-face or online.

For additional information on obtaining a patent, contact the U.S. Patent and Trademark Office via its Web site at `www.uspto.gov` or by phone at 800-786-9199 or 571-272-1000.

- **Retirement funds:** If you're currently working a full-time job, you probably have some sort of retirement fund established. This fund is as good as gold, and you can apply the cash within it to help you start up your new business. However, a couple of problems usually accompany early distributions of retirement funds. First, Uncle Sam will probably penalize you for doing so (check the rules for your particular kind of retirement account) and will then add insult to injury by taxing you on the income you pull out of your fund. Second, if you wipe out your retirement account, you have nothing to fall back on if your business fails (and no retirement funds when you're really ready to retire).

- **Stock offering:** Although the appeal (and value) of stock in a new business with no track record of success is perhaps limited, it's possible to sell stock to investors through either a public or private offering. You can probably accomplish stock offerings yourself, but the rules and regulations are extremely complex, and the penalties for breaking them — whether accidentally or on purpose — are severe. At minimum, bring in an attorney or law firm that specializes in securities law to advise you and your team. You may also consider working with an investment bank or venture capital firm to help steer the process and ensure its success.

Before you run out and buy that snazzy new company car, computer, or modular furniture unit, ask yourself whether the old one can serve you just as well for another year or two. Using the same old stuff you've always used may not be as exciting as shopping for something new, but you put the money you save to better use generating income for the business. And in a home-based business, generating income for the business means generating income for you.

For much more information on raising money for your new business, be sure to check out Peter's book (with co-author Joseph Bartlett) *Raising Capital For Dummies* (Wiley).

Putting Together a Business Plan

Whether you write it on the back of a napkin or fill hundreds of pages with full-color charts and photos of happy customers, your business plan can help you prioritize the actions you take to start up and run your business. Although businesses use formal business plans less often nowadays than they did in the past (today's businesses usually put together business plans for the benefit of loan officers at banks and potential investors), the process of putting together a business plan for your home-based business is an education in itself — one you can't get anywhere else.

Even though you have some flexibility in determining the exact format of your business plan (especially when it's an informal one that's strictly for your own use), if your intent is to use the plan for securing financing from a bank or investors, they expect to see certain information presented in specific ways. These expectations allow banks and investors to make informed judgments on the viability of your business and its potential for growth and profitability.

A formal business plan should contain, at minimum, the following elements:

- **Mission statement:** The company's mission statement sets the tone for the business, relating it to its values and goals. Mission statements are inspiring and serve to galvanize the employees to work hard to attain the company's goals. Paul and Sarah's mission statement fulfills all these criteria: "We're authors, broadcasters, and facilitators. Our mission is to explore new and better ways of living and working through the interface of nature and technology." Peter's mission statement is "The best books, on time, and on dollar."
- **Description of the company's products and services:** This element provides a complete description of all the products and services the company presently offers and plans to offer in the future. If your home-based business specializes in producing the best wedding cakes in the tri-state area, using the latest in confectionery technology, you'd lay it all out here. Be complete — leave nothing to the imagination.
- **Market analysis:** If you've already put together a marketing plan for your business, you already have the material you need to fill out this part of your business plan. The market analysis takes a close look at the markets in which you intend to sell your products and services and details the number of potential customers, the potential growth rate of the market, information about your competition, and the particulars of your marketing strategies. See the "Develop a marketing plan" section earlier in this chapter for an analysis of a marketing plan.
- **Financial projections:** Do you plan to go from $100 a month in revenues to $100,000 a month? This part is where you present your financial projections, including revenues, expenses, and profit or loss. Plan to include the three basic financial statements — a balance sheet, a profit-and-loss (P&L) statement, and a cash-flow projection — and be ready to back up your guesses and prognostications with hard data. (See the "Decide on an accounting system" section for more details about these financial statements.)
- **Management strategies for achieving company goals:** You have your products and services, your marketing strategies, and your financial projections. Now, exactly how do you intend to achieve your goals? This section presents the details of the strategies you select to achieve your company's goals and lays out when and how you plan to achieve them.

Although space doesn't allow us to present a sample of a formal business plan within these pages, you can view several at `www.businessplans.org`. Also check out *Business Plans For Dummies,* 2nd Edition, by Paul Tiffany and Steven Peterson (Wiley), for details on writing a successful business plan.

Farming out your business plan

Q: I want to start a business, but the bank needs a business plan before I can get a loan. I don't know how to write a business plan and am not good at writing. Is there a service that can write one for me?

A: Absolutely. You can hire a professional business plan writer. Your bank loan officer may be able to recommend one to you, or you can find one online. Many business plan writers now have their own Web sites. You can also look for business planning consultants at `www.bplans.com/pc` — look for someone who has general business background in the areas of accounting, bookkeeping, and marketing, and familiarity with financial statements, business jargon, and your local business community. Before you choose a writer, definitely ask for a few writing samples, and, if possible, have your bank loan officer review the samples to be sure they're of the type and quality the bank is seeking.

Professionals can generally prepare a business plan in two to four weeks. Fees range from $2,500 to $5,000, depending on the time required to research needed financial data, analyze the competition, develop sample marketing plans, and so forth.

Chapter 4

Marketing 101: Attracting Customers

In This Chapter

- Figuring out who your best customers are
- Assessing your customers' needs
- Selecting the best marketing methods for your business
- Getting started with a Web site and e-commerce
- Developing a marketing plan that meets your business's needs

You've worked hard to start your home-based business and get it going. You've set aside some space in which to operate, and you've picked up a business license. You've purchased and stocked products to sell, or you've prepared yourself to deliver first-rate services to what you hope will be an eager throng of potential clients and customers. But before you can start enjoying the fruits of all your hard work, there's one thing you have to do: Convince someone to buy your products and services. You see, the greatest business ideas in the world — the greatest products and services — are essentially worthless if no one is willing to pay you for them. For your business to be successful, you have to get good at marketing your products and services so that prospective customers and clients hear about you and are encouraged to buy from you.

In this chapter, we help you identify your best customers and assess their needs. We take a look at different marketing methods — including *referrals,* one of the most effective marketing tools — and help you create a meaningful marketing plan. We also check in on the latest information about starting your own Web site for e-commerce.

Identifying Your Best Customers

Here's a secret that may make a very big difference in the amount of money you stand to earn from your home-based business: *Some of your potential customers are better than others.* That is, some (the ones who are willing to pay top dollar for your products or services with little intervention on your part) will earn you a lot of money, and some (the ones who nickel-and-dime you to death, complaining all the way) will actually lose you money. Because potential customers come in all sizes, shapes, and spending profiles — and because customers don't come with their profiles stapled on their foreheads — your very difficult job is first to figure out which ones are the most likely to become your best customers and then to figure out how to attract and reach them. Because your time and marketing dollars aren't unlimited, the best use of your money is to target specific people — the people most likely to buy your products and services. Instead of running expensive radio or newspaper advertisements day after day, hoping to get the attention of the customers you seek, you may find that targeted advertising in a specific magazine or Web site delivers a much greater payoff.

What does your ideal customer look like? Here are a few questions to ask as you create a picture. (Don't worry if you can't answer all the questions right now — just give it your best shot.)

- Who do you think your best customers are?
- Are they individuals or businesses?
- If they're individuals, what do they like and what don't they like?
- What are their needs and problems?
- How can you best address those needs and problems?
- What's most important to your best customers?
- What's least important to them?
- How can you deliver more of the former and less of the latter?

Based on these questions, develop a written description of your best customers, and have some of your customers look it over to validate it or to make corrections. Here's a sample description of the ideal customer for a pet-sitting service:

> My ideal customer is a single, working adult with one or more pets, including dogs, cats, or birds, that require daily care and attention. My ideal customer often travels, has sufficient income ($45,000 or more per year) to afford to hire a pet sitter, and prefers to keep his or her pet in its home environment rather than in a kennel or other offsite care situation. My ideal customer loves his or her pets and wants them to have the best care possible.

The idea is to understand your best potential clients and customers inside out — to know what makes them tick and what motivates them. By doing so, you can easily figure out which marketing approaches (Web site, blog, direct mail, radio ads, search engine listings, display advertisement, social networking on sites like Facebook, LinkedIn, and Twitter, directory ads, such as electronic and print Yellow Pages, and so forth) have the highest probability of not only reaching your best customers, but also inducing them to want to find out more about what you've got to offer. (Check out the "Marketing: Taking Different Roads to Meet Your Goals" section later in this chapter for ideas on ways to market your products and services.)

Promoting a new business

Q: My sister-in-law and I have a home business together that offers complete medical billing for physicians. Our primary way of marketing is to visit physicians personally and present information on what we have to offer. Do you have any other suggestions on how to promote a new business without spending too much?

A: Our interviews with owners of successful medical billing services for *The Best Home Businesses for the 21st Century* and again for *The Best Home Businesses for People 50+* confirm that what you're doing now continues to be the best way to get started in this field. Most startups begin by knocking on doors or making marketing calls by phone. To make getting through to doctors easier, we suggest warming up your sales contacts by mailing brochures and letters and then following up with a personal contact for an appointment. Here are a few ideas that may help you get started:

- Talk with your own doctors and other healthcare providers whom you know personally, and ask for referrals.
- Collaborate with pharmaceutical salespeople, who regularly see doctors in their private offices. (Expect to pay a commission to reps who introduce you.)
- Don't limit your marketing contacts to medical doctors. You can also provide billing services to a wide range of other healthcare practitioners, such as acupuncturists, dentists, chiropractors, commercial ambulance services, dentists and orthodontists, home-nursing services, massage therapists, nurse practitioners, occupational therapists, optometrists, physical therapists, physician assistants, podiatrists, psychologists and other counselors, respiratory therapists, and speech therapists.
- Contact local professional societies about offering discounts to their members. After making contacts, follow up by phone to find out if you can provide additional information. Then keep your services top of mind (that is, in their minds) by sending periodic reminders in the form of timely tips and other useful information on postcards, flyers, or newsletters that you can send via mail, e-mail, or fax.
- Get new ideas and feedback on what you're doing from colleagues, such as on one of the groups on LinkedIn for medical billers.

Tapping In to Your Customers' Needs

Which do you think is the better approach — creating a product or service that you're not sure anyone will want to buy and then trying to sell it, or first finding out what people want to buy and *then* creating a product or service that responds to that want? Here's a hint: If you build a business around a product or service that you're not sure will sell, you're taking a very big risk.

Creating a product or service in a vacuum, without considering the input of your clients or customers, is a recipe for disaster because you're essentially designing a product or service that your prospects may neither need nor like. As a result, you have to market much harder — or offer a lot of incentives — to get your clients or customers to buy your products. Even then, they still may not buy.

Finding a need and filling it is one of the most basic marketing strategies. Your first step in marketing, therefore, begins before your product or service is available to the public, when you're designing and creating it. By tapping in to your customers' needs early in the process, you not only build a product or service that your prospects truly want and need, but you also set yourself up for marketing efforts that take far less personal energy, time, and money to implement.

Understanding the WPWPF principle

Many home-based business owners are in love with the products and services they sell, as well they should be. After all, they are their own best cheerleaders, creating infectious excitement whenever they have the opportunity to talk to someone about their business or their products or services. The problem is that some home-based business owners fall so deeply in love with their products and services that they fail to notice that their prospective clients and customers aren't equally in love. And when this happens, a great idea remains only a great idea — not a great product or service.

Paul and Sarah have developed a test for home-based business owners who love their products and services. It's called the *WPWPF* (what people will pay for) *principle.* Your products and services are only as good as what people are willing to pay for them. No matter how beautiful, clever, or well thought out they may be, if your clients and customers don't want them, they aren't worth even a fraction of the time and money you invested to create them, and you really don't have a business.

TIP

So what's the solution? How can you be sure that the products and services you've been dreaming about delivering to your clients and customers are the ones they truly want? It's actually quite simple: Ask them. Here are a few simple steps for defining your target market and then asking the people in that market which products and services they really want and need (and will therefore be willing to buy):

1. **Decide which market you're going to target.**

   Who, potentially, are your best customers — the people in the market you want to target? Do you want to sell your products and services to busy businesspeople, to retirees who spend their winters in Florida or Arizona, to preschool children, or to people who like to go on extended vacations to exotic lands? Whichever product or service you hope to create, first decide whom you're going to try to sell it to. All the steps that follow depend on this one, so take your time deciding which market you want to target.

2. **Ask the members of your target market which products or services they want and need.**

   You can do this in person, over the telephone, via written surveys sent through the mail, by e-mail, or through your Web site or blog. The key is to collect as much data about the wants and needs of your target market as you can — the more data, the better.

3. **Use the results of your survey when designing your products and services.**

   Using the data you collect from surveying your potential customers and clients, determine the design of the products and services you offer. Be sure that you address — and at least consider — every feature mentioned as important by the people you surveyed. Some may not make financial sense, but others may be essential to include, whatever the cost. Believe us: Not only do you end up with better products and services, but you also sell a lot more of them because they match the wants and needs of your customers and clients.

4. **Test the market.**

   After your products and services are available — but before you roll them out to the public at large — test them out on a few selected people, businesses, or not-for-profit entities. What's their reaction? Are they satisfied with the results? Do your selected customers have suggestions for improvements or changes? What about price? Are your products and services priced realistically? Will your potential clients be willing to pay what you ask? Incorporate the feedback you get by tweaking your product or service or the prices you plan to charge.

5. **Market, market, market.**

   By going through the preceding four steps, you can be reasonably assured that you have a product on your hands that you can not only sell, but that you also can sell a lot of. Now get ready for the ride of your life!

WARNING!

Never bring out a product before you find out for sure that your target market really wants it enough to pay for it. Doing so may mean wasting far too much time and money — delaying your ability to create a positive cash flow while creating negative public opinion about your company. Better to wait a few months to fully explore your customer needs and wants than to rush through a great idea that ends up going nowhere.

Carving out a niche

In most economies around the world, competition is a good thing. More competition is better for consumers, causing companies to push technology to the limits while reducing prices to gain advantage over other competitors. But although competition is almost always a certain win for consumers, it can mean big problems for the businesses that get caught up in it — especially small and home-based businesses.

Why? Because small and home-based businesses are often thinly capitalized; in other words, you don't have a lot of cash to spare, so your marketing dollars, as well as your time, need to be aimed well.

To avoid the problems that come with competition, carve out your own niche by providing your clients and customers with unique products and services that they can't obtain anywhere else.

TIP

Here are a number of tips for carving out a niche of your own:

- **Offer a product or service that no one else offers.** Do you remember the Pet Rock? If that little item is before your time, the Pet Rock — created by salesman Gary Dahl in 1975 — was a regular, everyday rock placed in a small cardboard box with a witty instruction manual titled the *Pet Rock Training Manual.* After appearing on *The Tonight Show,* not once but twice, Dahl sold more than 1 million Pet Rocks at a price of $3.95 each. Dahl's creation — definitely a product that no one else offered — took the nation by storm and made its inventor rich many times over.
- **Specialize in only one business area or industry.** You can't be everything to everybody, and if you want to be successful, you shouldn't even try. Instead of spreading yourself too thin with too many unrelated products and services, focus on the one or two kinds of products or services

that you do best. Peter figured this out a number of years ago when he decided to specialize in writing business books. Before then, in addition to writing business books, he had ghostwritten a book on how to pick up men through the personal ads (written from a woman's perspective!) and completely rewritten a book on dieting and nutrition. Today, the vast majority of his work is writing business books — often with busy businesspeople who come to him by way of referrals from happy clients.

- **Serve an unserved market.** Believe it or not, not every market has yet been tapped by companies eager to sell their products. If you take the time to identify these markets and serve them, you can carve out a niche that others will be hard pressed to match. Chances are you'll find yourself with little or no competition for months or even years.

When you carve out a niche in the market, you're doing nothing more than getting in touch with your potential clients and providing them with exactly the products and services they want and need. And when you offer that market something it really wants and needs, marketing your product becomes easier than you ever imagined.

Marketing: Taking Different Roads to Meet Your Goals

The topic of marketing covers an incredibly broad spectrum of activities, all with one final goal in mind: to spur clients and customers to buy your products and services. When you start your home-based business, marketing should take up most of your schedule. After all, your business isn't going to get very far down the road until you start selling your products and generating the money you need to give it life (and to pay yourself for all your hard work). As you gain clients and customers — and start doing paid work — you can reduce the amount of time and money you devote to marketing, but you should never forgot about it. When you own your own business and rely on it for your livelihood, it's important to keep a steady flow of new business in the pipeline, ready to pick up the slack as you complete your work for current clients. For most home-based business owners, plan on making an ongoing commitment of at least 20 percent of your time to marketing activities.

Why bother with marketing in the first place? Won't your products sell themselves? Few — if any — products truly sell themselves (and if someone trying to sell you on a business opportunity tells you otherwise, your internal lie detector should be on red alert). Selling your products and services requires constant marketing — you can't simply create something and hope it will sell.

Four approaches to marketing

When you're marketing your products and services, you have an almost unlimited number of approaches to choose from. Each approach can be grouped within the following four categories:

- **Personal contact:** Whether knocking on your prospective customer's door to pitch your product's advantages face to face, cold-calling on the phone, or buttonholing an acquaintance at your local grocery store, when you market your products directly to your customers one-on-one, you're making personal contact. If you have a great personality (always a plus when you're trying to sell something), if your product is complex, or if your product is best demonstrated live and in person (like that incredible kitchen knife that slices tomatoes and 3-inch-thick steel bars with ease), personal contact is definitely the way to go.
- **Contact through others:** Although you can personally sell only a finite number of products or services — after all, you only have 24 hours in a day — you can leverage your efforts and sell far more by selling through others. Selling through others involves creating a buzz around your products and services by getting people to talk about them (through word of mouth or through your promotional efforts), obtaining referrals from satisfied customers, and generating interest in the media.
- **Written communications:** Brochures, advertisements, newsletters, targeted e-mail messages, sales letters, proposals, digital greeting cards, and thank-you notes are all different ways of using the power of the written word to sell your products and services. If you're not comfortable selling your company's products and services personally, or if you would have difficulty giving your potential customers samples of your products and services (for example, giving a potential customer a sample of your car-detailing services without actually detailing his car), you should try selling your product through written communications. Again, properly used, written communications can leverage your own direct-selling efforts and generate far more leads and sales than personal contact alone could ever do.
- **Proof of what you can do:** Sometimes a demonstration of a product or service can spark sales like nothing else. Product samples, videotaped demonstrations, Web sites, house parties, product displays, audio tapes, photos, and trial subscriptions are all ways of showing what you and your business can do for your clients-to-be. When your prospective customers want to try your product before they buy it, or if you know that after your customers have a chance to actually use your products or services, they'll be hooked, showing them what you can do with proof of your services is the right approach.

Which approach works best for you depends on a variety of factors, including the nature of your business, the likes and dislikes of your typical customer, your customers' buying habits, and the complexity of your product or service. Be sure to keep each of these considerations in mind as you decide which approach to take in marketing your own products and services.

The good news is that you can promote your business in a variety of ways. If you decide to tackle even just a few of them, you can easily create a successful marketing campaign that can propel your home-based business to the front of the pack. In the following sections, we show you some of the most popular and effective ways to do just that.

Generating word of mouth

Word of mouth means getting people to talk about you, your company, and its products and services in a positive light. Of course, the more people talk, the better your company looks as a result, and the better it is for your business. That's exactly why any good promotional campaign starts off with a heavy emphasis on generating positive word-of-mouth excitement. There's nothing like a little bit of buzz to get your sales to take off.

Here are some of the best ways to get people talking about your business:

- **Networking:** Everyone has a circle of friends and acquaintances — both in work lives and in nonwork lives. Or you may belong to a community-service or fraternal or sororal organization, such as Optimists, Junior League, Rotary, BPO Elks, Lions International, or others. Your networks of friends and acquaintances are probably the first and best places to start a word-of-mouth campaign for promoting your business. They know you, they like you (at least, we hope so), and they're likely willing to tell *their* friends and acquaintances about you (who will then tell others, and on and on). If you're new to a community or to business, you can participate in a business referral organization; find a group on `meetup.com`. (See the following section on referrals for more information.) And whether you're new or well established, your chamber of commerce is a great way to network with other local businesspeople. Most chapters sponsor a variety of business mixers, networking lunches, and other events specifically geared to support your networking efforts.
- **Volunteering:** Why not give something back to your community by volunteering your time? Whether you help at a local school, crisis center, animal shelter, or other community-based organization, you can be sure to meet a variety of people who may one day become your clients and customers. Chances are members of the board of directors and some volunteers are influential people who, if they like you and what you do, can give you business or refer business to you (see the following section for more on referrals).

- **Offering sponsorships:** Sponsoring a kids' baseball team, local charity, parade, or other special event can be another good way to generate word-of-mouth promotional opportunities. Be careful, though, that you're not just one sponsor lost in a flood of others — if you are, your message will be ineffective. It's far better to choose your opportunities so that your business is featured and particularly noticeable to your target audience.
- **Using business cards and letterheads:** These basic pieces of stationery are the mainstays of most businesses' promotional efforts. Your letterhead and business cards can convey a lot of information to your prospective clients and customers and get people talking about your business. Invest a few dollars in a professional logo design, and you'll make a great first impression on your prospects while conveying the right kind of message to your current customers and clients.

Word of mouth costs your business little, but the payoff can be great. Look for opportunities to generate a buzz about your business wherever and whenever you can. If people aren't talking about your business, you can be sure they won't be buying from it, either!

Acquiring referrals

Getting *referrals* — when people you know direct clients and acquaintances to your business — is the number-one way that many home-based businesses obtain new business. Although current clients are your bread and butter, not to mention the best possible sources for vital repeat business, new clients provide opportunities to grow your business while covering for financial shortfalls if current customers decide to shop elsewhere — or not shop at all.

Referrals are extremely powerful because when referred customers come to you, they've already been presold on your business and your products or services. You've already got a piece of their goodwill — which is an extremely valuable commodity to have in your business dealings. Here are some other advantages:

- **Referrals are less expensive than many other kinds of marketing.** No costly Yellow Pages ads to run, no billboards to erect, and no extravagant mail-order campaign to launch. Referrals cost little or no money to obtain. And maintaining a favorable relationship with the people who give you referrals means simply doing good work for them and letting them know from time to time that you appreciate their business (perhaps with a discount on your products or services, a small gift, or some other token of your appreciation).

- **Referred customers trust you.** When people turn to their trusted friends and business acquaintances for advice on whom to hire for a particular job or to provide a particular product, they automatically tend to believe the recommendations they hear. As the saying goes, *you have only one chance to make a first impression.* When someone recommends you, you've already made a positive first impression with your client-to-be.
- **Referred customers are ready to buy from you.** When people ask their friends and business acquaintances for referrals, they're ready to buy. People wouldn't ask if they weren't. And because people trust the opinion of those they ask, most people go no further in their search for sources than the person or business recommended to them.

Identifying potential referrals

So where do you find referrals? Here are the most common places:

- **Family and friends:** If you don't yet have current clients, family and friends are a great place to start for getting referrals. Make sure that everyone you personally know is familiar with your new venture — what it is and what you do — and knows that you're looking for customers to help get it off the ground. Most will be more than happy to help.
- **Current clients:** If you're doing good work for your current clients (and you are, aren't you?), they will refer friends and business acquaintances to you when asked for recommendations. Just make sure you don't let your work with your current clients suffer as you take on new work — you need to walk a very fine balance in your business between delivering on your current work and developing new work.

  To help ensure that your clients will want to share you with others (don't laugh; some may want to keep you all to themselves), be sure to meaningfully thank them for the referrals they make and consider providing additional incentives for making them. Examples of incentives depend on the kind of business you have but can include half off their next order or a free automobile detail.
- **Business associates:** Vendors and other nonclient business associates can be another rich source of referrals. If you have a good reputation in your field, and if they like you, they'll gladly tell their business associates about you. Of course, they'll be equally happy if you send some business their way, too.
- **Other home-based businesses:** Many home-based businesses are one-person operations and, as such, can have a hard time dealing with the inevitable business peaks and valleys. Sometimes work is plentiful, sometimes not. In those times when another home-based business is overwhelmed, a good option is to farm the extra work out to a trusted and proven company — yours. Why not become the company of choice for other home-based businesses in your industry?

- **Web-based referral services:** Some businesses can benefit from Web-based referral services. Many of these services are run by professional or trade associations. Others are independent, such as Yelp (www.yelp.com) and TripAdvisor (www.tripadvisor.com).

Getting referrals for your business

Okay, now that you know where to find your referrals, exactly how are you supposed to get them? Unless you find a genie in a lamp on the beach, the best way is simply to ask. When you do good work for a client, thank her for choosing you, and let her know that referrals are welcome and appreciated. The following is a list of five other great ways to get referrals:

- **Do great work.** By far the best way to get great referrals is to do great work. People are proud of themselves when they find businesses that provide them with above-average services and products, and they want to tell others of their good fortune (and their good business sense). Do great work, and your clients and customers will be the best marketing tools you could ask for.
- **Build a mailing list.** A mailing list of all your referrals can be a powerful tool in your promotional efforts. Because they're already presold on you and your business, your referrals will generally welcome hearing from you on an ongoing basis. A variety of great Internet e-mail-based services allow you to send periodic newsletters to your referrals for a nominal fee (or perhaps even for free if you're a small user). Some of the most popular services include iContact (www.icontact.com), Campaign Monitor (www.campaignmonitor.com), Constant Contact (www.constantcontact.com), and MailChimp (www.mailchimp.com). With just one click, your message is sent to your entire mailing list — whether it consists of one person or a thousand — in a matter of seconds. Your clients can opt into and out of your mailing list easily and with the barest minimum of muss or fuss. You can also track a variety of statistics if you like, such as actual click-throughs, messages sent, forwarded, bounced, and delivered, and unsubscribed e-mails.
- **Keep your mailing list informed.** Many home-based business owners have discovered the value of keeping their referrals up-to-date with the latest news about their products and services. Not only do past and present clients enjoy reading such stories, but they also really enjoy reading about themselves. Make a point of playing up customer success stories as much as possible.
- **Always send a thank-you note.** People appreciate it when you take the time to thank them for sending you referrals. Whenever a new customer is referred to you, make a point of immediately sending a handwritten thank-you note to the referrer. It's far better to take the time to personalize your thank-you note than to just dash off a quick e-mail. You can also use a service like SendOutCards (sendoutcards.com) or Enthusem

(www.enthusem.com). Depending on the nature of your business, you can also send a small gift or a certificate good for a discount on your client's next purchase.

- **Make referrals yourself.** As your business grows, you'll soon find that people come to you seeking referrals. Pick out several high-quality and trusted companies to use for referrals, and be sure to let their owners know when you have sent a client their way. Not only will your clients be thankful for the referral, but the companies to which you make referrals will also be more likely to make referrals to you. And don't forget to post positive reviews on social networking business review sites, such as Yelp (www.yelp.com) and TripAdvisor (www.tripadvisor.com). Peter posted a review of his CPA last year on Yelp, and the CPA has since been contacted by many prospective clients who were impressed enough with the review to call.

Making use of public relations

In general, *public relations* (PR) means the release of information to the general public to favorably influence its opinion about you, your business, or your products and services. Because of the nature of PR — and the potential for information to be broadcast over a wide area through print or electronic media — its successful execution can lead to your message being communicated to an amazing number of people. If you handle your own public relations, the cost is minimal. If you farm it out to a consultant or PR firm, expect to pay $50 to $100 per hour or more.

Here are some of the most common — and effective — forms of PR:

- **Publicity (newspapers, magazines, Internet, and other media):** Have you ever seen a newspaper article about some hot new local business or a special-interest TV news story about the latest-and-greatest home-based business opportunity? It's no accident that that particular piece of news made it to your eyes and ears — the business being highlighted likely spent money to make sure it showed up on the media radar screen. The media thrive on interesting stories, especially human-interest ones with uplifting messages. By creating an interesting and positive story around your business — and getting it in front of the media — you can generate the kind of publicity you seek, drawing potential clients and customers in the process.
- **News releases:** *News releases* are brief summaries of company news that are specifically targeted at the media. The hope is that newspapers, magazines, radio, television, and other media outlets will find the news release newsworthy and give it exposure. Chances are, if the news is interesting, they will. The good news is that if the media pick up on your

news release and publicize it, you'll get wide distribution for free. To have the best chance of gaining the kind of reaction you seek from the media, be sure your news release is tailored to the particular interests of the media outlet you seek. A pitch to *Oprah,* for example, is going to be quite different from a pitch to an Internet radio show, which will be different again from a pitch written to your small, hometown weekly newspaper.

- **Blog entries:** You can submit information about your business to other people's blogs that relate to your market. To build and keep traffic, blog sites need to update their content daily; therefore, they welcome content that others write.
- **Letters to the editor:** Anyone can write a letter to the editor about most any topic. Doing so is easy and offers a unique way to get your message in front of thousands of readers at a price that's hard to beat: the price of a first-class stamp (or less, if you write via e-mail). If, for example, you own a home-based business that specializes in home security systems (alarms, deadbolt locks, and so on), you can comment on a recent article about a rise in crime rates while throwing in a plug for the products and services that your company happens to sell.
- **Speeches:** Have you ever thought about making a speech to a local service club — say, a Rotary or Lions Club — or to local business organizations? All kinds of business associations, clubs, and other organizations exist in every city, and they tend to have lots of meetings. Guess what every organization needs for every meeting? A speaker. Whether you speak to your local chamber of commerce, the Society for Human Resources Professionals, or a local software *special interest group* (SIG), you have a great opportunity to promote yourself and your company by sharing your expertise with others. And you just may get a free lunch or dinner out of it, too (but beware: they don't call it the rubber-chicken circuit for nothing).
- **Seminars:** Seminars are a way to generate new customers and clients — and make a few bucks in the process. Home-based financial planners, for example, often use seminars to generate business. Here's how they work: You send out announcements for a free seminar, usually held at a nice local hotel, to prospective customers and possible referral sources. Rent out a meeting room at the hotel (much better than trying to jam 65 people into your living room), and arrange for the seminar to be catered with a light meal and refreshments. During the course of the seminar, you provide attendees a lot of usable information and pass out brochures, pamphlets, and other promotional material — all emblazoned with your company's name and contact information. After the seminar, guess who the attendees' first choice is whenever they have questions about the subject matter of the seminar or need help setting up their own personal financial plan?

Collaborating without getting lost

Q: We're a new small business. We offer public relations, marketing, and fundraising. A local advertising agency has outsourced several small jobs to us. Now the owner wants to include our names on his marketing materials but doesn't want to use our company name. Is this standard business practice? It seems like he's using our services to market his business.

A: Business-to-business collaboration is *one of the major trends* increasingly common among small businesses today. In researching our eBook *On Your Own But Not Alone,* we found that 65 percent of the business owners we interviewed — all of whom had been in business for more than five years — were teaming up in some way with other small businesses, and most wanted to do even more in the future. One message was clear, though: In creating such collaborations, there's no standard business practice unless it's to say, "It's all negotiable."

We found ten types of strategic alliances that range from networking to virtual organizations. Many types of collaborations, such as joint ventures and mutual referral agreements, involve each company promoting its own identity. In others, like satellite subcontracting and interdependent alliances, the company that gets the business usually is the one whose company name is used on a particular contract. Here are the types of alliances we found:

- Networking
- Mutual referrals
- Cross-promoting
- Interdependent alliances
- Joint ventures
- Satellite subcontracting
- Consortiums
- Family/spouse collaboration
- Partnerships
- Virtual organizations

Kurt Zell, for example, has a production company through which he subcontracts work to independent camera and sound professionals. He gets the business and brings in independent professionals who work as part of his organization. They're paid by Zell's company, not by the client. In relationships like this, it would be highly unethical for a subcontractor to market his own business to clients brought in through the contractor.

In your situation, the ad exec evidently believes that including your names and expertise on his marketing materials will help him get more business. For you, this arrangement could mean an inflow of new business with no marketing costs. But you must determine whether you see a downside to such an arrangement. If so, strive to negotiate a more desirable arrangement.

Among your options would be to suggest that you contribute to the cost of producing his business cards and marketing materials in return for including your company name. Then you can agree to pay a referral fee for any business that comes directly to you from these materials or simply agree to bring the agency in on any business project arising from these materials. Alternatively, you can include his services on your promotional materials as a way of helping you attract larger projects that include advertising

One of the great things about public relations is that if you have a bit of time to spend, you can generate your own PR materials and make your own contacts. And the more PR work you do, the better you'll get at it. Not only will you become more confident in your abilities and savvy in how the system works, but you'll also make contacts in the media and in your community that you can keep coming back to.

Taking advantage of direct marketing

Direct marketing means making direct contact with potential clients, most often by mailing or e-mailing them promotional messages. However you do it, the point is to get your message squarely in front of a decision-maker in a way that will capture his interest in just a few short seconds. Any longer and your prospect will likely throw your message in the trash — at no small expense to you and your business. Here are just a few ways to direct market:

- **Direct mail:** Although direct mail — or, ahem, junk mail — can be a major headache for many who receive it, when it's targeted precisely to potential customers and clients, it can be a cost-effective way of getting your message in front of the people most likely to buy your products and services. You can target your prospects very precisely by renting mailing lists of people within specific demographic groups. Do you want to reach human resources managers only? No problem. People who live within a particular zip code? Easy. People who recently bought a house? Piece of cake. For a fairly reasonable fee, you can buy hundreds or even thousands of up-to-date mailing labels for exactly the kind of people you want to reach with your message. Regardless of how much people complain about receiving direct-mail solicitations, enough of them usually respond to make them worthwhile. For more information on direct-mail marketing, check out the Direct Mail Association Web site (`www.the-dma.org`).
- **Circulars and flyers:** With a computer and a printer or photocopier, you can create all the circulars and flyers you could ever want, make thousands of copies, and blanket your clients-to-be with them. Drop them in your direct-mail envelopes, or pass them around your neighborhood. With a little practice, you can create circulars and flyers in minutes, and the price is very easy on the budget. You probably won't get as good a response as you would from a direct-mail campaign, but it's certainly worth a try.
- **Giveaways and contests:** One of the tried-and-true methods of attracting the attention of potential clients is to give something away — the more attractive the prize, the more attention you'll get. And that's really the whole point of promoting your business: to attract your potential clients' attention long enough to show them the benefits of your products and services.

- **Incentives:** Businesses commonly use incentives to get prospective clients and customers to buy. Whether you offer two for the price of one or give a coupon for 10 percent off the next purchase, incentives are a standard tool in the marketing campaigns of many regular businesses, and they work just as well for home-based businesses.
- **Newsletters:** If you're ready to get a bit more sophisticated in your direct-marketing efforts, consider creating a newsletter. Businesses create newsletters to provide customers and clients with value-added tools and information while also serving as a platform for promoting the company's products and services. If you run a pet-sitting business out of your home, you can create a one- or two-page newsletter with the latest trends in pet care, along with plugs for your business. If you're a lawyer who specializes in employment law, you can keep your clients up-to-date on the latest developments in the field. Sending your newsletter by e-mail or fax lowers your costs and time investment.

  TIP: If you have neither the time nor inclination to create a quality newsletter yourself, consider hiring a home-based desktop publishing professional to do it for you.

You can spend as little or as much as you want on direct marketing, but the results you get will be directly proportional to the amount of money and effort you put into preparing your direct-marketing pieces and precisely selecting the individuals who receive your message. Investing some quality time and money now will pay off big-time later.

Investing in advertising

When many people think about marketing, they're thinking about advertising. Advertising your products and services can be an effective way to get the word out, but it can also be expensive (and, frankly, a waste of money for many home-based businesses). The key is to be sure that your advertisements are specifically targeted and that you advertise in places where your potential clients are most likely to read or hear your message. Consider advertising in the following places:

- **Yellow Pages ads:** For many businesses, running a Yellow Pages advertisement is essential. It can be expensive — in the thousands of dollars for an ad large enough to stand out — but effective. Can you imagine a successful plumbing, appliance repair, or tree-trimming business — home based or not — that doesn't rely heavily on the Yellow Pages?
- **Business directories:** Business directories are another good way to get the word out about your company, as long as your potential clients and customers are likely to see your listing. Most directories have traditionally been available in printed form, but an increasing number are now

found on the Internet. With just a few mouse clicks, your clients-to-be will be able to find out more about your company and discover what it has to offer them.

- **Web site or blog:** Creating a Web site or blog to market your business and its products and services is a must for most businesses today, small and large. The good news is that starting up and maintaining a Web site or blog is easier and less expensive than ever. (See the "Going tech with Web sites, blogs, and e-commerce" section later in this chapter and Chapter 13 for more information.)
- **Web site advertisements:** Although banner advertisements have long been the standard method for advertising businesses on the Web, a relatively new innovation is taking hold: targeted advertising on search engines such as Google (in Google's case, called AdWords) that is geared to specific keyword searches. If you're a home-based plumber, for example, you can have your business show up at the top of the list whenever someone does a keyword search for *faucet repair.* You don't pay unless the person doing the searching clicks your listing. Relative to print, radio, and TV ads (which are quite expensive), Web site advertisements are a bargain. Better yet is getting links to your site from as many other high-traffic Web sites as you can.
- **Your own radio or TV show:** Would you like to get your message out to thousands of people every week? Why not host your own radio or television show? If your business is interesting enough to generate public interest, you have a real shot at it.

Going tech with Web sites, blogs, and e-commerce

More businesses than ever are moving to establish a presence on the Internet, and being e-commerce-capable is rapidly becoming the standard worldwide. Despite challenges facing an organization that decides to market itself on the Web (getting your site noticed in a sea of millions is just one challenge), having a Web site or blog is still a great idea for many home-based businesses. If your company doesn't yet have its own site, chances are it soon will. The simple fact is that building and maintaining a Web site or blog is now considered to be essential to any organization's marketing plan — just as important as printing brochures; placing ads in targeted publications; networking with potential clients; and performing other, more traditional marketing activities.

At its heart, a company Web site or blog is nothing more than a glossy, full-color brochure — with a twist: The Web site is available to potential clients instantly, anywhere in the world, at any time, day or night. It can be interactive (as in the case of a blog, where you can post your thoughts anytime and then have visitors post their responses), and it allows you to respond to visitor queries, communicate with clients in real time through online chats and message forums, and provide customers a place to research your products — and buy them.

Today, any business can have a Web site or blog, including home-based businesses. Our advice is that if you believe your sales will benefit by establishing a Web presence for your business, make creating a Web site or blog a priority.

Growing a repair business

Q: Is my business doomed? I do carpentry and household repairs, and although I have some business, it's just not enough. I don't have any money left to do the kind of advertising I know I should do. I'm not much of a salesman. Is there hope for me?

A: Yes, there's hope. Many people don't have much sales and marketing experience before starting their first home business and can feel quite overwhelmed by the relentless chore of finding enough business. Surveys show that getting business remains the number-one concern of small and home-based business owners year after year.

Advertising is expensive because, to be effective, it must appear again and again in publications where your targeted customers are looking when they need your services. In a business like yours, if you can afford to, we advise getting an enhanced Yellow Pages listing and localized listings on Yahoo! Get Local and SuperPages. And (for free) you can list on craigslist for your city at `www.craigslist.org`. In addition, you can actively market yourself in several other low-cost ways, including the following:

- **Build a list of all the people who have regular interaction with potential customers who want and need services like yours right now — not "someday."** For example, real estate agents who have just sold new homes or who have clients trying to sell a home but needing to make improvements to get their price may fill the bill. Or how about home inspectors who have discovered problems in the homes they inspect? Contact these people by phone or in person, and let them know about you and your service. You aren't selling when you contact them; you're just getting acquainted and making sure they know how to reach you.
- **Put these people's names into a database, and send them something monthly.** Consider, for example, a tips newsletter, a postcard about a special offer, or a news clipping related to home improvement.
- **Offer mini-workshops or seminars at hardware stores on do-it-yourself home improvements.** You may be surprised by how many people realize they need help after hearing about what they "can" do themselves — especially if your mini-workshops or seminars are free.
- **Arrange to leave a specially produced booklet or newsletter at hardware stores.** If you're not already familiar with the software necessary to produce a professional-looking booklet or newsletter, consider hiring a desktop-publishing professional to do it for you.

Is creating a Web site a good idea?

Q: I'm a photographer and sell most of my work through art fairs. Recently, more and more people are asking me if I have a Web site. I don't, but I'm starting to wonder if I should. What would the advantages really be, and would they be worth both the time and the money?

A: Having a Web site for any business is fairly common today. We interviewed hundreds of home-based businesses for *The Best Home Businesses for People 50+* and found that the majority of them have Web sites, which is about double the percentage we found when we interviewed people for a book that came out in 2000. But there are some holdouts.

You won't be surprised to find out we think having a Web site is worth it. On the up side, we found many people, from interim executives to former brick-and-mortar shop owners, who get their business or do their business from the Web.

Because photographs are visual, selling yourself and your work via a Web site is a natural. You can sell your images on your own Web site. However, we believe you should put up a Web site only when you're able and willing to keep it up. A Web address that yields a "Cannot find" message or is obviously out-of-date works against you, particularly if you're using your site to attract photography clients.

So if you're not ready for your own site, you can sell your images on such sites as Photographers' Portfolios at `www.vsii.com/portfolio/homeport.html` and Portfolios Online at `www.portfolios.com`.

We suggest visiting the sites of other photographers and talking with them about their experiences. For example, nature photographer Ernest Hori has a site at `www.horizenfoto.com`; portrait photographer Mary Ann Halpin has one at `www.maryannhalpin.com`; and Joseph Sohm shows his work at `visionsofamerica.com`.

Even if your business is a local, high-touch one, a Web site or blog is important because

- **It increasingly serves in lieu of a printed or mailed brochure — one that can be updated immediately.** A Web site or blog is a much faster and generally more convenient way for your potential customers to get information about your products and services. Instead of waiting to receive a brochure in the mail, they can type in your Web site address and obtain the information they're looking for in seconds.
- **With a clear majority of homes and businesses having Internet access, increasingly people are going online to check out businesses they've heard about or been referred to.** To not be there when they click is to ensure losing business. For this reason, it's a good idea to use your business name as your Web site address. Only a little more than 10 percent of all Web sites are found in search engines, so you want to make finding your business on the Web as easy and intuitive as possible.

- **The Web is becoming the new Yellow Pages.** Getting listed in search engines and exchanging links with sites that people are likely to turn to when looking for your kind of business is good business for you.

But what if you know nothing about creating a Web site or blog? How do you go about making one happen? Will you have to spend thousands of dollars to get your Web site up and running, or do you have more affordable options? We address these and other questions in detail in Chapter 13.

Developing a Marketing Plan — Now!

Whenever you want to achieve a measurable goal within a specific period of time, you greatly enhance your chances of doing so by having a plan. Plans make your goals real: They organize and prioritize your actions, and they tell you how close you are to achieving your goals.

A *marketing plan* summarizes all your marketing goals and strategies, along with the actual methods you can use to achieve them, and states milestones and deadlines for achieving your goals. It's not the same as a business plan, which takes a much broader look at your business goals and plans, including marketing. In essence, a marketing plan answers the following questions:

- Who are your target customers and clients?
- What are your unique product attributes and advantages in the marketplace?
- Where will you focus your marketing efforts?
- When will you implement each step in your marketing plan?
- How much revenue do you expect your marketing plan to generate, and how much will it cost you to generate that level of sales?

If you've read through some of the earlier sections of this chapter, you're probably already thinking of lots of ways to start marketing your products and services. You may be ready to start up a Web site, seek referrals, or create an e-mail newsletter for your current customers and clients.

REMEMBER

Your marketing plan belongs to you, and you can make it as simple or as complex as you want. If you're just starting, a one-page or even a one-paragraph plan may be just right. As your company gets bigger, you may see benefits in expanding your plan to meet its growing needs.

The following sections review the five key parts of a good marketing plan.

Part 1: Overview

Also known as an *executive summary,* the *marketing plan overview* provides a glimpse of your overall plan without bogging the reader down in the details that are presented later in the document. Upon reading the overview, a reader can get a pretty good idea about your overall marketing strategy, market focus, product focus, and the tactics and programs you plan to put into effect. *Projected revenues* — the estimated amount of money you intend to bring into the business during the period of the plan, as well as the budget required to achieve that level of sales — are also important parts of the marketing plan overview.

Part 2: Marketing objectives

Marketing goals and objectives define the targets that you hope to achieve in your marketing efforts. Your goals may be modest (to increase sales 10 percent a year for the next three years, for example) or quite ambitious (to be the company of choice whenever anyone in the nation needs a dog groomed).

This section of the marketing plan should, at a minimum, include

- An overall objective for your marketing efforts (for example, to become the preferred source of Internet solutions for doctors and dentists)
- Several specific marketing objectives, such as units sold, *market share* (the percentage of the overall market that your company commands), or distribution channels (planning that 25 percent of your sales will be through Target stores, for example)
- Basic financial objectives, such as total sales and profit for the year

Part 3: Situation analysis

This part of the marketing plan reveals what's going on in the marketplace: who your competition is, which products are similar to yours, what their relative success is, what the market trends are, and so on. The idea is to develop a good understanding of your customer base, its needs and wants, and your strengths and weaknesses relative to the competition. Be sure to include the following:

- **A summary of the *demographics* (the characteristics of a population, such as age, gender, income, and so on) and economic, technological, and social trends that impact your customers:** You can get this information through the Internet or the reference section of your public library.

- **A list of your key competitors, including strengths, weaknesses, products and services, market share, and other key information:** See Chapter 7 for how best to collect this kind of information.
- **A brief discussion of your target customer, as well as his or her wants and needs:** You should know your customer as well as you know the back of your hand — perhaps even better.
- **A summary of your key products and services:** This summary needs to include a discussion of their advantages and disadvantages versus the competition.
- **A discussion of your current distribution channels (if any):** This discussion needs to address how they help or hinder the product marketing process.

Part 4: Marketing strategies

For every key marketing objective listed in your plan (see the "Part 2: Marketing objectives" section), you should have one or more marketing strategies for achieving it. Include a minimum of the following:

- **Specific features of your products and services that you can use to help you market them, such as convenience, speed, ease of use, and so on:** Consider why people will buy your products and services instead of someone else's.
- **A pricing strategy for your products and services:** To find out more about the fine art of product pricing, check out Chapter 7.
- **Specific strategies to promote your products:** For ideas on promoting your products, see the "Marketing: Taking Different Roads to Meet Your Goals" section.
- **Specific strategies for getting your products and services into the hands of your customers and clients:** These strategies include using e-commerce and developing relationships with distributors, for example.

Part 5: Financials

This part of the marketing plan takes all the words in the previous sections and turns them into numbers — specifically, dollars and cents. An annual marketing plan gives financial information for an entire year and may be broken down into months or quarters. Be sure to include the following:

- **Detailed projections of anticipated revenues and percentage growth (or decline) — by product or service — from the previous period:** For example, you may anticipate revenues of $55,000 for the year, reflecting 10-percent growth from the previous year.
- **Detailed projections of expenses required to obtain the projected revenues:** For example, you need to account for expenses such as attending industry conferences, including roundtrip airfares, hotels, taxis, and the cost of meals.

TIP

When putting your marketing plan into action, consider using Paul and Sarah's 5/5/5 approach to marketing. The *5/5/5 approach* involves using five different avenues for reaching prospects and initiating and following through on five different activities every day, week, or month, depending on how much business you need (daily, if you have little or no business yet; weekly, if you have some but need more; monthly, if you have ample business and want to be sure you sustain it). This approach is the best way we've found to be sure you're doing the level of marketing activity you need to succeed. You can get further details in their book *Getting Business to Come to You.*

ASK PAUL & SARAH

Putting an idea into action

Q: I've drawn up a plethora of sketches of blue jeans, and now I'm satisfied with one I think the public would rush to purchase. How do I proceed with manufacturing and finding a buyer?

A: Some business experts may view the idea of a solo novice designer like yourself going head-to-head in a highly competitive field of giants like Levi's and Lee to be a pipe dream. But we've seen too many people defy the odds to discourage you from proceeding if you're sufficiently passionate, committed, and determined. The novice designers we've seen succeed have done so in two ways: by carving out a highly specific niche, such as designing specialized clothing for yoga devotees, orthodox Jewish professional women, or people with physical disabilities; or, for a mainstream item like jeans, by starting small and building up an avid following for a unique design that makes their line desirable to sales reps and retail stores.

So before leaping into mass production here or abroad, we suggest offering your jeans directly to what you hope will be a mad rush of avid buyers by making (or hiring someone to make) several dozen pairs and selling them yourself. You can do this at swap meets or sidewalk booths (as Ash Hudson did with his wildly popular Conart T-shirts) or by placing them in a few select boutiques (as Anna and Sarah Levinson did with their brightly colored Ripe Cosmetic nail polishes). After your jeans begin selling rapidly and attracting growing numbers of customers, you can arrange for mass production and contact reps or buyers — if they haven't sought you out already.

You can contact reps through the Manufacturers' Agents National Association (MANA) at One Spectrum Pointe, Suite 150, Lake Forest, CA 92630; phone 877-626-2776; Web site `www.manaonline.org`. Another source of assistance for creating and distributing your product is a site called Launch Your Line (`www.launchyourline.com`).

Chapter 5

Creating a Sustainable Income in Challenging Times

In This Chapter

- Picking out businesses that succeed during challenging times
- Developing a business that can make it through the good times and the bad
- Taking a look at businesses that work well during improving times

Starting a new home-based business doesn't come with any guarantees that it will succeed. No matter how many hours you put into it, or how much money you throw at it, if you don't have the right business idea at the right time for the right customers at the right price, it may not become a sustainable source of income for you over the long run — it's that simple.

REMEMBER

The trick is to come up with a business idea that matches your passion with the realities of the marketplace.

In this chapter, with both past and recent history in mind, we identify home businesses you can start and do well with during an economic downturn, as well as those that do better in economic good times when people are earning enough money to buy creative and everyday products and services from others instead of doing without or making or doing them for themselves. We also take a look at a few businesses that can survive both good and bad economies.

The point is no matter what the economic environment may be, you can find plenty of home-based business opportunities out there that match your passion with an income that can sustain you and your family for as long as you like.

Recognizing that People Behave Differently in Bad Times

What people will pay for and how much they'll pay for it varies according to both their own personal economic situations and the state of the economy as a whole. For example, in bad times, three out of four people buy more basic goods and services but less of everything else. Sales of premium-quality items and services like HBO and Showtime movie channels go down with the economy, as do everyday expenditures on haircuts and shots for the family dog. The numbers of coupons used and everyday value items bought, however, go up.

Still you may ask, "Is an economic downturn really the time to start a home business?" The answer may surprise you because it's "yes." First, consider past experience. The Great Depression of the 1930s gave birth to Hewlett-Packard, Polaroid, Revlon, and Texas Instruments, all of which have survived more than one economic downturn since. The downturn of the 1980s gave rise to Microsoft, Genentech, The Gap, and The Limited. In fact, more than half of the Fortune 500 companies started in downturns. What about a downturn makes the creation of new and successful companies possible? First, such company startups have to consciously make cost-effective decisions and be innovative in their products and processes. Second, many of their competitors may have disappeared. Third, you can acquire technology at commodity prices during economic downturns, which lowers the overall cost of getting a business underway.

REMEMBER

People today are having to relearn a life lesson that their grandparents and great-grandparents learned long ago — that they can't always count on a growing economy. Sure, everyone hopes the economy will do well, but with competition from countries like China (already number one in auto sales), India, Brazil, and Russia, the future will most definitely be different from the past. Whether the economy goes up as fast as it went down or continues to slide, you need to start a business that can ride the waves of the economy. For a few examples of great businesses that last, make sure to check out Chapter 17.

Identifying Businesses That Work Well in a Down Economy

The economy naturally cycles between boom and bust — it always has and it always will. Regardless of what kind of economy you find yourself in when you read this book, however, you can find plenty of business opportunities that work in any kind of market. In this section, we focus on the opportunities that are particularly effective during down economic times.

Assuring affordable energy

Everyone needs affordable energy — it's a basic human necessity to survive today. Here are some businesses that serve this basic human need and, thus, are successful even in times of economic turmoil:

- **Alternative energy installation and consultation:** In the second edition of this book, we wrote about "living off the grid" as a trend that would feed the demand for businesses installing devices that captured solar, wind, hydro, and geothermal energy. Now with continually increasing energy costs, improvements in these technologies, and more government subsidies that lower their costs, the demand for alternative energy is growing among households and businesses in cities and towns across the country, as well as among farmers eager for methane digesters. Find out more about these alternative energies at Home Power Magazine's Web site, `www.homepower.com`.
- **Energy and building performance auditing and rating:** After the shock wears off when a home or building owner gets a jarring fuel bill — whether it's for electricity, propane, or natural gas — he seeks ways to cut his costs, which is one reason why the demand for energy auditors continues to grow. New construction is another reason. Building codes everywhere require — or soon will — energy efficiency. Both developers and building owners win from using the services of an energy auditor because energy efficiency can increase a building's value by an estimated 20 dollars for each dollar in annual energy savings. If you're interested in energy auditing, check out Green and Save (`www.greenandsave.com`), a company that offers both training to become an energy auditor and affiliation with its force of energy auditors, who are scattered throughout the country.
- **Chimney sweeping:** In addition to the fact that many people choose to use their chimneys to help heat their homes during economic downturns, the increasing number of wood pellet stoves adds to the chimney sweep market. Fire safety also prompts a continuing need for chimney sweeps because creosote builds up in chimneys and stovepipes and because birds and raccoons like to make homes in chimneys, resulting in 25,000 fires a year. Check out this business at the National Chimney Sweep Guild's Web site at `www.ncsg.org`.
- **Smart meter installation:** *Smart meters* are electricity meters that help reduce energy use; they're becoming more and more popular with homeowners and business owners alike as both groups of people try to cut fuel costs and utilities. Some utilities use independent contractors to install smart meters, which is where you come in. Find out more about smart meter installation and its increasing prevalence across the globe at `www.smartmeters.com`.

Helping others reduce and reuse

Tough times bring a variety of diverse business opportunities out of the woodwork, especially businesses that focus on helping people become more resourceful and environmentally friendly in their lifestyles and homes. Some of the best and fastest growing of these opportunities include the following:

- **Environmental remediation or cleanup:** Even in a down economy, problems like mold, lead paint, asbestos, moisture, radon, contaminated soil, and buried hazardous waste demand attention. Home and building owners may discover such problems themselves, or the issues may turn up in the environmental assessments that most commercial real estate transactions involve. For this reason, the need for environmental remediation and cleanup businesses is always present. People in the environmental remediation business assess the nature and extent of certain environmental risks on homes and other buildings and then get their hands dirty cleaning up the less-than-hospitable environments. A number of organizations offer training and certification in environmental remediation, including the Environmental Information Association (`www.eia-usa.org`). Whichever organization you choose for training, make sure it's approved by the Environmental Protection Agency.
- **Green services:** Businesses providing green services are already hatching like rabbits around the world, and the consequences of climate change and energy costs will continue to spur their growth even more. When we did the first edition of this book, we didn't conceive of many of the newer ones that have emerged since then, including bike-sharing programs, businesses that provide bicycle commuters a place to store their bikes, bike-repair services, organizations that provide places to change from riding clothes into business clothes, and companies that offer central order pick-up zones where shoppers can collect packages delivered from multiple stores in one place. Other green services we've featured before have become more commonplace. For example, more and more people are choosing green burials and need to have pressboard or cardboard coffins made.
- **Remodeling:** The most active market for people in construction in a down economy is remodeling because when economics require people to stay where they are, instead of moving up, they remodel. A growing remodeling specialty is serving the ballooning numbers of seniors who choose independent living over institutional care but find that their homes need various alterations. For example, they may need a first-floor master bedroom or newly adapted bathrooms and kitchen. Another growing market is green remodeling to make homes and businesses more energy efficient, environmentally friendly, and sustainable. Key remodeling resources include the National Association of the Remodeling Industry (`www.nari.org`) and the National Association of Home Builders Remodelers Council (`www.nahb.com`).

Fulfilling day-to-day business needs

The majority of businesses need support services of all kinds every day — regardless of whether the economy is good or bad. Hence, businesses that fulfill these day-to-day support needs for other businesses can expect not only to work well in bad economic times but also to thrive in good ones. Here are some of the most lasting business-support opportunities:

- **Bookkeeping:** Bookkeeping has been around since ancient Babylonia. When times are tough, businesses frequently outsource this service to cut back on staffing costs, which increases the demand for independent bookkeepers. In addition to relieving business owners of the daily duties of handling the books, bookkeepers can also reach into the realm of forensic work by helping identify errors that creep into accounting software. Some bookkeepers have other specializations, too, such as payroll or accounts receivable. Still others serve only specific types of clients like chiropractors, retail shops, or restaurants. Clearly, the opportunities in this field are many. Check out the American Institute of Professional Bookkeepers for more information about becoming a professional bookkeeper (`www.aipb.com`).
- **Business support services:** The business support services field encompasses all forms of administrative work needed by small companies and professionals — anyone in fact, who's without the time, desire, or resources to do her own administrative work. Support services include preparing spreadsheets or databases; word processing; editing, formatting, and proofreading documents; transcribing; drafting correspondence, proposals, and reports; and much more. Like with bookkeeping, businesses frequently outsource their support services to independent assistants during economic downturns. Some people who provide support services to other businesses call themselves "virtual assistants" because they can do much of their work electronically. Sites that bring together companies and individuals seeking to get discrete tasks done and people looking to do them are Amazon's Mechanical Turk (`www.mturk.com/mturk/welcome`) and Short Task (`shorttask.com`). The International Virtual Assistants Association has a mentor program and offers certification (`www.ivaa.org`).
- **Computer consulting:** Almost all businesses depend on technology, but most small business owners don't have the inclination or possess the skills to deal with the problems of installation, upgrades, compatibility, repairs, malware, spyware, viruses, worms, or the crisis that follows when the company Web site goes down. Thus, computer consultants keep busy even during down economic times. They may even get calls from business owners who are eligible for their manufacturer's technical support but need support faster than the manufacturer can provide. Resources for computer consultants include the Institute for Certification of Computing Professionals (`www.iccp.org`) and the Independent Computer Consultants Association (`www.icca.org`).

- **Tax preparation:** Nearly one out of every two adults uses a tax preparer or accountant to prepare his or her taxes, according to a recent nationwide survey. The inevitability of taxes and their ever-increasing complexity keep tax preparers busy during all types of economies. Most states don't require a license to become a tax preparer, but those people wanting to obtain credentials in this field can, with some self-study, become an enrolled agent by passing a federal exam. *Tax reviewers* are specialists in the tax preparation field — they help people resolve costly mistakes and problems with IRS collections. Check out `www.taxsites.com` for a list of tax preparation–related resources.
- **Web services:** The Web is an area that provides constant business opportunities, and it will continue to do so far into the future. It will change from Web 2.0 to 3.0 and inevitably result in tons of work for Web designers, specialty programmers, search engine optimizers, content writers, Web promotion specialists, and Webmasters. Everything you see and do on the Web required someone to design it and others to maintain it. The Web holds countless opportunities for people interested in starting their own businesses. For example, you can specialize in a type of work, such as creating tools to use on social networking sites, or you can serve a single industry or profession. O'Reilly Media offers a wide range of book titles, training, and conferences that introduce you to virtually every Web service topic you need (or want) to know about (`www.oreilly.com`).
- **Paralegal services:** These services provide practical services to attorneys and clients at lower fees. Independent paralegals draft wills, draft divorce papers, review legal documents, such as leases, and depending on state law, may do so with or without the supervision of an attorney. Some paralegals do contract work for law firms by working from home virtually. The demand for paralegals is projected to grow more than 20 percent over the next six years. Check out the American Association for Paralegal Education for more information (`www.aafpe.org`).

Meeting healthcare needs

The cost of healthcare in the United States is quickly approaching unsustainable levels, and, as a result, healthcare organizations are increasingly outsourcing work to less-expensive home-based businesses. At the same time, necessity and technology are giving rise to alternative ways to deliver standard healthcare — online doctors and telephone triage nurses, for example — which means new opportunities for a growing number of work-at-home professionals.

Despite the recent economic downturn, the prevalence of alternative or supplementary healthcare providers has grown. Examples of this alternative or supplementary medicine include acupuncture, biofeedback, Chinese medicine, chiropractic, homeopathy, hypnosis, naturopathy, and yoga. Although the appeal of alternative medicine has been to supplement conventional medicine in the past, these days an increasing number of patients appear to be seeking it to save money. Lucky for you, you can run most of these alternative practices out of your home office or deliver them directly to the homes of patients. Check out www.healthlinks.net for more information.

The bottom line is that patients in poor economies seek less-expensive healthcare alternatives, such as the following:

- **Disease management:** If helping patients with chronic conditions while largely or wholly working at home appeals to you, consider the growing field of disease management. Disease management programs are growing because, first of all, they save money and, second of all, more people are suffering from conditions requiring supervision, such as asthma, congestive heart failure, diabetes, coronary artery disease, end-stage renal disease, high-risk pregnancies, depression, and chronic obstructive pulmonary disease.

  Disease managers phone patients on a scheduled — or at least regular — basis to discuss whether they're taking their medications, what they're eating, and how they feel overall. Sometimes patients use testing devices to convey data to their managers' computers; face-to-face education may also be involved. Disease managers specialize in one disease or condition and have experience in general healthcare, too. Disease managers may be independent operators who contract with insurance companies as patient agents, with assisted living operators, or with patients directly. Check out the Disease Management Association of America's Web site (www.dmaa.org) for more information.

- **Patient champion:** Although some hospitals have designated staff or volunteers who serve as patient advocates, *patient champions* are part of an emerging professional health field that fulfills this advocate role with independent practitioners. Patient champions receive compensation for their savvy tenaciousness, their ability to communicate with medical personnel with respectful firmness, and their lack of discomfort in being in hospitals and around sick people.

  Patient champions must have permission from their patients or their legal representatives to discuss the health or treatment of their patients in compliance with the Health Insurance Portability and Accountability Act of 1996. Patient champions who specialize in children must know about guardianship rules and child rights. One way you can gain experience in this field is to secure work as a *mystery shopper* for the more than 150 companies that measure and improve the levels of service of healthcare providers (go to www.mysteryshop.org for more info). Check out the Health Advocacy Toolbox at www.cthealthpolicy.org/toolbox for more information about this growing field.

Here are six more, quick-fire healthcare possibilities you can do from home. Covering them in great detail is beyond the scope of this book, so, for more information, refer to the Web sites we provide here:

- **Claims assistance professional:** Helps individuals collect their insurance claims (Alliance of Claims Assistance Professionals: www.claims.org)
- **Doula:** Offers birth coaching both before and after delivery (DONA International: www.dona.com)
- **Midwife:** Delivers babies (Midwives Alliance of North America: www.mana.org)
- **Lice remover:** Picks lice out of people's hair, primarily children (Lice Squad: www.licesquad.com)
- **Stress manager:** Helps people reduce stress in their daily lives (Project Nature Connect: www.ecopsych.com)
- **Telephone triage nurse:** Staffs telephones, taking calls from individuals experiencing health emergencies and evaluating and deciding whether to send the patient to an emergency room or advise a next-day appointment (American Academy of Ambulatory Care Nursing: www.aaacn.org)

Providing alternative-living services

People are increasingly adopting alternative lifestyles — perhaps even more so during the recent economic downturn. This increased interest in alternative living translates to a growing need for businesses to help people adopt their new lifestyles. Interestingly enough, you can provide many of these new services from home. Here are just a few of the promising alternative-living services home-based businesspeople are starting to provide:

- **Custom bicycle making:** The making of bicycles has gone beyond the high-end custom, super-light, carbon-fiber cycles that can cost more than $2,000 to practical cargo bikes, which are suitable for delivering freight, and ecobicycles, which provide electric-powered ways to make home and local deliveries. For example, Dave Ewoldt from Tucson builds bike trailers for transporting cargo in his side yard. He also teaches others the skills they need for light bike manufacturing (check out www.attractionretreat.org/TI/Trailers for more info). You can find ideas on designing your own practical bike carts at bikecart.pedalpeople.com. You can also take orders for custom-made bikes from a Web site like bikes.urbanoutfitters.com.
- **Hauling:** Today's hauling services aren't just beat-up trucks who come and take away the stuff you don't want. The new face of hauling consists of rickshaw vans and trike bikes that deliver small loads (usually less

than 600 pounds) to stores and restaurants. *Trike bikes* are three-wheeled vehicles with a platform or storage box over the rear wheels; they're sometimes battery-assisted. In replacing trucks, they conserve energy and space on crowded streets. As gasoline prices continue to rise, so will the use of this type of hauling. Even hauling away old appliances and furniture, garden trimmings, and construction debris has a spiffier look with blue and white enclosed trucks or bikes and uniformed personnel. You can get a franchise to be a hauler at `www.1800gotjunk.com`. But you don't need a franchise to do hauling; you can start a home-based hauling company from scratch. To add to your income as a hauler, you can sort through the junk you haul and sell anything valuable before taking the rest to the dump.

- **Home repair services:** Who doesn't need a handyperson close by? In today's economy, while real estate agents are twiddling their thumbs, handypeople who are knowledgeable, reliable, and trustworthy are booked up weeks ahead. As a handyperson, you can repair, install, or do whatever else your clients need done to their homes at affordable rates. Keep in mind that California state law limits the handyperson to doing only jobs worth up to $500, and other states limit the kind of tasks a handyperson can do. Even so, a home-based business in this field can be very successful and is ideal for people who can solve problems quickly. Check out `www.handyman-business.com` and `www.bejane.com` for more info.
- **Horseshoeing:** Like many people, we assumed that blacksmiths like the ones in Western movies went the way of horse and buggies long ago. But actually more horses are living in the United States now than in the 19th century, and most of them need shoeing. People in this specialized field of making horseshoes are known as *farriers*. Farriers need to understand the anatomy and physiology of horses' legs because they also care for injuries and diseases of horses' hooves. The physicality required of this trade can result in wear and tear on the human body, so it isn't something you can expect to do into your senior years. Check out the American Farrier's Association for more details (`www.americanfarriers.org`).
- **Inventing:** Recessions are a golden age for inventing. After all, the photocopier, electric shaver, and car radio all came into being during the 1930s. In today's economic recessions, inventors and their inventions have the added benefit of Web access. First, they can turn ideas into products by using crowdsourcing sites like The Cambrian House (`www.cambrianhouse.com`), Kluster (`www.kluster.com`), and The Crowdfund Company (`www.crowdfundcompany.com`). Inventors can use crowdsourcing to brainstorm, rank ideas, find funding, and solve problems by taking advantage of the ideas of many people. Then, to sell their products, they can use social networking sites to make contacts with corporations who may end up buying directly from the inventors.

As an inventor, however, you need to be cautious about companies that ask for an upfront fee to promote and market your invention but do not deliver what they promise. Before employing the services of any company, check out whether other inventors have had complaints with the company. The U.S. Patent and Trademark Office (`www.uspto.gov`) has a public forum for making complaints publicly available.

- **Massage and Yoga:** People haven't spent any less money on massages during the recent economic downturn, probably because in addition to making people feel better, evidence shows that massages lower tension and fatigue (two things most people have been feeling a lot of lately). In fact, many companies are now bringing the services of massage therapists and yoga instructors into the company because they provide a low-cost employee benefit that results in workers who are more alert and accurate. Many individuals also use massage and yoga as lower-cost alternatives to medical and pharmaceutical treatment for common chronic health problems, such as tension, fatigue, neck and shoulder pain, and stress. For more information, check out the American Massage Therapy Association (`www.amtamassage.org`), the Associated Bodywork and Massage Professionals (`www.abmp.com/home`), and The Yoga Site (`www.yogasite.com`).
- **Mobile services:** Mobile services save customers time and money on gasoline; plus, they're a way to gain an edge on location-based competitors. Examples of services now being taken to where the customer is include auto glass repair or replacement, auto body repair, dent removal, screen repair, bicycle repair, dog grooming, hair cutting and styling, knife sharpening, medical services, and notarizing. For an extreme example, someone has even created a mobile wedding chapel on the back of a fire truck. This chapel goes anywhere for $2 a mile and $200 for the preacher's services, who happens to also be the driver. And at least three German firms offer mobile bike repair. The shops are, of course, attached to bikes. Can you think of anything you can turn into a mobile service by using a van, a trailer, a car, a retrofitted vehicle, or even a bicycle? If you can, you may have just found your next home-based business!
- **Psychic services:** The more people are stressed by a shrinking economy, the more they turn to psychics, astrologers, palm readers, Tarot card shufflers, numerologists, and other paranormal specialists. Psychic services can generate fees of $80 to more than $300 an hour. Two types of people predominate this field — those who have strong subjective impressions of clients and are able to communicate them and people who are skilled at reading astrological charts and reporting what the charts reveal. Check out the American Federation of Astrologers, Inc., for more on this branch of the psychic field (`www.astrologers.com`).

- **Selling products on the Web:** When we can't find something we need at a local store, like many people, we turn to the Web where we invariably find whatever it is we're looking for. Shopping online easily develops into a habit. So whether you have an information product, such as eBooks, or items you've handcrafted, you can sell them on the Web via your own Web site, your eBay account, a storefront on Yahoo!, or an online mall or gallery like `www.etsy.com`. Craigslist (`www.craigslist.com`), a kind of online classifieds, gives you access to the world and, thereby, self-selected people who want what you have. As you start selling online, follow these three tips: (1) Carefully search the Web to find other sites that are selling what you want to sell to find out what they do well and what you can do to give yourself an edge. (2) Provide extraordinary and prompt customer service, even though doing so may mean having access to your store or auction account nearly 24/7. (3) Before investing in an e-commerce platform on your Web site, test your products on other marketplaces.
- **Sewing:** When the economy is down, people want to alter or repair their clothing rather than buy new stuff, so sewing is always a way to make money when times are tough. Sewing for money can take many forms. For instance, many people want to sew their own clothing, so you can teach sewing in classes or private sessions. People with special physical problems, such as spine curvature, mastectomies, severe arthritis, preemies, and wheelchair-bound people want and need clothing that's suited to their requirements, so you can make special clothing for special groups of people. Other markets for custom sewing and design include making clothes for special occasions like weddings and proms, party costumes, theatre costumes, custom uniforms, and clothing for members of religious groups with rules for what they can and cannot wear. The Home Sewing Association (`www.sewing.org`) lists sewing instructors and offers free lessons on how to sew.
- **Tabletop manufacturing:** If you would have bought an Altair or IMSI personal computer in the 1970s, you may be ready to embrace tabletop manufacturing. *Tabletop manufacturing* is basically three-dimensional printing. Using melted plastic, powder, gel, and — depending on the machine — other materials, tabletop machines can make auto parts, bone implants, sculptures, and more. Eventually, these machines may produce parts for Pontiacs, Oldsmobiles, and other orphan vehicles when the mandatory period that car companies have to supply parts expires. Tabletop machines for under $5,000 are available today, but they're limited to making small objects. Check out `fabathome.org` and `www.desktopfactory.com` for more information; once equipped, you can bid for work at `www.100kgarages.com`.

Selling affordable luxuries

Although the overall luxury-goods market is one of the first things to feel the pain in down economic times, affordable luxury goods and services become even more popular. After all, everyone likes to treat himself to something nice every once in a while. Consider some of these business opportunities tailor-made for home-based businesses:

- **Direct selling:** Direct-selling organizations grow during economic downturns. Although the Web — particularly social networking — can support direct sellers, three-quarters of all direct selling is done one-on-one in person or at party events (group selling) at people's homes. Such party events are a low-cost way for your customers to socialize and have a good time — with a chance to shop, of course. While the range of products sold covers the gamut — from air filters to wine — the largest categories of merchandise being sold are personal-care items like cosmetics, jewelry, skincare, clothing, weight-loss products, and vitamins. All these items are affordable luxuries. For most people, direct sales is a part-time business with low startup costs. In fact, be wary of companies charging more than a few hundred dollars to get started. Some sites to look at are www.dsa.org and www.mlmsurvivor.com. (Also check out Chapter 2 for a lot more information about direct-selling opportunities.)
- **Skin care:** Although people sacrifice spending on many items during economic downturns, they continue to spend money on anti-aging skin care products. Some companies even report increases in sales on skin care products, including those with luxury ingredients like crushed gemstones and nanoparticles of gold. If you're a licensed esthetician and wish to lower your overhead with a home-based salon, check whether your state and local zoning regulations permit you to do so (www.beautytech.com/st_boards.htm).
- **Travel services:** Economic downturns and high gas prices may restrain the urge to travel, but they don't eliminate it. To fill this ever-present urge, people replace vacations to faraway places with "staycations" or "nearcations." Destinations near major population centers attract vacationers and day-trippers. The types of travel businesses suitable to poor economic circumstances are original local tours like the Brooklyn Pizza tours (www.asliceofbrooklyn.com) and bed and breakfast inns (check out the Professional Association of Innkeepers International at www.paii.org for more info).

  Medical tourism is a growing specialty as people discover they can obtain expensive medical procedures at a fraction of what they cost in the United States by traveling to other countries (www.medicaltourismassociation.com). *Ecotourism* is another bright spot in the travel industry. The International Ecotourism Society (TIES) defines ecotourism as "responsible travel to natural areas that conserves the environment and improves the well-being of local people." TIES offers online courses that lead to certification in sustainable tourism management on its Web site (www.ecotourism.org). People have a huge appetite for travel even in challenging times, so the key is finding out how to make travel possible and affordable.

Creating a Business That Can Ride the Economic Waves

Throughout the first part of this chapter, we identify the home-based businesses we believe have the best potential to prosper in economic downturns. But one lesson we've learned from the past is that no one has a foolproof crystal ball. New opportunities from new technologies will continue to arise, some technologies that showed promise won't gain market acceptance, and established businesses will fade or require such retooling that they won't be recognized by the same name. That's the process, the opportunity, and the price of an economy in an era in which change is normal and in which some dreams disappear as new ones arise.

But even though you can't know exactly what the future holds, you can build a lasting business that will be able to ride the waves of the economy for years to come. In the sections that follow, we explore some of the approaches you can take to do so.

Choosing to serve nondiscretionary needs

The recession that began in September 2008 provided us with information about what people are willing to cut from their expenses and what they continue to spend their money on. An American Pulse survey by BIGresearch revealed that the top ten items people considered to be necessities in late 2008 were, in rank order:

- Internet service
- Basic cellphone service
- Basic satellite or cable TV service
- Clothing (if purchased at discount)
- Hair care
- Fast-food meals
- Casual sit-down meals

- Charitable contributions
- Vacations
- Fast casual dining

The more your home business serves something people regard as a necessity, the more you raise your chances of success in any economy. Consider that the top three items on this list wouldn't have been there in the last deep recession of the early 1980s — a lesson of how vital it is for businesses to adapt.

In line with what the survey found, spending on personal care, such as hair salons, barber shops, and skin care providers, actually rose 4.5 percent from April 2008 to April 2009. Spending on other personal services not identified as necessities — such as trips to spas, entertainment, dining in fine restaurants, and purchases for the home — decreased.

Cushioning yourself locally and virtually

Some home businesses are inherently local, meaning that your customers are located within your community or within driving distance of your community. For instance, no one has discovered a way to install a home theatre, provide midwife services, or do pest control via the Web, so those businesses have to be local. On the other hand, you can provide Web design services or business-support services for clients anywhere in the country or even the world. In addition to determining the kind of marketing you do, your choice of whether to build up your business locally or virtually determines from where your income comes. In the economy we believe is emerging, home businesses that can derive income from both within one's community and from elsewhere via the Web have more potential to be resilient.

Fortunately, the Web enables more and more businesses to serve both local and distant customers. You can expand many primarily locally focused businesses, such as sewing and tutoring, simply by providing services and selling information and products online.

Crowdsourcing locally and virtually

Crowdsourcing enables businesses to capitalize on a Web version of an old adage that has proven correct again and again when tested with research: There's wisdom in crowds. Crowdsourcing starts with putting up an announcement or making a call on a Web site, asking a large number of people to get involved in or respond to some task. Wikipedia (for information), YouTube (for videos), and Flickr (for photos) are all forms of crowdsourcing.

The advantage of crowdsourcing is that groups of people are better in predicting outcomes than most experts. For example, Wikipedia is comparable in accuracy to the *Encyclopedia Britannica,* and businesses both large and small use YouTube, one of the most popular sites on the Web, to communicate with the world. Crowdsourcing works when the group is diverse and the members don't influence one another and when, for no or little money, the members provide content or solve problems.

REMEMBER

Participating in crowdsourcing can benefit a home business far more than looking things up in a dictionary. For instance, you can get others' help in naming your business at `namethis.com/name_this/` (by participating as a member, you can also earn money) and get help making decisions at `www.hunch.com` and `www.quirky.com`.

Another form of crowdsourcing can lead to new business by enabling people with specific skills to bid on projects that customers put up on the Web. A few online marketplaces for creative services include `www.crowdspring.com`, `kluster.com`, and `99designs.com`. Travel agents can bid for clients at `www.zicasso.com` and `www.orbitz.com`.

TIP

For other recent examples of crowdsourcing, check out `en.wikipedia.org/wiki/Crowdsourcing`.

Telescoping your niche

Consider this rule of thumb: When times are good, specialize in a niche you cultivate; when times aren't so good and money is tight, telescope that niche. *Telescoping* is our term for extending or adding to the range of services you provide to existing customers without undermining your reputation for the business specialty you've developed. Telescoping your niche means offering to do work for your customers that they ordinarily would've had to do for themselves or would've had to turn to another specialist for. Because your customers are already working with you, why not have them turn to you for additional services you know you can provide? For example:

- If you're a tax preparer and notice a client is downsizing his bookkeeping staff, you may offer to do his bookkeeping as an outside service.
- If you're a real estate agent and your potential client is concerned about whether her home will sell, you can also offer to stage the home so it's presented in the way most attractive to buyers. Staging results in a quicker sale and a higher price, which makes your customer (and you) very happy.
- If you're a travel agent helping a bride and groom with travel arrangements for a destination wedding out of the country, you can offer to coordinate with the wedding organizer in the distant locale.

As you can see, telescoping enables you to expand what you offer in a down economy and then to narrow your services again when the economy improves.

Trading time and goods when currency is short

In addition to everyday bartering, which we discuss in Chapter 11, other forms of nonmonetary exchange can keep your business going when times are tough. These alternative means of exchange can play a valuable role for many businesses in both good times and bad — getting your business started when cash is short; obtaining goods and services your cash budget may not cover; and developing relationships in your community. The primary types of alternative exchange are

- **Time banks:** A *time bank* tracks the time its members spend doing something for other members. As one member provides a service for another member, he accumulates "time credits," which he can then "spend" on time for what he needs from other members.

  Unlike with bartering, in which everything exchanged is valued at market price, in a time bank, all time is valued equally. Each one hour of service provided equals an hour of credit one can use for another service. So, for example, a bookkeeper who charges $35 per hour can get advice from a lawyer who bills at $250 per hour. Their time is valued equally, which makes for a great deal for the bookkeeper and an improvement on what an attorney gets for doing pro bono work or having empty hours on the calendar. Another benefit is that because the values are equal in time bank exchanges, they aren't taxable.

  REMEMBER

  Time banking is occurring in communities worldwide. One may already be set up in your community. If you're interested in starting one, check out the following Web sites to find out more information:

  - `www.timebanks.org`: Offers a start-up kit and a lot of other helpful information about time banks
  - `www.besttimebank.org`: Provides information on how to get an IRS ruling to make a time bank nontaxable

- **Community currency:** Local currencies, also called *complementary currencies*, are another means of alternative exchange. As communities adopt them today, community currencies are gaining more and more media attention, but they go back many years. For example, the *Swiss Wir* was started during the Great Depression and is still going strong today.

Most U.S. community-currency programs were inspired by and based on the model of Ithaca HOURs in Ithaca, New York; Paul Glover started this currency in 1991. Find out more about it at `www.ithacahours.com`. Local currencies are one of the programs of the E.F. Schumacher Society, an organization devoted to building local economies (`www.schumachersociety.org/about.html`).

- **Local exchange trading system (LETS):** LETS is a type of local exchange system that eliminates coins, tokens, notes, or any other form of printed money usually required for exchange of local goods and services. Instead, members of LETS centrally track and record transactions, usually by using computer software available specifically for this purpose. For example, a massage therapist may earn credit by giving a massage to another LETS participant and then use that credit to acquire a service from a handyperson or any other participant. To find out more about LETS, check out `www.gmlets.u-net.com`.

Paul and Sarah describe more about these exchange systems in their eBook, *Charging What You're Worth.*

Saving money and keeping your overhead down

One of the best ways to build a sustainable business is to keep your costs (also known as your *overhead*) down. When's the last time you took a close look at your expenses with an eye to becoming lean and mean? We suggest you take a good look now, and here are some of the best places to start:

- **Phone expenses:**
  - Consider using voice over IP (VOIP) services, such as Skype, Net2Phone, Google Voice, and Vonage, rather than a land line, but realize that land line services may be more audible at times and that you lose VOIP service during power failures. So you may want to have one land line on hand.
  - If you have a land line, check to see whether you can obtain a Yellow Pages listing with only a residence line.
  - Make outgoing calls on a residence line even if you need a more expensive business line to have a Yellow Pages listing.
  - Compare telephone long-distance rates on sites like `www.abelltolls.com` to find the best deal for you.

- If you need to decrease your marketing budget, use less costly or no-cost ways of marketing yourself (marketing over the phone or the Web, for example), but don't decrease your overall effort. The most successful companies maintain or increase their marketing during economic downturns.

- **Auto expenses:**
  - Use sites like autos.msn.com/everyday/gasstationsbeta.aspx and gasbuddy.com that compare gas prices by zip code to get the best deal.
  - Fill up your gas tank when it's half empty because half-empty tanks contain less air. The presence of air in your gas tank causes evaporation, so the more air you have, the more gas you lose to evaporation.
  - Fill up your gas tank in the early morning when the gas is densest. Because fuel storage tanks are buried in the ground, as temperatures rise, the gas expands, and the gallon of gas you get in the morning costs less than the gallon you get in the afternoon.
  - When filling your tank, choose the slow mode by squeezing the gas nozzle. The slow mode minimizes the vapors you create when you pump — the more vapor you have, the less room you have for gasoline.
  - Don't buy gas when the gasoline truck is at the station filling the storage tanks. As the truck pumps the gas in, dirt that usually sits on the bottom of the storage tank is stirred up, and you'll likely suck some of it into your gas tank, which can make your vehicle run less efficiently and can damage fuel injectors.

- **Utility bills:**
  - Compare the costs of alternative ways to heat your home and office. Paul and Sarah find wood pellets a lot cheaper than propane, for example. You can compare your heating alternatives at the Department of Energy's Web site (www1.eere.energy.gov/calculators).
  - Apply e-coating film to your windows. This do-it-yourself project keeps the heat in during cold weather and out during hot weather.
  - Use a programmable thermostat to save energy costs; a programmable thermostat allows you to lower or raise temperatures at various times of day or night based on need.
  - Replace conventional light bulbs with compact fluorescents. Better yet, as they become affordable, choose LED bulbs, which last ten times longer than compact fluorescent bulbs.
  - Check out — and use — the numerous energy-saving tips on sites like www.coned.com/customercentral/energysavings.asp.

Businesses Best Suited for an Improving Economy

Although each of the businesses we describe in the following sections can also work in times of economic downturns, we consider them more vulnerable to economic forces than the businesses we list in the previous sections. We aren't suggesting that you rule out the following businesses during a down economy, but we are suggesting that you look long and hard at these opportunities before committing to them.

At the same time, when the light at the end of the tunnel begins to get brighter, keep in mind that these businesses often offer great opportunities as the economy gains strength and prosperity returns.

Offering services to other businesses

The first expenses that many businesses cut out of their budgets when times get tough are outside services. However, when the good times return (which they always eventually do), the need for business-to-business services surges. Here are a few examples of great businesses to get into as the economy improves:

- **Business coaching:** Business coaches help companies improve performance by working with managers, giving them feedback on their management styles, and developing skills they need to do well in their companies and get ahead in their careers. They help key personnel communicate more effectively, make intelligent decisions, and deal with burnout. Recent estimates show that about half of all companies now use coaches to some extent, and a study by Booz Allen Hamilton showed a $7.90 return for every dollar invested in executive coaching because it produces better teamwork and higher retention. Most business coaches charge between $100 and $500 an hour, so it's one of the highest paid and fastest growing areas of coaching. Visit the Worldwide Association of Business Coaches (`www.wabccoaches.com`) for more information.
- **Consulting:** The wide world of consulting appeals to a wide variety of people because it offers you a way to turn your expertise, experience, and years of accrued wisdom into a livelihood when salaried jobs are either no longer available or no longer appealing. Sometimes becoming a consultant is as easy as having your former employer retain you on a contract, enabling you to develop other clients while you bring in income that may be less or more than you earned as an employee. Indicative of the many possible consulting opportunities out there, more than 150 associations of consultants offer membership to consultants of different fields, including business review and planning, computing,

creativity, crisis control, organizational development, financial advice, introduction of new technology, marketing, strategic planning, training, business turnaround, and all forms of technical assistance.

Regardless of which field they're in, effective consultants are part counselor, parent figure, shrink, stern disciplinarian, and, of course, problem solver. Be sure to check out *Consulting For Dummies,* 2nd Edition, by Bob Nelson and Peter Economy (Wiley), for more information.

- **Customer support:** If you enjoy talking and you think choosing your own hours sounds good, you can join hundreds of thousands of Americans who work semi-independently as "agents" in the customer support industry. Companies recognize that gaining a new customer costs five times more than retaining an existing one, so they invest a lot of money in customer support and increasingly are contracting with United States–based companies to carry out this vital aspect of their business. If you have a successful work history of relating to customers, you can be up and running in this field within two weeks after completing the necessary training.

  The largest customer support training companies are LiveOps (`www.liveops.com`), Working Solutions (`www.workingsol.com`), and Arise Virtual Solutions (`www.arise.com`), which also engages people who do technical support. Each of these companies has its own way of operating — you may need to incorporate yourself or you may have to work as an independent contractor — and entry costs vary. If you prefer to be employed, take a look at Alpine Access (`www.alpineaccess.com`).

- **Editorial services:** Editorial services take many forms — copy-editing, line editing, developmental editing, proofreading, indexing, and more. In addition to working as an independent contractor for print publishers and corporations, the digital age has brought new editorial opportunities. Each year hundreds of thousands of self-publishers share their information, opinions, and stories with the world in both print and eBook form. Many of these self-publishers turn to independent editors for help; still more need to be enlightened to the value of well-edited material. Every journal, business report or proposal, and technical training manual, whether it's published in print or electronic format, virtually requires editorial work.

  An as-you-wait editing service (`www.gramlee.com`, for example) is entirely Web based and can easily be done in a home office. In this specialty, your customers submit documents to you electronically and you return them within two hours, editing complete. If you don't have publishing experience and editing is a new career for you, copy-editing and proofreading are among the easiest fields to break into. The U.S. Department of Agriculture Graduate School offers a self-paced course in editing and proofreading (`www.grad.usda.gov`). Find several editorial groups at `www.linkedin.com`.

- **Grant and proposal writing:** Most of the many nonprofit organizations that accompanied the economic downturn of 2008 either failed or succeeded based on their abilities to obtain grant funding. Typically, people who form nonprofits don't have the time, desire, or skill set needed to write effective grant proposals. However, as one proposal writer told us, "Any writer with good skills can do this work, whatever your background. As with lawyers, it doesn't matter who your client is — if you can write logically and can understand the subject enough to explain it, you can write a grant proposal." In addition to nonprofits seeking government or foundation funding, local governments also use grant proposal writers to gain funds from state, federal, and foundation funds.

  Grant writers usually work on an hourly or project basis; some funders pay grant writers a percentage of the proceeds of the grant if it's awarded. However, most grant writers don't work on a contingency basis. The American Grant Writers' Association offers courses in grant writing; check them out at `www.agwa.us`.

- **Interim or contract executives:** One consequence of the retirement of the baby boomer generation and the much smaller generation that's replacing it is that corporations are more willing to contract out for top executive roles. Thousands of companies are seeking interim, contract, or short-term executives for positions like CEO, CFO, and CIO, as well as managerial roles in marketing, purchasing, and other departments. Some of these interim assignments are part time, and some are full time; either way, they're usually limited to periods from several months to several years. You can seek out client companies yourself or enroll with services that broker or place interim executives, such as Interim America (`www.interimamerica.com`) or Your Encore, Inc. (`www.yourencore.com`).

- **Technical writing:** Constantly changing technology brings with it the need for manuals and other materials that introduce it to consumers, sell it, explain how to use it, service it, assemble it, install it, and so on. The pace of innovation has been accelerating for more than a hundred years, and it'll likely continue to do so as innovation shifts abroad, particularly to China, which is investing heavily in science and technology. Companies often contract out for technical writing projects, some of which can extend over several months or more. Technical writers can also find work making technologies created abroad understandable and usable by English-speaking sales engineers and technicians. Check out the Society for Technical Communication (`www.stc.org`) for more information about this field.

- **Translation services:** Translation services are essential in a global economy — contracts, instruction manuals, software menus and commands, scripts for dubbing, subtitles for films, and much more all require translation. Accurate machine-based translation is still years away, but the Web allows a translator to respond instantly to a request for services. MyGengo (mygengo.com), for example, hires home-based translators, who begin work almost immediately when a client types or pastes content into the MyGengo Web site. Working for a site like this is one option for translators, but most U.S. translators operate as independent home businesses. Translating technical documents in growing technology fields and Web content are two high-demand specialties for translators. If you prefer oral interpretation and are willing to work from places other than your home, courts and hospitals need accurate interpreters to work onsite. Check out the American Translators Association (www.atanet.org) for more information.

- **Web writing:** The Web has opened up new markets for writers. Some pay quite well, as is the case when you write blog and Web site content for many companies or organizations; others require a lot of work to produce much income. Sites like www.dailyarticle.com, www.constant-content.com, www.associatedcontent.com, and www.helium.com broker writers' works. Some of these sites require writers to transfer all rights of their material; others let the writer specify a license for reusing her content. The site www.scribd.com has a store where writers' can sell their work, and, of course, eBook writing is a growing market. Writing projects that offer the best pay are business writing, such as annual reports, company newsletters, and speeches for executives, ghostwriting, and copywriting for selling and promoting products and services. To get started as a professional Web writer, choose a topic or focus that motivates you to become an expert in that topic; then develop that expertise. Check out www.publishersmarketplace.com and www.writersdigest.com for more information.

Appealing to clients who have money to spare

No matter what the economic climate may be — sunny, stormy, or partly cloudy — people love to shop. And when clients have money to spare, you can bet that money won't stay in their wallets for long. The following are two big items people are likely to spend money on when they have extra money to spend:

- **Functional art:** Functional art brings together the aesthetic with the practical. It satisfies two appetites — the quest for beauty and the internal desire to get a value for the money you invest for items in your home and business. Artists who create functional art apply their skills to creating everyday objects imbued with a handcrafted beauty and artistry that manufactured products can't attain. In addition to creating original work, functional artists also turn existing items that were once simply functional into something artistic, like transforming file drawers or cat litter boxes into unique furniture or accessories, for example.

The key to functional art is that when people perceive something as handmade art, they're willing to pay a higher price for it than they would for any machine-tooled version of the same item. For current examples of such handcrafted work, check out www.functionalartgallery.com and www.etsy.com; for current trends in taste, check out www.hgtv.com.

- **Home theater installation:** Unlike the sales of most consumer electronic products, sales of home theater components not only held their own during the recent economic downturn — they increased. Many people try to install their own theatres but find the task overwhelming or the result unsatisfying. For example, even when you sufficiently connected the components and attuned them to one another, the TV may not be placed in the right light, or the speaker placement may not produce the desired surround-sound effect. These people often turn to experts in the field for help.

  Many installers report getting a significant portion of their work from customers whose previous installers' work was inadequate. So you can see that even people who have already had home theaters installed (or have installed them themselves) often turn to experts in home theaters for assistance when they need it. If you have experience in one of the relevant skills for home theatre installation (electricity, networking, electronics, and so on), an understanding of how sound works combined with a penchant for precision, and decent customer service skills, you can build a business largely fed by word-of-mouth referrals. Check out www.highdefforum.com for more information.

When people have extra money to spend, they're also likely to spend money on products and services designed to help them with day-to-day living or family events. Here are some quick-fire examples for you to consider (along with some resources to check out if you're interested):

- **Animal training:** Training dogs and other animals (Association of Pet Dog Trainers: www.apdt.com)
- **Cake baking and decorating:** Creating custom cakes for special occasions like weddings (International Cake Exploration Societé: www.ices.org)
- **Candle making:** Making handmade candles (International Guild of Candle Artisans: www.igca.net)
- **Chair making:** Making classic chairs in the heirloom quality (The Windsor Institute: www.thewindsorinstitute.com)
- **Creativity coaching:** Helping individuals reach their creative goals (Creativity Coaching Association: www.creativitycoachingassociation.com)
- **Daily money management:** Helping seniors and others manage their daily finances (American Association of Daily Money Managers: www.aadmm.com)

- **Dog walking:** Walking five or more dogs once or twice a day (International Association of Canine Professionals: www.dogpro.org)
- **Errand services:** Running errands and doing nearly any other chores — small or large — that people can't or won't do themselves (International Concierge and Errand Association: www.iceaweb.org)
- **Family child care:** Providing child care to the children of others in one's own home (Monday Morning America: www.mondayam.com)
- **Feng shui practice:** Helping people evoke harmony in their surroundings (Feng Shui Institute of America: www.windwater.com)
- **Financial planning:** Counseling clients on managing debt, buying a home, handling college costs, planning for the future, and more (Association for Financial Counseling, Planning, and Education: www.afcpe.org)
- **Home staging:** Making a home look its best when it's placed for sale on the market (StagedHomes.com: www.stagedhomes.com)
- **Housing counseling:** Counseling buyers of first homes, seniors considering reverse mortgages, and people experiencing economic difficulty (The Center for Housing Counseling Training: www.housingtraining.org)
- **Image consulting:** Helping clients improve their appearance and personal style visually and vocally (www.imagemaker1.com)
- **Interior decorating:** Designing for the interior of homes, businesses, and other buildings (American Society of Interior Designers: www.asid.org)
- **Landscape gardening:** Designing and installing landscape gardens (Professional Landcare Network, or PLANET: www.landcarenetwork.org)
- **Life coaching:** Helping people develop their individual potentials (Peer Resources: www.peer.ca/coachingschools.html)
- **Mediation:** Assisting people in settling disputes (Mediate.com: www.mediate.com)
- **Money coaching:** Helping clients overcome limiting financial beliefs and behaviors (Money Coaching Institute: www.moneycoachinginstitute.com)
- **Pest control:** Identifying, blocking, or eradicating pests (National Pest Management Association: www.pestworld.org)
- **Pet grooming:** Bathing, ear cleaning, styling, nail clipping, stripping dogs and cats (PetGroomer.com: www.petgroomer.com)
- **Pet sitting:** Caring for pets when their owners are away, either as an agency or as a pet sitter (National Association of Professional Pet Sitters: www.petsitters.org)

- **Professional organization:** Organizing possessions, clothing, files, and more for clients (National Association of Professional Organizers: www.napo.net)
- **Vegetable garden installation:** Installing vegetable gardens for other people (Your Backyard Farmer: www.yourbackyardfarmer.com)
- **Virtual juror:** Working as an online juror and providing juror feedback to attorneys who are preparing cases (VirtualJuror.com: virtualjuror.com)
- **Web-based teaching:** Providing online education of all kinds (Flexjobs: www.flexjobs.com)
- **Wedding planning:** Coordinating weddings at a better cost than clients could plan their own weddings (The Association of Certified Professional Wedding Consultants: www.acpwc.com)

Information resources for following economic trends

Because new and small businesses are the engine of the U.S. economy, governments and several private foundations provide resources to help you succeed. If you've decided a home business is the path you want to take, the following resources can help you get on your way. Often you can locate local offices on the Web sites of national organizations.

Helpful publications and Web sites include

- ***Bizpreneur News:*** A free, semimonthly e-newsletter that offers information about managing and marketing business ventures; providing good customer service; increasing sales; developing a Web presence; and gaining insight on legal issues, taxes, and finances (www.smallbizpreneurs.com)
- **BuzGate.org:** A gateway Web site offered by government and nonprofit small business assistance agencies that gives free help to small businesses (buzgate.org)
- **Elm Street Library:** A library of books and eBooks by Paul and Sarah Edwards that enable people to find sustainable independent livelihoods and the skills needed for success (elmstreetlibrary.com)
- ***Entrepreneur Magazine*:** A continuing resource for business ideas that contains a Home-Based Biz section with many helpful articles (www.entrepreneur.com)
- **James J. Hill Reference Library:** A free reference library that provides services and fee-based research to businesses (jjhill.org)
- **Ewing Marion Kauffman Foundation's Web sites:** Web sites that publish research on small business, provide a wealth of articles, promulgate policy ideas, and offer learning programs and materials (www.entrepreneurship.org and fasttrac.org)

(continued)

(continued)

Helpful agencies and organizations include

- **Chambers of Commerce:** Groups that provide networking opportunities in most communities (chamber-of-commerce.com)
- **Hollings Manufacturing Extension Partnership:** A nonprofit organization funded by the Small Business Administration (SBA) to help small and medium manufacturers improve their businesses (www.mep.nist.gov)
- **Minority Business Development Centers:** Organizations that help minority and women-owned businesses become certified to bid on government work and provide help in getting technical and financial assistance (www.mbda.gov)
- **My Own Business:** A nonprofit organization that offers a free course on how to start your own business (myownbusiness.org)
- **Regional Economic Development Associations:** Associations that offer sources of information about the regional economy and sources of technical assistance
- **Service Corps of Retired Executives (SCORE):** Organization that provides individual counseling by volunteer retired executives and many free resources like online workshops, articles, and newsletters (www.score.org)
- **Small Business Administration:** Federal government agency that offers assistance to small businesses in a wide variety of loan and training programs (www.sba.gov)
- **Small Business Development Centers:** Organizations that provide individual attention in the form of counseling on matters ranging from business planning to identifying sources of funds (www.sba.gov/sbdc)
- **U.S. Chamber of Small Business Center:** Organization that provides helpful articles in a small business library (uschamber.com/sb)

Part II
Managing Your Money

The 5th Wave   By Rich Tennant

In this part . . .

Money definitely makes the world go 'round — in life and in business. Home-based businesses are no exception. In this part, we explain the fundamentals of financial management, starting with how to keep track of your money. We consider how to price your products or services to maximize your return and then examine health insurance and retirement. We wind up this part with an in-depth look at taxes and deductions.

Chapter 6

Keeping Track of Your Money

In This Chapter

- Separating your business and personal finances
- Establishing a business bank account and accepting credit card transactions
- Deciding on a bookkeeping system
- Keeping an eye on your finances
- Understanding invoicing, collections, and cash flow
- Establishing good credit and fixing bad credit

If there's one thing that keeps people from starting their own home-based businesses, it's probably concern over money. Where will the money you need to start up your business and keep it running come from? Will there be enough to allow you to quit your current job, support your family, or at least pay some bills? How will you know whether you're making money — or losing it?

The key to answering all these questions is *financial management.* Financial management is one of the main points of focus for any home-based business, and proper financial management requires a good system of bookkeeping, as well as constant attention to the numbers. Your business's finances aren't something you should leave to chance. In this chapter, we take a look at how to manage your finances so that your finances don't manage you.

Organizing Your Finances

In most large businesses, tracking cash — where it comes from, where it goes, and how it's used — is one of the most important administrative functions. Large corporations like Coca-Cola, Wal-Mart, and ExxonMobil may have thousands of people working in their finance and accounting departments. Clearly, tracking cash is important to them!

Should you hire an accountant?

Do you need an accountant to help you keep track of your business's finances? The answer to this question depends on how capable you personally are in handling your own bookkeeping, accounting, taxes, and financial strategies, and on how complicated your business is. Some business owners love to take care of the administrative tasks involved in running their own businesses; others hate it. Some home-based businesspeople are naturally skilled at doing financial tasks; however, the talents of others are better suited to delivering products and services to their customers. In addition, doing your own bookkeeping and accounting takes time and discipline — you have to regularly update your records and periodically check them for errors.

If, for example, your finances are fairly simple, you're computer savvy, and you have sufficient time and interest to keep your records up-to-date by yourself, you can use a software package such as Quicken or QuickBooks to do your own bookkeeping. Simply input your receipts and expenses, and the program performs every accounting function and trick you can imagine. You can generate all kinds of financial reports and graphs (which your lenders will want to see when you need to borrow money to grow), write checks, and collect the information you need to do your taxes.

If, however, your business isn't simple, or if you've got a unique business setup (for example, if your home-based business is a C corporation instead of the more common sole proprietorship), getting the help of a professional bookkeeper or accountant may be worth your time and money. When looking for professional assistance, avoid choosing someone out of the Yellow Pages or from a random Internet search — you never know what you're going to get. Instead, ask your home-based business friends or colleagues in the area for referrals to a good accountant or bookkeeping service — preferably one that specializes in handling businesses like yours.

Cash serves many functions in a business: It's a way to keep score, a way to measure the profit generated by different products and services, and a way to reflect the equity built by the company's investors and owners. Plus, cash serves as more than just a yardstick for performance; it also enables companies to pay employees and purchase supplies and services.

Indeed, cash is the focal point of most organizations — both large and small. When you have a small home-based business, cash — or the lack thereof — can quickly make or break you.

Why do you have to worry about keeping your business finances organized? Isn't that shoebox in which you keep all your personal receipts sufficient for your home-based business, as long as you have enough money to pay your bills and yourself? Not quite. Keeping your finances organized and accurate is important because you need adequate financial information about your business to do the following:

- To know where your business stands — whether it's profiting or losing money and whether expenses are out of line with income
- To apply for loans and receive credit from vendors and suppliers
- To prepare your federal and state income taxes
- To provide accurate and up-to-date financial info to interested buyers in the event that you decide to sell your business

Can your shoebox do all that? We don't think so! But it's not all about what your shoebox can or can't do. It's also about the value of your time. Consider how long it may take you to do something you don't do well and what your hourly rate is. Now compare that amount of time and money to how long it would take an expert to do the same thing and what his or her rate would be. In many cases, you actually save money by hiring a professional accountant or bookkeeper. Time really is money, and you need to dedicate the majority of your time to what you do best — and what brings money into your business.

Setting Up a Business Account

When you set up your company's finances, the first step is to establish a separate bank account for your home-based business. Although the Internal Revenue Service (IRS) doesn't require you to separate your business finances from your personal finances, take our word for it: It makes things a lot easier when you prepare your taxes. If you don't establish this separation from the get-go, you may spend hours and hours first trying to identify the business expenses in your personal checking account or credit card receipts and then pulling them out and classifying them.

At minimum, you need a checking account for your business, although a savings account and even a retirement account may be good ideas, too. Setting up a new checking account is easy, particularly if you've already established a personal account at the bank or other financial institution where you choose to set up your business account. Drop by your friendly local bank, fill out a form or two, deposit a bit of money (or transfer it from an existing account), and pick out your check design. In minutes, you'll be all set. Remember, though, that most banks require your company's employer identification number (EIN) if you're setting up an account for anything other than a sole proprietorship, so have your EIN handy.

WARNING!

If you set up a new account in the name of your business (not in your own name) — particularly if the account isn't with the institution where you do your personal banking — you may find that the bank places holds on checks you deposit over a certain amount of money, say $500 or $1,000, making your funds inaccessible until they clear the originating bank. These holds can remain in place for a couple of days to a week or more, and needless to say, they can cause you and your business major problems if you need your cash right *now.* The good news is that your bank will likely lift the requirement to put holds on deposits to your business account after your business establishes a record of stability (a process that can take anywhere from a few months to a year or more). If your bank doesn't automatically lift the requirement, be sure to ask your bank manager to lift it.

TIP

One more thing: Consider applying for a credit or debit card that you use only for your business. Visa, MasterCard, Discover, and American Express all offer cards that are specifically geared to the unique needs of small business users. These companies can provide quarterly spending reports by employee — breaking down your charges into specific categories, such as retail, restaurant, lodging, and telecommunications — and give discounts on business services, extended warranties on equipment purchased with the card, and many other benefits. Debit cards issued with a Visa or MasterCard insignia are particularly flexible because they can be used as either debit (or, often, ATM) or credit cards, depending on the situation and your personal preferences. The choice is yours.

Accepting Credit Card Sales

If you sell products, you probably want to be able to accept credit card payments. In fact, as a way to improve your cash flow, you may want to require that your clients pay you by credit card *before* you deliver their product orders or services.

Although many home-based businesses don't need to be able to accept credit card payments, others — particularly home-based businesses that sell products — do. If you have the kind of business that's suitable for taking credit card sales — perhaps you sell dollhouses, computers, or rare records through your Web site — you gain many of the following advantages when you accept credit cards:

- Customers — particularly those customers who would rather not wait to send a check or payment through the mail before you ship their orders — appreciate the convenience of being able to use their credit cards to make an immediate purchase.
- People who use credit cards to purchase items tend to spend more money per transaction than non–credit card customers.

- You get your cash from the transaction much more quickly than when you invoice your customers and let them pay later, improving the cash flow of your business. A credit card payment is immediately directly deposited into your bank account.
- You reduce or even eliminate internal paperwork that results from invoicing customers and following up on delinquent payments.
- Your business appears more established and credible than businesses that don't accept credit cards.

Being able to accept credit cards is definitely a good thing. As with many other good things in life, however, accepting credit cards isn't free. In fact, you have to pay a price for the privilege.

Knowing the costs of credit card transactions

How much will accepting credit cards cost you and your business? The answer depends on what kind of business you operate (retail, mail order, or Internet), who processes your transactions, and how much money you submit for processing (the overall dollar amount of your transactions).

Here are the typical costs you can expect to pay to the company that provides your credit card processing:

- **Setup charges:** Including application fees, these fees range anywhere from free to $300 and more. Plus, you have to pay software licensing fees and purchase equipment if you plan to use a point-of-service terminal instead of just using your computer's Internet access. If the setup charge is free, expect to pay higher transaction fees to make up for the free setup.
- **Transaction fees:** For each transaction, you're charged a flat fee that may range from $0.20 to $0.50 per transaction.
- **Discounts:** These fees are percentages taken from each order, and they range from less than 2 percent to 5 percent or more.
- **Monthly charges:** These charges include a statement fee, a monthly minimum if the discount and transaction fees don't equal a monthly minimum, and leasing fees if you lease instead of buy equipment.

REMEMBER

Accepting credit cards is definitely not a free service, but if the level of your sales justifies it, it's a small price to pay — and can be offset by the price of just one or two bad checks. However, before you sign up for a service, carefully compare a variety of different providers. Prices and services vary widely, and you can definitely find some deals better than others.

Establishing a merchant account

Before you can accept credit cards, you have to find a bank, credit card company, or other merchant account provider that will grant you *merchant status* or allow you to open a *merchant account* — that is, authorization to accept credit card payments. This process isn't quite as easy as you may think; in fact, for a new business or one that credit card companies consider to be risky, gaining merchant status can be downright difficult. Here's a list of the kinds of businesses that credit card companies consider particularly risky (and that may make getting approval more difficult):

- Adult Web sites
- Dating services
- Prepaid telephone cards
- Online casinos
- Massage services
- Online pharmacies
- Mall kiosks (seasonal/independent)
- Ticket brokers

If you've been in business for some time (at least two or more years), you're not involved in a particularly risky business, and you have a good credit history, you should have no problem getting merchant status. Of course, until you apply, you'll never know for sure.

WARNING!

One caution: Different companies charge vastly different prices to create and maintain a merchant account for you. Do your research thoroughly, and compare prices. You may also be able to get better terms going through a membership organization or company, such as Costco, that provides access to merchant accounts. Some companies falsely represent themselves as independent sales organizations (ISOs), and eager merchants have been scammed. To determine whether the ISO you're talking with is legitimate, ask for the bank the ISO is affiliated with and then contact it to verify the status of the ISO. You can also check with your local better business bureau to find out whether any complaints have been filed against the ISO, and the extent and nature of the complaints if any have been filed. Carefully read any contract or agreement you're asked to sign. If you have any questions, it may be worth your time and money to have a lawyer review it for you.

Obtaining credit reports

If a customer asks you to provide a line of credit, it's always wise to first check out the customer's creditworthiness — that is, the customer's ability to pay back your loan. You can purchase credit reports on businesses from firms like Dun & Bradstreet Business (`www.dnbcreditreport.com`) and Credit.Net (`www.credit.net`). For credit checks on consumers, the major credit reporting agencies — Equifax (`www.equifax.com`), Experian (`www.experian.com`), and TransUnion (`www.transunion.com`) — provide this service to businesses. Visit these companies' Web sites or give them a call for more information.

Using the PayPal option

As a direct result of the explosion of the eBay online auction service, PayPal (`www.paypal.com`) and a number of similar financial services companies have sprung up to facilitate the resultant transactions. In addition to offering the ability to accept cash transfers from customers with their own PayPal accounts, PayPal allows your customers to pay you by using their credit cards. You can then either keep the funds in your PayPal account or electronically transfer them to your business's bank account.

Using PayPal to accept your customers' credit cards offers some compelling advantages over the more traditional process of qualifying for and establishing a merchant account, including the following:

- You don't have to fill out a lengthy application or jump a bunch of hurdles to be able to accept credit cards for your business. Simply establish a PayPal account (which takes at most a few minutes), and you're ready to go.
- Although not free, the fees that you pay to accept credit cards with PayPal may be significantly less than what you'd pay a bank for running charges through a merchant account (currently from 1.9 to 2.9 percent, depending on monthly sales volume, plus $0.30).

  You also avoid paying separately for a gateway service. If you're processing a lot of credit card payments, these savings can really add up.
- Unlike merchant accounts, PayPal charges no monthly fees for leasing credit card software or generating transaction records.

TIP

Our advice? Give the PayPal option consideration when you're starting out. It's far easier than establishing a merchant account, and the cash is just as green when it hits your bank account.

Choosing the Best Bookkeeping System for Your Business

Keeping track of your business's financial transactions is a must — there are simply too many good reasons why you can't ignore it. Your business's finances aren't going to get less complicated as your business grows; in fact, the opposite is likely to be true. Start your business off on the right foot, and make accounting for your financial transactions a regular part of doing business.

Although you may enjoy playing with Microsoft Excel, we suggest that you pick up one of the many excellent accounting software programs available on the market today instead of creating your own spreadsheets from scratch. Programs such as Quicken, QuickBooks, and Peachtree Accounting can take care of your business's every financial need — now and into the future.

For example, QuickBooks, Simple Start Free Edition — a capable and easy-to-use software program for businesses with up to 20 customers that you can download for free — allows you to do the following basic tasks (more advanced tasks, such as producing estimates, require an upgrade to a more capable paid version of QuickBooks):

- Print checks, pay bills, and track expenses
- Invoice customers and track payments and sales taxes
- Generate reports, including profit-and-loss statements, statements of cash flows, balance sheets, sales reports, and more
- Manage payroll and payroll taxes
- Track information for taxes and share information with an accountant
- Follow along with extensive tutorials and help functions

The accounting method you decide to use ultimately depends on the nature of your business and on the amount and complexity of the financial transactions you incur. If you're at all in doubt as to how to proceed with your bookkeeping or accounting system, talk to an accountant for help in setting up the right way.

You'll have a great feeling when you get your business off the ground and receive your first payments for your products or services. After all your hard work and planning, these payments are what you've been waiting for. Chances are you'll be busier than you ever imagined and may easily get so caught up in taking care of customers that you forget to take care of your business.

However, successful businesses don't just happen — they require constant attention. Like a wonderfully productive vegetable garden, businesses need to be carefully tended and watched for signs of trouble. In business, one of the best ways to keep an eye on the health of your business is to review the wide variety of financial reports available to you. Make a regular habit of generating the reports you need and reviewing them. Don't just assume that everything is fine — prove it to yourself regularly.

Balancing check registers and bank statements

You can do the most basic form of financial analysis once a month when you balance your check registers against your bank statements. Most bank statements summarize the total dollar amount of the deposits you made during the month, as well as the total dollar amount of the money you disbursed from your account. After you've double-checked to make sure the bank statements are in agreement with your check register, subtract the amount of your checks from your deposits to give yourself a quick and dirty idea of what direction your business is heading financially — north or south.

Spending far more than you're taking in? Then you know you have to find ways to bring in more money while also controlling expenses. Bringing in far more money than you're spending? Terrific! Figure out how to do more of what you're already doing.

Analyzing the two most important financial statements

Financial statements take the data you've entered into your accounting system and organize it in a way that allows you to quickly gauge the financial health of your company. Although financial statements may seem a bit intimidating to many — especially for new home-based businesspeople — accounting and bookkeeping software make the process easier than ever before. It's really as simple as one or two clicks of your computer's mouse.

Two of the most popular and useful financial statements are the income statement and the balance sheet. Each has its own unique role to play in your financial analysis and, ultimately, in the way you run your business.

The income statement

The *income statement* (also known as a *profit-and-loss statement,* or P&L) measures the *profitability* of your business — in other words, how much money is left over after you add up all your business revenues and subtract all your business expenses.

Income statements reveal three key pieces of information:

- A business's sales volume during a specified period
- A business's expenses during a specified period
- The difference between a business's sales and its expenses — its profit (or loss) — during a specified period

Table 6-1 shows what a typical income statement looks like.

Table 6-1 Susan's Antiques: Income Statement

Income Statement — Twelve Months Ended December 31, 20XX	
Revenues	
Gross sales	50,000
Less: Returns	(1,000)
Net sales	**49,000**
Cost of Goods Sold	
Beginning inventory	50,000
Purchases	10,000
Less: Purchase discounts	(2,000)
Net purchases	8,000
Cost of goods available for sale	58,000
Less: Ending inventory	(48,000)
Cost of goods sold	**10,000**
Gross profit	**39,000**
Operating Expenses	
Total selling expenses	(5,000)
Total general expenses	(10,000)
Total operating expenses	(15,000)
Operating income	24,000
Other income and expenses	5,000
Total other income and expenses	5,000
Income before taxes	**19,000**
Less: Income taxes	(10,000)
Net income	9,000

In the example in Table 6-1, Susan's Antiques had $49,000 of net sales revenue and a cost of goods sold of $10,000, leaving the company with a gross profit of $39,000. However, this gross profit was further reduced by the expenses of selling products and running the company (advertising, printing, rent, salaries, bonuses, and so forth) and by income taxes. The result is a net income of $9,000.

The balance sheet

The entire world of accounting hinges on a simple mathematical truth, known as the accounting equation:

Assets = liabilities + owners' equity

Assets include cash and things that can be converted to cash. *Liabilities* are obligations — debts, loans, mortgages, and the like — owed to other organizations or people. *Owners' equity* is the net worth of the organization after all liabilities have been subtracted from the organization's assets.

The *balance sheet* reveals these three categories. Table 6-2 shows a sample of a typical balance sheet.

Table 6-2 Susan's Antiques: Balance Sheet

Consolidated Balance Sheet — as of December 31, 20XX	
Assets	
Current Assets	
Cash and cash equivalents (checks, money orders)	12,000
Accounts receivable	25,000
Inventory	30,000
Total current assets	**67,000**
Fixed Assets	
Equipment	20,000
Furniture, fixtures, and improvements	15,000
Allowance for depreciation and amortization	(2,000)
Total fixed assets	**33,000**
Total assets	**100,000**

(continued)

Table 6-2 *(continued)*

Consolidated Balance Sheet — as of December 31, 20XX	
Liabilities and Owners' Equity	
Liabilities	
Current Liabilities	
Notes payable to bank	10,000
Accounts payable	5,000
Accrued compensation and benefits	19,000
Income taxes payable	6,000
Deferred income taxes	3,000
Current portion of long-term debt	1,000
Total current liabilities	**$44,000**
Long-term debt	10,000
Deferred income taxes	10,000
Total liabilities	**64,000**
Owners' Equity	
Common stock	20,000
Additional paid-in capital	10,000
Retained earnings	6,000
Total owners' equity	**36,000**
Total liabilities and owners' equity	**100,000**

The value of the assets of Susan's Antiques is exactly balanced by its liabilities and owners' equity. Because of the accounting equation, there's no other option. The balance sheet demonstrates the fact that assets are paid for by a company's liabilities and owners' equity. Conversely, the assets are used to generate cash to pay off the company's liabilities. Any excess cash after liabilities are paid off is added to owners' equity as profit.

Happiness Is a Positive Cash Flow

For a new business — especially a new, home-based business that you depend on to generate income in both your work and your personal lives — generating a positive cash flow as quickly as possible after startup of the business is absolutely critical. Every new business goes through an initial period during which expenses exceed revenues (thus generating a negative cash flow), but the sooner you can make your cash flow positive, the better for the short- and long-term financial health of the business (and the easier you'll sleep at night).

Happiness in business truly is a positive cash flow. The following sections help you put your company into the black and out of the red.

Should you lease or buy?

Q: I'm thinking about acquiring a new van for my business and upgrading my computer system. Should I lease or buy?

A: The choice to rent, lease, or buy has many important business considerations. For example, leasing may enable you to get a better van or computer than you could otherwise afford. Because leasing is normally equivalent to 100-percent financing, it may allow you to keep more working capital on hand. Leasing may also allow you to pay for the items out of your earnings instead of having to use your savings or get a home equity loan.

But, of course, you need to qualify for a lease, which means you must have good credit, although you probably don't need as flawless of credit for leasing office equipment and furniture as you do for leasing a van. As a general rule, if you're leasing under your business name, you can expect to be required to have been in business for at least a year. But computer companies like Dell and Gateway all have consumer leasing programs based on credit history.

Leasing has a cash advantage over a purchase on credit because a lease usually requires little or no down payment, whereas a credit purchase may require 20 to 30 percent down. However, a disadvantage of leasing is that it's more expensive than buying because it includes charges to cover overhead and profit. If dealers are offering zero-interest financing, leasing is decidedly more expensive.

Technological obsolescence is another reason often cited for leasing, though some leases include annual automatic upgrades. At the end of a lease period, you can give back the equipment that may now be considered obsolete and have little market value. You may also get additional tax benefits from leasing, but because tax laws are continually changing and have many exceptions to exceptions, consult with your tax specialist before deciding about leasing.

Taking all this info into account, you can see we can't give you a stock answer as to whether renting, leasing, or buying is best. If you do decide to lease, consider the following:

- The exact nature of the financing agreement (Does it have liens or restrictions?)
- The amount of each payment (Are there any add-on and document-processing fees or termination penalties?)
- The person responsible for insurance, maintenance, and taxes (usually, the lessee)
- What happens to the leased item at the end of the lease
- Renewal options
- Cancellation penalties, if any
- Disadvantageous terms and conditions
- Length of the lease period

(continued)

(continued)

Generally, it's cheaper if you arrange your own vehicle financing instead of going through a dealer, which marks up the loan rate. You can determine the cost of a loan in advance by using sites like Bankrate.com (`www.bankrate.com`), E-Loan (`www.eloan.com`), CapitolOne Auto Finance (`www.capitalone.com`), or LowerMyBills.com (`www.lowermybills.com`). To calculate leasing costs, you can get a lease quote at `www.leasesource.com`, as well as purchase their pricing services.

Whether you buy or lease, but particularly if you lease, consider getting *gap insurance* included in your lease. This insurance protects you if you find yourself in a situation in which a week or two after you get your vehicle, it's stolen or totaled, and the insurance company plans to pay you only $18,000 on a $26,000 vehicle. Gap insurance covers the difference.

Something to consider about leasing computers is that you may be restrained to add memory or make other changes because you have to restore each computer to its original condition at the end of the lease period.

Treating cash as king

Most home-based businesspeople who have chosen the sole-proprietorship form of business (see Chapter 10 for more on the most common forms of business) use their money to pay not only business expenses, but also personal expenses, when they're the primary wage earners. In other words, the money from your self-proprietorship business enables you to fulfill both your business and your personal obligations, such as office rent and car payments.

As a business, you have many different forms of money available to you, including cash, checks, money orders, and credit cards — and some are better than others. For most businesses, being paid in cash — either before delivering a product or service or upon delivery, at the latest — is by far the top preference, followed by checks. Here are the different ways you can be paid, in order from the most to the least preferred:

- **Cash:** Assuming it's not counterfeit, being paid in cash is ideal. It's 100-percent liquid, you can spend it immediately if you like, and you can be sure it's not going to bounce or have a one-week hold placed on it when you deposit it to your business bank account. (If *your* bank puts a hold on cash deposits, find a new bank — fast!)
- **Checks:** In many cases — particularly for large payments of many thousands of dollars — being paid in cash just isn't practical, so using checks makes the most sense. However, checks aren't as liquid as cash; you have to take them to the originating bank or deposit them in your bank account (where they may be held until they clear) to be able to obtain

cash. Doing so takes time. Not only that, but checks also introduce the possibility that the customer's account may not have sufficient funds available to pay the obligation or that the checks are bogus. Insufficient funds are a very real concern, and you have to be sure your customer has the capacity to pay you before you accept a check.

- **Credit cards:** Credit cards are another step down the ladder of preference for receiving money. Credit card companies take a piece of every transaction you give them to process. But if a card turns out to be stolen or bogus, or if your customer decides to dispute the charge because he's unhappy with the product or service you delivered, you may be out the amount of the entire transaction.
- **Online payments:** These payments include those paid through services such as PayPal, Authorize.Net, and Amazon Simple Pay for customers who don't have credit cards or who may be credit-adverse (who account for about 10 percent of online sales). Online payments are riskier than the preceding payment alternatives because of the risk of inputting your information into a Web site that's bogus or has been specifically set up by hackers to gather your sensitive financial information, username, and/or password.
- **Credit:** When you sell someone a product or service and let him pay for it later, you're extending credit to your customer. Although this practice is quite common in business, it's by far the least preferred way to be paid. It may be weeks or even months before you finally get your money — perhaps well after you've sold and delivered your products or services — and you run the risk of never being paid at all. If you do decide to bill your clients for your products and services, be sure to check out their credit histories first. If in doubt, require your clients to pay you in cash, by check, or with a credit card.

REMEMBER

Creating a positive cash flow starts with bringing cash into your business. The longer you take to convert whatever form of payment you decide to accept into cash, the longer you have to wait before your cash flow is positive. And don't forget: *Happiness is a positive cash flow.*

Kick-starting your cash flow

Do you always seem to be a day late and a dollar short? Even though you're bringing in good money, is it already spent as soon as it arrives? If you answer yes to these questions, you likely have a problem with cash flow. Assuming you're charging enough for your products and services, either you're not collecting your money quickly enough or you're spending too much money too quickly.

But don't fret; here are some ways to put your cash flow on the right track:

- **Get your money upfront.** If at all possible, ask for payment before you deliver your products or services. There's no better way to get your cash flowing in the right direction than being paid sooner rather than later.
- **Don't pay your bills any sooner than you have to.** Your cash flow will thank you if you wait to pay your bills until you're required to do so. If, for example, your utility bill requires payment 30 days after you receive it and you pay your bills with an online banking account, schedule your payment to be delivered the day before it's due (don't schedule payment on the exact due date — if the payment fails, you won't have enough time to fix the problem before your payment is late). If you're paying by check, wait until day 25 before you write out your check and drop it into the mail. Waiting to pay your bills doesn't mean holding your payments longer than the date when payment is due. Late payments may, at best, create ill will between you and your vendor or supplier and, at worst, damage your credit.
- **Make sure your invoices are timely — and accurate!** Send invoices as soon as you deliver a product or service — preferably with the delivery itself. And make sure they're accurate. Many payments are delayed or rejected because of honest but preventable mistakes in invoicing.
- **Bill more often.** The more often you bill your clients or customers, the more often you'll be paid. And the more often you're paid, the better your cash flow is. Instead of billing your clients quarterly, why not bill them monthly? If you're supplying products, try breaking your deliveries into smaller chunks that you can bill sooner and more often.
- **Give prompt-payment discounts.** Everyone loves price discounts, and if you offer discounts to clients who pay their bills quickly, you're sure to have many takers. You may get a little less money as a result, but this drawback is offset by the fact that you get your money sooner rather than later.
- **Manage your expenses.** The flip side of bringing cash into your company is sending it out. The less cash you spend, the better your cash flow is. Spend money on your company only when necessary. Instead of buying the latest and greatest computer every year, for example, try to make the one you have last as long as you can — replacing it only when necessary.
- **Manage your accounts receivable.** In other words, make sure to keep track of what's owed you and take action to collect late payments. Customers and clients have plenty of reasons why they haven't paid the money that's due to you, however, you'll never find out why if you aren't keeping track of your clients' payments. Accounting software programs such as QuickBooks can easily generate a *receivables aging report,* which tells you the status on all your payments. If payments are even a day late, take immediate action to get paid.

Understanding collections

There comes a time in the life of every home-based business owner when a client either forgets to pay you for the products or services you sell her or outright refuses to do so. It's one thing if the products and services you sold your client were never delivered, were supplied late, or were poor in quality. Most customers have a problem paying you in those kinds of situations, and they may express their displeasure by holding on to the cash they owe you. It's another thing altogether, however, if you did what you agreed to do when your client placed her order.

But why wouldn't your clients pay you the money they owe you? Or why would they drag the process out so long that it becomes almost more trouble getting your money than it's worth? Here are just a few of the possibilities:

- The check may be in the mail — really.
- Your client may have forgotten to pay you.
- A mistake in your invoice may prevent your client from paying you.
- Your client may not be satisfied with the product or service you provided.
- Your client may be trying to improve his own cash flow or make a last-ditch effort to save his business before declaring bankruptcy or going out of business.

Each of these issues can be addressed, but you have to find out which reason pertains to your situation before you can address it. Collecting money owed you isn't the best part of having your own business, but it is necessary.

Follow this six-step plan and you should get even the balkiest client or customer to pay up:

1. **Personally call your client.**

   Before you do anything else, get on the phone with your client to find out what the problem is. If it's minor, you can take care of it right then and there, over the phone. In the vast majority of cases, this initial phone call is all it takes to nudge your clients into paying you. If, however, calling your client doesn't get payment to you right away, you need to take further action.

2. **Send a past-due notice immediately.**

   Don't wait after a payment is due to send out a past-due notice. If payment is due 15 days after you invoice, and you don't receive it, send out a past-due statement on day 16. If payment is due 30 days after you invoice, send out a past-due statement on day 31. Don't be shy — it's your money, so go after it. In addition to sticking the past-due statement in the mail, try faxing and e-mailing copies. You can use software to remind you when it's time to act on a payment. For example, QuickBooks has a reminder feature.

3. **Stop work.**

   If your client or customer drags things out longer than is acceptable to you, you may have to stop work to get her attention. If you sell products, stopping work means suspending deliveries of any further orders until your client pays her bill. If you deliver services, stopping work means putting any current projects on hold until payment is made. Stopping work shows your client or customer that you're serious about getting paid, and it's sure to solicit some sort of response. Before you undertake this step, however, be sure to give your client fair warning that you plan to take this action if you don't receive payment by a particular date.

4. **Enlist the services of a collections agency.**

   If you've gone through all the previous steps and still haven't been paid, it's probably time to assign the tardy account to a collections agency. A *collections agency* specializes in motivating customers to pay their financial obligations. Subject to federal, state, and local regulation, collections agencies use a variety of tactics to get your clients' attention — including phone calls, letters, and even lawsuits — and to get them to pay. You pay a price for this service, however. Expect to pay anywhere from 10 to 50 percent of any monies collected by the agency. Although an agency takes a healthy cut, the probability of getting some payment likely increases with an agency in your corner.

5. **Mediate.**

   Taking a client or customer to court isn't our idea of fun. Before you're forced to take that last, most drastic step, you have one more way to get out of your impasse: mediation. A *mediator* is an impartial third party whose job is to help you and your customer work through your problems and reach a reasonable solution — one that is a win for both parties. If your client has simply decided not to pay you, mediation may not be fruitful. However, if your client is upset because of some perceived shortcoming in your performance, you may have a chance of resolution through mediation. You can find mediators by doing a simple Internet search or in the Yellow Pages, listed under *Mediation Services.*

6. **Take them to court!**

   Taking your clients to court is always the last resort. Not only does taking a client to court take up a lot of your precious time (and, if you need a lawyer, your money), but suing a client also puts the last nail in the coffin that was your business relationship. If, however, despite all your efforts, you still haven't been paid, and you decide that it's in your interest to do everything in your power to get the money that is owed you, by all means, take your client to court.

In many cases — for relatively small amounts of money owed — taking your client to court means going to *small-claims court,* which, by design, offers a simple and inexpensive way for you to have your case heard by a judge. The amount of money that qualifies as a small-claims action differs from state to state, and from country to country. In Alaska and Texas, for example, a small-claims action can't exceed $10,000, whereas $1,500 is the limit in Kentucky. And although you can sue a client for up to $25,000 in small-claims court in the Canadian provinces of Alberta, British Columbia, Nova Scotia, and Saskatchewan, you'll find a limit of $5,000 in Newfoundland and Labrador.

The extent to which you pursue your money is up to you. In some cases, you may decide that it's easier to write off the money (and the business relationship) than to pursue it to its ultimate conclusion. In other cases, you may decide to do whatever is necessary to get paid.

Getting a Loan

Studies show that one of the primary reasons so many businesses fail in their first year of existence is because they're *undercapitalized* — in other words, they don't have sufficient cash to meet their ongoing obligations over the long haul. Depending on what kind of business you have, putting enough money aside to allow you to make it through your first year can be a daunting proposition. But it shouldn't stop you from starting a successful home-based business — because you can always apply for a loan.

For many home-based businesspeople, the first choice in lenders is a time-honored one: F&F (friends and family). If friends and family aren't able to meet your business needs, though, you need to look elsewhere for the cash you need to sustain your business as you get established and build sales.

In the following sections, we explain some of the most commonly used sources of loans for home-based businesses.

Discovering different kinds of credit

Banks, credit unions, savings and loans, and other financial institutions are always coming up with new-and-improved loan products. Keep in mind, though, that you may have trouble obtaining a loan in the name of your business until it has established a track record of success over some extended period of time. If that's the case for you, check out the different kinds of credit we describe in this section to find one that may work for you.

Some of the most common forms of credit for home-based businesses, along with their pluses and minuses, include the following:

- **Credit card:** Many home-based businesses are financed — especially when they're first starting up — with credit cards. In fact, a recent survey showed that almost three in five of all small business owners use credit cards to at least partly finance their business operations. Not only are credit cards easy for most people to get, but they're also convenient and easy to manage. All this convenience comes at a price, however. Credit card interest rates can be obscenely high — now routinely 30 percent— and they're so easy to use that you can quickly find yourself bumping up against your credit limit. Although you'll likely be able to write this interest expense off when you do your taxes, you can quickly find yourself in over your head if you aren't careful. A study for the Ewing Marion Kauffman Foundation found that for every $1,000 in unpaid credit card debt, the risk a startup business will not make it goes up by 2.2 percent. Used judiciously, credit cards can be a terrific business tool — and may be all the credit you ever need.
- **Personal loan:** Individuals can get *personal loans* from banks, credit unions, finance companies, and similar sources based on their own personal income and creditworthiness. Assuming you have sufficient income and a good credit rating, you have a good chance of qualifying for the loan you need. After you have your loan, you're free to spend the money as you please, making personal loans quite flexible. If you decide to apply for a personal loan, be sure to do so while you're working at your regular job — *before* you leave to start your own business. Your income is likely to be higher, at least initially, improving the chances of approval as well as increasing the amount of money your bank will be willing to loan to you.
- **Business loan:** Banks and other financial institutions make *business loans* to finance business startups, cover ongoing operational needs, or finance business expansions. New businesses are inherently risky — they often have little or no *equity* (value) built up, usually lack a sufficiently long track record of success, and have a statistically high rate of failure within the first few years after founding. So business loans can be difficult for home-based businesses to obtain. Although rates can be reasonable — usually only a few points over the prime rate established by the Federal Reserve — the hoops you have to jump through, as well as the ongoing reporting and bank reviews, may be enough to send you looking elsewhere for funding. You may even have to pledge your personal assets as collateral in the event of a loan default. To get a business loan, at a minimum, you need a business plan, and you need to establish a good working relationship with your banker. If you and your business have what it takes, however, business loans can be your best solution. If

you're interested in business loans, check out peer-to-peer lending (P2P) facilitated by companies like Lending Club (`www.lendingclub.com`) and Prosper (`www.prosper.com`). The rates are typically lower than a bank loan or credit card.

- **Line of credit:** A *line of credit* is a business loan with a unique twist: Instead of a lump sum for the full amount of the loan, you're given approval to borrow funds up to a certain limit in whatever amounts or as often as you like. The advantage of a line of credit is that you don't have to use any of the money available to you until you need it, which means you don't have to make loan payments until you actually tap your credit line. With a regular loan, you get a check in the full amount of the loan, and you start making monthly loan payments soon thereafter. On the down side, a line of credit often has a higher interest rate than a standard loan, and its use may be more restricted.
- **Home equity loan:** A *home equity loan* is similar to a personal loan, with one major difference: You're required to pledge your home or other real property as collateral in the event that you default on your loan obligations. Because your equity bears the burden of risk — a fact that can weigh heavily on your mind if your business gets into financial trouble — home equity loans for substantial amounts of money can be obtained relatively easily. Loan terms can run 15 years or more. You likely have a choice of a lump sum or setting up a line of credit that you can draw on — and pay back — as necessary.
- **Microloan:** A growing number of states, counties, and cities are establishing *microloan* programs (usually defined as loans of $25,000 or less) to assist the startup and expansion of small businesses. The Utah Microenterprise Loan Fund (`www.umlf.com`), for example, has made loans from $1,000 to $25,000 to more than 560 small businesses over the past 15 years. For an up-to-date listing of organizations that provide microloans, check out the Association for Enterprise Opportunity Web site at `www.microenterpriseworks.org`.
- **SBA loan:** *SBA loans* are business loans that are backed by the U.S. Small Business Administration. Because the lending bank has less of a risk in the event of default, home-based business owners can obtain them more easily than a standard business loan. Interested? Talk to your friendly local banker or visit the SBA Web site at `www.sba.gov`.

So what kind of loan should you get? The answer depends on your particular situation, financial goals, the amount of money you plan to borrow, and your own personal credit history. Take some time to discuss your different options with your loan officer, financial advisor, or CPA. Remember, however, that you should always minimize how much you borrow and be diligent about paying back your loans as soon as you can.

Getting the loan you want

The best way to get the loan you want is to first understand what factors go into a decision to extend or deny credit to an applicant. The standard rule that most banks, credit unions, savings and loans, and other financial institutions use is called the *Five Cs:*

- **Capacity:** Will your business have the financial wherewithal to make loan payments — in full and on time — as required by your agreement with the lending agency? Will your cash flow support this additional burden of debt on your business? If you answer no to these questions, you need to figure out how to improve revenues while tightening up on expenses. Do so *before* you apply for your loan, not after.
- **Capital:** *Capital* represents the ratio of your company's debt to its assets or equity. Unfortunately, most business startups — including home-based businesses — have relatively high debt loads versus equity or assets. This is normal. You can, however, improve your chances of getting the loan you want by minimizing the debt you carry and maximizing equity and your own investment in the business.
- **Character:** Are you personally a good credit risk? Do you have a history of meeting your own financial obligations, including repaying loans on time and avoiding defaults or bankruptcies? A shaky credit history is an indication to a lender that your character is less than sterling. If you have shaky credit, be sure to do whatever you can to repair your own credit before you apply for a loan. Obtain a credit report from one of the major credit reporting agencies — Equifax (`www.equifax.com`), Experian (`www.experian.com`), or TransUnion (`www.transunion.com`) — and take action on any problems that may show up.
- **Collateral:** What kind of property can you pledge in case you default on your loan? Car loans require your car to be pledged as collateral. Home mortgages require that your house be pledged as collateral. What are your options for collateral? In many cases, lenders may require that you pledge your assets or property to secure your loan. Your ability to provide sufficient collateral will greatly enhance your chances of getting the loan you want.
- **Conditions:** Conditions include the health and growth potential of the markets within which you operate, the demographics of the typical buyers of your products and services, and many other economic factors external to your business. Although you can do little to influence or control the behavior of your markets or your customers, you can influence exactly which markets and customers you plan to target.

As you prepare to apply for a loan, review each of the Five Cs, and make an honest assessment of how you measure up. Which areas can you improve in? Find them and try to improve them now — before you apply for your loan. There's no reason why — if you do your homework — you can't get the loan you want for your business.

Fixing your bad credit history

Although everyone would love to have a great credit history, not everyone does. And, unfortunately, a bad credit history can prevent you from getting the loan you want and the money you need. The good news is that you can turn a bad credit history into a good credit history. It takes time and patience, but the rewards can be well worth the time and effort.

In her book *Money Troubles: Legal Strategies to Cope with Your Debts* (Nolo), Robin Leonard presents an eight-point plan for repairing your credit and improving your chances of getting a loan. Here's that plan in a nutshell:

1. **Secure a stable source of income.**
2. **Create a budget you can and will live within.**
3. **Open a passbook savings account (and add money to your account on a regular basis).**
4. **Apply for a savings passbook loan.**
5. **Pay back this loan over a six- to nine-month period.**
6. **Obtain a secured credit card.**
7. **Use this credit card sparingly (and pay off balances quickly to avoid potentially high interest charges).**
8. **Apply selectively for other cards (including gasoline companies, department stores, and other nonfinancial institutions).**

If your credit is seriously damaged, and this plan isn't enough to solve the problem, consider working with a credit counselor or credit repair agency. For more information, contact the National Foundation for Credit Counseling at `www.nfcc.org`.

Chapter 7

The Price Is Right: Deciding How Much to Charge

In This Chapter

- Understanding what your prices have to cover
- Evaluating your potential customers and figuring out how much they'll pay
- Researching your competition to get a better idea of what you should charge
- Applying pricing strategies that lead to sales

Pricing plays an extremely important role in the ultimate success of your business. Do it right, and your business will flourish; do it wrong, and your business will likely die a slow, miserable death. Because your business will live or die as a result of the pricing decisions you make, this topic deserves your undivided attention.

Here's how pricing works, in a nutshell: If you set your prices too high, your clients will seek less expensive sources for the products and services you provide, and you'll soon find yourself going out of business from lack of sales. Set them too low, however, and although you'll be swamped with customers — everyone loves a bargain, after all — your profit margins will be too small to sustain your business as it grows. The key is finding a compromise between these two extremes that pays you what you're worth while generating sufficient business to keep you working as many hours as you want.

You can set prices for your products and services in a variety of ways. In many cases, though, finding the right price comes down to good old-fashioned trial and error. In other words, do some research, check the competition, set a price, and see what happens. If sales aren't high enough, you can decide whether to lower your prices as an incentive for potential buyers to part with their cash. If sales are too high and the resulting profits are too low, you can choose to raise your prices to improve your margins (see the "Changing your prices" section later in this chapter).

Remember that the best pricing strategies are ones that strike a balance between generating the sales you need to survive and earning a reasonable profit that will allow your business to grow in the future. This chapter helps you understand how to develop the pricing strategy that's best for you, your business, and your customers and clients. We help you sort out the costs that you have to cover when you set your prices and help you get a feel for what your customers will be willing to pay. We also give you ideas for how to research your competition and review a number of different approaches to pricing that will aid your sales efforts. Finally, we consider the reasons why you should (or shouldn't) consider discounting your prices and how to take a stand when doing so is in your business's best interest.

Figuring Out What Your Prices Must Cover

Although the motivation behind your business may be to help others get things done or to provide them with the products they need to run their own businesses successfully, you can't have a business — at least not for very long — if you don't charge your customers some amount of money for your trouble. But you can't just charge them any old price; your price has to be low enough to attract the attention of prospective customers but high enough to allow you to generate a profit.

Since the beginning of business as you know it, the whole idea of pricing products and services has been to pay for all the expenses incurred in running a business while leaving a reasonable profit. Unfortunately, many home-based businesspeople don't fully understand the expenses they actually incur in running their businesses. Not only that, but they also sometimes forget that their home-based businesses should pay a decent salary and generate a reasonable profit — just like non-home-based businesses.

Imagine that the finances of your home-based business are a house. Just like any other sturdily built house anywhere in the world, it needs a roof, a foundation, walls, doors, and windows. Your finance house, also called your *money house,* also has a first floor and a second floor. Figure 7-1 shows this money house.

The following list describes the major components of this money house and how they relate to the finances of your home-based business:

- **The foundation — your salary:** Whenever your company sells a product or service, a portion of the cash you take in is set aside to pay you and any employees who have a regular salary.

- **The first floor — your overhead:** The cash you take in also pays for your *overhead,* including all the expenses your business requires to operate, regardless of whether or not you're selling any products. Insurance, rent, and telephones are examples of overhead expenses.
- **The second floor — your direct costs:** *Direct costs* are expenses that you incur on behalf of specific projects or products. If you drive to another town for a meeting or purchase wood to build a cabinet for a customer, for example, you're incurring direct expenses.
- **The roof — your profit:** *Profit* is what you're in business to try to make; it's what's left over when you've brought in all your cash for selling a product or service and subtracted out your salary, overhead, and direct expenses. Profit is your reward for taking a risk (yes, starting your own business does involve taking a risk, even if you've signed up for a "proven" system), and it plays an important role in building your business.

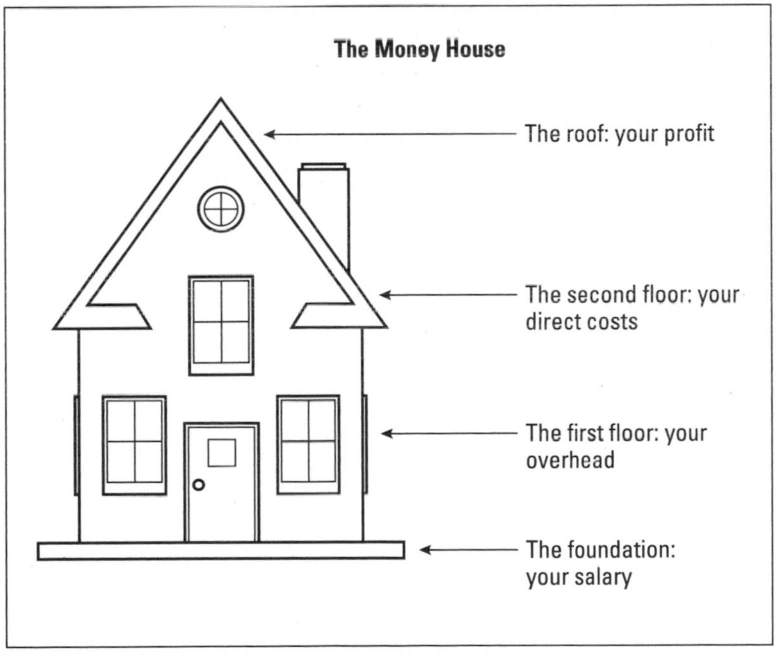

Figure 7-1: The money house.

Just like a large business like General Motors, IBM, or Pfizer, your home-based business can make a profit or incur a loss. Home-based businesses are real businesses, and the profit you make in your business is just as real as it is for any other business. People view profit in many different ways. Some people identify the revenue beyond what they expect to pay themselves as a higher salary. For others, it's having the money to spend on extra things, such as investing in one's business without borrowing (usually a better idea than taking out loans to grow your business) or taking a long-deserved trip to a ski resort or the beach. But for most people, profit is additional earnings.

In the following sections, we take a closer look at the kinds of financial elements that make up each part of your money house, and we explain how they all work together to determine the prices you charge for your company's products and services.

Paying salaries

When you set up your business as a sole proprietorship, you likely won't pay yourself a salary because, under a sole proprietorship, the money you make in your business is automatically counted as income to you for tax purposes. When you set up your business as a partnership or corporation, however, you may find that paying yourself a salary makes a lot of sense.

But how much should you pay yourself? When deciding how much salary to draw from your business, you first have to decide which of the following three lifestyles you want your business to support:

- **Survival:** In this mode, your business is just getting by, and you have little or no extra money to set aside to pay yourself. Ideally, you still work your regular day job or have a spouse or significant other to help support you while you're working to build your sales.
- **Comfortable:** Comfortable means things are going pretty well — well enough to allow you to quit your regular job and work at your home-based business on a full-time basis. You can choose to continue with the status quo — and be quite comfortable where you are — or work to increase your sales and see your business really take off.
- **Much better than average:** At this salary point, you're making more money than most people in your community or even in the nation. Attaining this level of income requires a lot of hard work and perhaps no small amount of luck. But for many, the rewards are worth the extra effort.

Establishing your overhead

Overhead consists of all your home-based business's nondirect costs and nonsalary expenses. In essence, your overhead expenses are the costs of doing business — the expenses that your business incurs even when you aren't creating products or delivering services to customers. Here are some examples of common overhead expenses:

- Computers, copiers, printers, telephones, and other office equipment
- Desks, chairs, and other office furniture
- Internet and e-mail connections
- Web site hosting fees
- Other marketing costs
- Letterhead stationery and business cards
- Office supplies
- Travel for business operations, marketing, or other nonproject purposes
- Phone line(s)
- Water, electricity, and other utilities
- Newspaper, journal, and magazine subscriptions
- Insurance
- Licenses
- Rent or mortgage
- Repairs and maintenance

TIP

Because overhead doesn't directly produce revenue (or, ultimately, profit), smart business owners work hard to minimize overhead expenses, keeping them at the lowest possible level while still providing the highest-quality services and products. To minimize your overhead expenses, you need to carefully assess every expense before you execute it. Before you spend a dime on any overhead item, take a moment to decide whether or not you really need it. And don't forget: Your overhead (and direct) expenses are generally tax deductible. Check out Chapter 9 for more details on the tax implications of your expenses.

Incurring direct costs

Direct costs are the expenses you incur as you create products or deliver services; if you aren't making products or delivering services, you have no direct costs. Generally, the more direct costs, the merrier, because they directly become part of the products and services you deliver to your clients, increasing the overall amount of money you bring into your business (and ideally increasing your clients' satisfaction at the same time). Here are some examples of direct costs:

- Materials and supplies consumed in the manufacturing process
- Travel at your client's request
- Time spent in client meetings
- Postage and phone calls for specific projects
- Fees to consultants contracted to assist on specific projects
- Equipment dedicated to producing a specific product or delivering a service to a particular client

If you aren't creating products or working on client projects, you don't incur direct costs. (But you do still have to pay for your overhead — whether or not you're producing and selling your products and services — and this overhead can quickly add up.)

Striving for profit

Although *profit* may seem like a mysterious and complex concept if you're new to owning your own business, it really boils down to a fairly simple idea:

The difference between a company's revenues and its costs

To figure out your company's profit, add together all the cash your company brings in from selling products and services and any income you earn from other sources, such as interest-bearing bank accounts and investments, and then subtract your salary, overhead, and direct costs from your total income. If the profit is negative (because the money you spend for your business is more than the money you bring into your business), it's called a *loss.*

Although we suspect you may already know this little tidbit, remember that profits are good and losses are bad.

Profit is the roof on the money house we build earlier in this chapter. It's the motivation that drives many businesses to ever-greater heights. In the case of a home-based business, profit is the reward to the owner for risking his or her capital in the marketplace. If allowed to accumulate within the business, the profit becomes the *equity* — the money put aside in savings — that gives the company real value.

Starting a training business

Q: I've been teaching various aspects of computer applications for several years. I've developed one-day seminars on topics like the Internet that I give at local colleges. The classes close out immediately, and many of my students follow me to different colleges to take all the different seminars I give. They also bring their friends. In other words, the seminars are well received and popular. Can I give these seminars at business conferences?

I also do in-house corporate training, and I hope to make contacts for future contracts for training. Generally, I get paid $200 for the day. Would I get paid more to do a business seminar? How would I go about getting such jobs?

A: Yes, you can speak at business conferences and do in-house training. I understand, however, that one of the major seminar producers in the United States now pays only $300 a day, and this job involves lots of travel. But the conference and corporate pay rates are typically better. To make a go of it, you need to develop marketing materials (a Web site with video and Web cam messages) and individually solicit meeting planners. You can fortify this material with great testimonials, perhaps on tape.

Sizing Up Your Potential Customers and How Much They'll Pay

Pricing your products and services is more than simply sticking price tags on them — pricing is an integral part of the overall strategy for your home-based business. In fact, it may well be one of the most important components (one reason we devote an entire chapter to the topic). Not only is pricing important because it determines to some extent exactly how much cash your business brings in, but it's also important from a marketing perspective and from the perspective of the overall health of your business and its ability to survive the long haul.

Set your prices too high, for example, and your sales will be few and far between. The result? Little or no cash into the business and an overall financial loss as you continue to expend money that isn't being offset by income. Not only that, but you'll also spend an awful lot of time twiddling your thumbs as you wait for your phone to ring. On the other hand, set your prices too low, and you'll set yourself up for a going-out-of-business scenario as you expend far too much time and money for too little return on your investment.

Before you launch headlong into your new home-based business, take a close look at your prospective customers — who they are and how much they're willing to pay for your products and services. What if your targeted customers don't seem willing to pay the price you need to turn a reasonable profit? You have little choice but to rethink your entire business strategy, either by creating more value for your clients-to-be to justify a higher price or by moving to an entirely different product or service that you *can* sell at the right price.

Take a moment or two to picture the kind of person who will buy your products or services. As you imagine your typical client or customer, ask yourself the following questions. To help you answer these questions, check out your competition to get a feel for what products and services they offer and how much their customers are willing to pay (see the next section for more tips).

- **What's your product or service worth to your prospective customers and clients?** Will your customers and clients see what you're selling as high value, low value, or something in between? Have you targeted the right market for your products and services? If not, what is the right market, and are there enough buyers to make it worth your while? Are you providing the right products and services to your target market? If not, what are the right products and services, and can you produce them cost-effectively?
- **What price are your prospective customers and clients willing to pay?** Is the price low, high, or somewhere in between?
- **Are you charging enough for your products and services to establish and grow a healthy business?** Will the price your customers and clients are willing to pay allow you to cover your business expenses — including the value of your time — and leave some money for profit? Will these prices enable you to grow your business, or will they cause your business to shrink — or, over a period of time, fail?
- **Do you have the right mix of price versus hours worked?** Are your prices set high enough to make a reasonable return on your investment of time and money, or are they so low that you have to work around the clock to make enough money just to keep your business afloat? Remember, there are still only 24 hours in a day!

Pricing can play an important role in your business's success or its failure and deserves your focus and attention — both in initially setting prices for your products and services and then in monitoring them over time to ensure that they're creating the return you desire. Find the right pricing, and you ease the way to increased sales at a high return — something that every home-based business owner is happy to have.

Researching Your Competition

So you've probably gathered that pricing is really important to the success of your business. But if you're new to your home-based business and have little or no previous experience selling the products and services you now offer, what's the best way to decide what prices to charge?

By far the quickest and easiest way to determine whether your prices make sense is to research your competition and see what they're charging. After you understand what other businesses like yours charge, you have a much better idea of the prices you should charge. Want to attract more business than the competition? Just charge a little less than they do. Want to position your company as a premium brand? Charge a little more than the competition.

TIP

Lucky for you, the Internet has made researching your competition much easier than it's ever been. Researching competition used to mean spending a lot of time leafing through the Yellow Pages and making phone calls. Today, however, with a few clicks of your mouse, you can find all kinds of free information about what prices your competitors' products are selling for and about the companies you compete against — information that you can use to structure your own competitive strategies and tactics.

Here are some places to start your online search for information:

- **Amazon:** `www.amazon.com`
- **Big Book:** `www.bigbook.com`
- **Business Wire:** `www.businesswire.com`
- **CanadaOne Directory:** `www.canadaone.com`
- **Craigslist:** `www.craigslist.com`
- **eBay:** `www.ebay.com`
- **Google:** `www.google.com`
- **Hoover's Online:** `www.hoovers.com`
- **Public Register's Annual Report Service:** `www.prars.com`
- **U.S. Chamber of Commerce:** `www.uschamber.com`

TIP

Fuld & Company is an international leader in obtaining competitive intelligence on businesses for a variety of clients. The company has developed the I3 Internet Intelligence Index, available for free on its Web site at `www.fuld.com`. The Internet Intelligence Index contains links to more than 600 competitive-intelligence Internet Web sites, covering an incredibly wide variety of information.

ASK PAUL & SARAH

The best business media

Q: Before I start work each morning, I like to read the newspaper over breakfast. I find this routine both relaxing and motivating, as I'm able to scan the articles for ideas, leads, general inspiration, or information. Unfortunately, I have time to read only one paper before work beckons. Which do you think offers more relevant information for a home-based business owner: a local newspaper or a national newspaper such as *USA Today* or *The Wall Street Journal*?

A: The answer depends on the nature of your business and your clientele. If your customers are businesses, your best bet is *The Wall Street Journal.* Even owners of small businesses most often read this newspaper. However, if your business serves only local customers, your local newspaper is, in almost all cases, your best bet. Another alternative, if you live in a city large enough to have one, is a local business journal that blends both local and business news. If your business addresses a broad consumer market on the Internet, through mail order or through wholesalers, a national paper like *The New York Times* or *USA Today* may better help you keep your finger on the pulse of popular consumer issues and tastes.

After choosing the one paper to read every morning, use the following time-saving techniques to help you keep up with your industry's ever-changing issues:

- **Read industry-specific newspapers online.**

  Most newspapers provide a significant portion of their content online. You can periodically peruse relevant topics in newspapers you don't subscribe to, which is a great way to keep up with an industry-specific town's newspaper. If you're in the computer industry, for example, you can peruse the *San Jose Mercury Times* site periodically (`www. mercurynews.com`). If you deal with government, you can pop over to `www.washingtonpost.com`. If you're in the entertainment business, try `www.latimes.com`. Such Web visits can be a great way to take a work break!

- **Create your own custom newspaper using a site like `www.crayon.net`.**

- **Subscribe to a weekly business news magazine, such as *BusinessWeek* (which you can also read online at `www.businessweek.com`), instead of reading a daily paper.**

Pricing Strategies That Deliver Sales

In an ideal world, the prices you apply to your products and services would enhance — not hinder — your ability to sell them. Pricing is a fine art (some say a mystical art), and the psychology of marketing, along with how you present your products and your prices, determines much of the way your clients-to-be react to them.

For example, when your products and services are desirable and in short supply, people are willing to pay far more for them than when they're undesirable and available in overwhelming amounts. This example illustrates the basic law of supply and demand that you probably learned about in school. Think for a moment about what happens when a few toys end up on the top of every child's list of wants during the holiday season. As a surge of parents hits the stores, the toys inevitably become hard to find, and parents become willing to pay top dollar to get them — often, whatever it takes to ensure the happiness of their children. And for the toys that don't make the top of the list? They're plentiful and often on sale.

What does this idea of supply and demand mean for you? It means determining the best price points for your products and services. In the following sections, we explore different ways to develop pricing strategies that ease the way to sales.

Creating value for your clients

Above all, your clients and customers want to feel like they're getting the best value for their money — regardless of whether the prices you charge are high or low. So by increasing the *perceived value* of your products and services (value is a subjective judgment, after all), you can increase the prices you charge for them and increase your profit at the same time!

Here are some of the best ways to create and increase the perceived value of your organization's products and services:

- **Go above and beyond.** Exceeding your customers' routine expectations dramatically increases the perceived value you deliver to them. Think for a moment about how you feel when someone goes out of his way to give you the best possible service. Aren't you willing to pay a little more to get more of that particular kind of service in the future? The better work you do, the higher your perceived value and the higher the prices you can charge.
- **Be different.** Many markets are crowded with competitors, each one offering products and services that seem to differ little from the competition. When you differentiate yourself from the rest of the pack — whether through novel packaging, a unique sales approach, or the product or service itself — you increase your value to your clients and customers.
- **Focus on customer service.** The bad news is that every industry has more than its share of businesses that don't provide good customer service. The good news is that this shortfall gives you a terrific opportunity to provide the service that's lacking in your industry. Take advantage of it, and you greatly enhance the perceived value of your organization's products and services. Believe us — most people vastly prefer buying their products and services from companies that provide good service than from ones that don't.

- **Add value.** If you and a competitor offer the same item for the same price, why would a customer decide to buy exclusively from you? Well, in truth, they wouldn't — unless, of course, you add value to the transaction. Perhaps you provide better after-sales support, or maybe you're willing to take returned items for 30 days after an item is sold rather than the 10 days your competitor allows. By adding value to the items you sell — value as perceived in the eyes of the buyer — you create value for your clients (and they'll value you for it).
- **Build long-term relationships.** All business is about relationships, and your customers and clients value the long-term relationships they develop with you and other trusted vendors. By building relationships with your clients and customers, you become more than a place to buy something — you become a trusted friend and adviser, someone to turn to when your customers have questions or need help. Help a few times, and you'll have a customer for life!

REMEMBER

Always keep your customers' perceived value of your products and services in mind when you develop and set your prices. Adding value in your customers' eyes gives you much greater flexibility in the prices you ultimately choose.

Setting your prices: Five approaches

Pricing is integral to the marketing process, and it can have a dramatic impact on whether potential customers choose to buy from you or from someone else. The right price can generate more sales, and the wrong price can send potential customers and clients looking elsewhere to fulfill their needs.

The following list describes five of the most common approaches that home-based businesses use to set their prices. As a part of determining your pricing strategy, carefully consider which approach (or combination of approaches) makes the most sense for your business.

- **Startup pricing:** If you're just getting started in your business, offer your customers an introductory rate that's set at a point somewhere between what other, established businesses charge and the amount you would be paid if you were doing the work on salary for an employer. Just don't forget to increase your pricing to bring it in line with the rest of the market after you get past the startup phase and establish a track record. To avoid unpleasant surprises, don't forget to let your early customers know that prices *will* rise in the future. Otherwise, they may not be very happy when your prices go up.

- **The going rate:** In some businesses, almost every company charges a *going rate* for particular products or services. For example, the typical carpet-cleaning business in your community may charge $199 to clean three rooms and a hallway. You can choose to set your price at the going rate and differentiate your business through things other than price, such as better customer service or extra service that your competition doesn't provide. As some business owners have discovered, finding something that differentiates you from the competition can be as simple as a brightly painted van that advertises your business everywhere you go or an easy-to-remember phone number (for example, 1-800-CARPETS — of course, that's already been taken, so use your imagination to come up with your own idea).
- **Splitting the difference:** When you survey your competition, you may find that they offer a range of prices for the same products or services: some high, some low, and some in between. By splitting the difference between the top and the bottom of the range, you can be sure that your price is neither too high nor too low. After seeing how your customers react, you can make further adjustments later (see the "Changing your prices" section later in this chapter for tips on how to do so).
- **Bargain-basement pricing:** If you really want to generate a lot of business quickly, you can dramatically undercut your competitors' prices. However, before you try this approach, understand that some potential clients may be wary of buying products and services that are priced substantially below the competition. To offset this wariness, you need to find some way to make them feel like they aren't taking a risk by hiring you (great references from previous clients can do wonders here). Understand, too, that you may not be able to keep up this approach for long without doing serious financial damage to your company.
- **Premium pricing:** At the other end of the spectrum from bargain-basement pricing is pricing at a premium, *above* your competition. This approach works well when you, first, differentiate the products or services you sell from those offered by your competition and, second, add value your clients and customers can see and appreciate. Consider a fancy dog-washing service that doesn't just come to your home but that arrives in a brand-new, stainless-steel trailer, customized with all the latest tools of the trade, hot water, and big fluffy towels for your dog, Spot. Because you want only the very best for your pet, paying a few extra dollars for first-class service like this is a no-brainer.

REMEMBER

After you set your prices, keep close tabs on what your competition is doing. Are they raising their prices? Lowering them? When your competition moves, be prepared to adjust your prices accordingly.

Selling the eBay way

Many home-based businesspeople have found success on eBay (www.ebay.com), the popular auction Web site. Why eBay? Because it's the most successful auction site with the widest reach to a global audience of buyers. In recent years, eBay has introduced fixed-price listings for sellers who want to sell their products for a set price without going through the hassle and uncertainty of an auction. Some home-based businesspeople have discovered that they can get more than enough business just by selling on eBay, while others have used eBay as a stepping stone to bigger-and-better things. Whatever your long-term goals may be, selling your products on eBay is an extremely easy thing to do, and your listings can reach a nationwide, and even worldwide, audience — exposing your products to a much larger number of potential buyers than if you sold them only in your local area. This increased exposure translates to higher prices and more profit in your pocket.

Here are a few recent eBay success stories:

- A few years ago, Cristiane Bastos opened an eBay store, called Butterfly Twins, where she started selling Rosa Chá bikinis from Brazil. The bikinis were quickly gaining in popularity at the time because they were prominently featured in the *Sports Illustrated* swimsuit edition. As her eBay business grew, she added one-piece swimsuits and Havaianas flip-flop sandals to her sales mix, followed by high-end items, such as Oakley, Revo, and Nike sunglasses and athletic watches. By carefully researching which of her items were selling best, and which eBay listings drew the most customers and best prices, Cristiane optimized her approach, and sales quickly shot up 600 percent.
- For years, Scott Griggs had a traditional bricks-and-mortar store in which he sold his model trains. However, the high overhead costs involved in running a store put a lot of pressure on Scott's bottom line, squeezing his profits in the process. Finally, when it was clear that keeping his store open would eventually push him over a huge financial cliff, Scott closed the store and moved his model train business to eBay. Today Scott posts 3,500 to 4,000 auction listings on eBay each month, along with another 2,000 or so eBay store listings each month.
- After being a buyer on eBay for a number of years, Tara Barney decided to pursue an idea she had to become a seller of jewelry she made that matched the color schemes of her favorite children's clothing lines. The result was a new eBay-based business — Tara's Treasures. Using a feature called Custom Pages, Tara created her own look and feel for her brand — when customers encounter one of her pages on the eBay Web site, they immediately know they're on the Tara's Treasures site. Tara's business has done so well that Tara upgraded to a Premium Store on eBay to handle the increased volume and to analyze her buyers' shopping patterns.

Although eBay can be a great place for home-based businesses to sell their wares, doing so comes at a cost. eBay charges a variety of fees that fall under two broad categories: insertion fees and final value fees. You pay *insertion fees* to run your auction or fixed-price listing — whether or not you sell the item. You pay *final value fees* only when you sell the item; these fees are a percentage of the price for which you sell your item. You can find much more information about eBay fees at pages.ebay.com/HELP/SELL/fees.html.

If you don't feel like dealing with eBay yourself, a number of companies are out there to sell your items on eBay for you. Of course, you have to pay such companies a fee for their services. But some people use them to save time and to attract more buyers (thanks to the greater amount of traffic many of the service sites attract).

Changing your prices

After you decide on a specific price for a product or service, your clients expect to pay that price for the foreseeable future. No one likes buying things from a company that changes its prices every other week (or, in the case of gasoline, every other hour). However, at some time, you may need to change your prices, either up or down. If the changes translate into price increases, you may have to overcome the resistance of your clients and customers. But if the changes are price decreases, I doubt anyone objects!

In the following sections, we look at price increases and price decreases — and how each impacts your business.

Increasing your prices

Price increases aren't usually pleasant events for the company making them — no company wants to tell its clients they have to pay more money for the same product — but they're often necessary. Some of the most common reasons for price increases are

- **You've underpriced your products.** After you set a price and begin to sell your products and services, you may discover that the money you're bringing in isn't enough to cover the expenses of the business and generate a reasonable profit. In this case, when you can't or don't want to reduce your expenses to bring your costs in line with the money you're bringing into your business, you have no other choice (assuming you want to stay in business) than to increase your prices.
- **Your expenses have increased.** If your costs of production increase, you can either reduce your profit or increase your price. The choice is up to you (although if your expenses have dramatically increased, you may have to do both).
- **You need to cover a client's hidden expenses.** If you're performing services for a client and discover additional costs from working with that client that you didn't anticipate (for example, your client requires you to attend meetings twice a week instead of just once a month as you planned), you have to find a way to recoup them without reducing your profit. The easiest way is to increase your price.
- **You want to test the marketplace.** Sometimes you simply want to test the marketplace with a higher price to see whether the quantity of units you sell increases, decreases, or stays the same. Airlines, food manufacturers, and others test the marketplace all the time. Who knows? You may discover that your customers are more willing to pay a higher price for your products and services than you thought.

- **You don't want the work.** If you don't want to do work for certain clients at the low prices you've agreed to, the best way to get out of this situation is to raise your prices far beyond your normal rates. If the customer decides to pay more, great — you just won the lottery! If not, you won't miss it. Peter has been known to increase his prices when he's booked up with a lot of projects. When someone is willing to pay the (much) higher fare for a new project, he makes room in his schedule to accommodate it.

REMEMBER

Don't be embarrassed by your prices or hesitate to raise or lower them when doing so makes sense for your business. If you decide to increase your prices, however, be as forthcoming as you can be, and give your customers plenty of notice so they can adjust.

Decreasing your prices

In some cases, you may have a good reason to decrease your prices. Though you may not have to decrease your prices as often as you increase them, you're bound to have to do so from time to time. The main reasons for decreasing your prices are

- **You've overpriced your services.** If you've overpriced your services, you can choose to keep the extra money as profit (making for a very nice windfall, thank you very much), or you can give it back to your customers in the form of lower prices, refunds, or rebates.
- **Your expenses have decreased.** If you've decreased your expenses, you may want to lower your prices. Then again, you can always keep the fruit of your decreased expenses as profit and increase the amount of money you put into savings. Doing so will motivate you to continue to find new ways to cut expenses.
- **You want to reward long-term clients.** Long-term clients always like to know you appreciate them. You can show your appreciation (and build their loyalty) by reducing prices for them, either on a one-time basis or permanently — perhaps in the form of a discount card, special gift, or other premium.
- **You want to get new work.** One way to get new business is to drop your prices for new customers as a way to introduce them to your company and your products and services. Two-for-one specials for new customers, percent-off coupons, and the like are all ways to get new customers to try out your company — and, ideally, stick around.
- **You want to extend a professional courtesy.** Doctors, lawyers, and other professionals are noted for extending lower prices to colleagues as a professional courtesy. Why not extend lower prices to your colleagues, too? How about discounting your products and services for other home-based business owners?

As with any other price changes, make sure you lower your prices as part of an overall strategy, not just as a reaction to some momentary event. If in doubt, leave your prices where they are until the case for changing them is more compelling. Not sure whether it's time, yet? Then it probably isn't.

Deciding whether to discount

When you're starting out in your home-based business, you need to get the ball rolling. Your prices can help you do so, or they can stop the ball dead in its tracks. In the beginning, getting work — regardless of how much you charge — may be more important than charging just the right price. After you build up experience and references, you can better call the shots regarding your pricing.

In the beginning, you want to get known. You want to develop a buzz about your company and its goods and services. You want people to start talking about you and your company. As they do, and as more and more clients seek you out, you have the leverage to charge them what you're worth. In other words, if you're going to discount your products and services, the time to do so is when you're getting your home-based business established — not after you've developed a solid reputation, base of experience, and prices people have begun to rely on.

By far the biggest mistake home-based businesspeople make is *chronic undercharging*. Chronic undercharging creates a downward spiral that slowly eats away at the foundations of your business — the longer it goes on, the weaker your business becomes. Eventually, the bottom falls out altogether, and you're left with nothing but unpaid bills.

Chronic undercharging creates the following problems in home-based businesses:

- **Low-ball clients:** You tend to attract customers who are much more interested in paying as little as possible than in buying the best product or service out there.
- **Low-margin work:** You spend far too much of your time on low-margin work and far less of your time on high-paid projects that offer the greatest return for your time and money. Because there are still only 24 hours in a day, you're working more hours for less pay — a going-out-of-business plan if we've ever seen one.
- **Burnout:** You force yourself into a situation in which you focus far more time on your business than you do on maintaining and improving your relationships with friends and family or on keeping yourself healthy and happy — a classic road to burnout. Burnout isn't unique to home-based businesses, but it can be a very real problem — especially for people who are juggling the demands of kids and family or a job that they haven't yet left behind.

Discounting is okay as long as you do it consciously and in line with long-term strategy. It's not okay when it becomes a knee-jerk reaction to every potential client who hesitates for a moment when you quote a price. If you're going to discount your services, consider some of the following approaches:

- Offer every tenth pound of coffee for free.
- Give a 25-percent discount on your client's first order.
- Offer volume discounts.
- Give a discount for paying before a certain date.
- Offer a variety of products and services at a variety of price points — high, low, and in between. When faced with a client or client-to-be who wants you to discount your prices, you're far better off cutting the products or services delivered than cutting your unit price for those services.

  So, for example, when a client balks at your quotation of $1,000 to develop a turnkey Web site, don't say: "What if I drop my price to $750? Do we have a deal?" Instead, say: "No problem. Here's a complete list of all the different features you get in my $1,000 plan. Which features do you want to delete to meet your budget?"

Taking a stand on prices

When you've established a price and your prospective client doesn't want to pay it, at some point, you have to take a stand. You can't just give your products or services away, right? Often, you simply want to maintain your prices exactly where they are and deny requests to lower or discount them. Here are some strategies to help you hold the line on your prices when you think it's in your best interest to do so:

- **Understand your limits.** When you want to take a stand and hold the line on your prices, first you need to understand the limitations within which you can work and the minimum prices you're willing to accept.
- **Learn to say no.** Far too many people cave in the moment their customers show even one iota of resistance to their prices, no matter how well thought out and reasonable they may be. But, lucky for you, we've found a very easy cure to this kind of reaction: Just say no! Know your limits, and when someone wants you to go beyond them, be ready, willing, and able to say no.
- **Be ready to explain why.** When you say no to people who think their requests are reasonable, you have to be able to explain why. Most people like to hear some rationale when someone else denies their "reasonable" requests. Responses like "I'll lose money on the deal at that price" or "That's a going-out-of-business plan for me" may be sufficient.

In contrast, responses like "Because I got up on the wrong side of the bed this morning" or "I always charge you more than the rest of my customers" may not leave the best impressions with your customers.

- **It's not personal — it's business.** Separate your personal feelings from the need to conduct your business in a way that ensures its survival. Although you may like the feeling of cutting your prices and giving away your products and services to anyone who asks, you'll quickly go out of business with that approach. Remember: You've got a business to run — it isn't a charity.
- **Be prepared with a counterproposal.** Whenever you tell a prospective client or customer no, be prepared with an alternative that you can say yes to. For example, if you don't want to agree to dropping your price from $100 to $75 a unit, as requested by your client, you may be able to say yes to $95 — a figure that may well seal the deal for you.

You're going to face times when you have to take a stand and hold the line against dropping your prices. Although you may lose potential customers in the process, your business will be healthier for it. And a healthy business is a business that thrives and grows — building long-term income for you and an ongoing partner for your clients.

Chapter 8

Getting Health Insurance and Planning for Your Retirement

In This Chapter

- Identifying the best benefits for you
- Deciding on a healthcare strategy that meets your needs
- Considering other benefits

Most full-time employees take their benefits for granted. Sick leave, holidays, tuition assistance, healthcare, worker's compensation, 401(k) savings plans, and more are an expected part of any full-time job. However, when you start your own home-based business, you quickly discover that benefits aren't something to take for granted. In fact, some benefits aren't even available to home-based businesspeople at all, and those that are have real and substantial costs.

For many prospective home-based businesspeople, their biggest concern about leaving their full-time jobs behind to start their own businesses is losing their benefits, especially benefits related to healthcare.

They have good reason to be concerned, too. A hospital stay for a routine surgery to remove an inflamed appendix or to fix a damaged knee joint can quickly run into the tens of thousands of dollars. And if you have the misfortune of having to undergo extensive treatment and hospitalization for a more serious condition, such as cancer or an automobile accident, you can expect to owe hundreds of thousands of dollars. Just a month's prescription for certain name-brand drugs can cost hundreds of dollars or more.

In this chapter, we take a look at the benefits available to home-based businesspeople. Because health insurance is the primary concern for most prospective owners of home-based businesses, we take an especially close look at that particular benefit: what to look for in a healthcare plan and how to get the coverage you need.

Providing Your Own Benefits

Healthcare in the United States is so expensive that a recent study published in the *American Journal of Medicine* found that 62.1 percent of all bankruptcies in the United States have a medical cause. Even more chilling is the fact that 75 percent of these medical debtors had health insurance. After years of having benefits provided by your employers — generally without even having to ask for them — you're taking a very big step into the great unknown when you start your own home-based business. For example:

- Do you qualify for medical coverage? And if you do qualify, can you afford it?
- What if you're injured and can't work — what then?
- Will you be able to set up a retirement fund? Are there limits to what you can contribute?

These questions — and many, many more — are valid concerns for individuals planning to make the move into self-employment, and you shouldn't quit your day job before you have this particular aspect of your work life figured out. It's important for you — and for your family and loved ones — to address these concerns sooner rather than later. After all, you can lose not only your business but everything in your personal life if a medical disaster strikes when you're unprepared.

When you're the boss, you have to find the best benefits you can get for your hard-earned money, recognizing that what's best for someone else may not be best for you. Finding what's best for you in terms of benefits generally requires a lot of research on your part, but the payoff is an enhanced quality of life, and it's well worth the expense.

The best solution for your benefits involves two key factors:

- Pricing your products and services high enough to make sure you cover the cost of health insurance
- Not letting yourself get taken in by what appears to be inexpensive and adequate coverage but what is really inadequate

Working for yourself doesn't necessarily mean fewer benefits. If you do your homework, and if your prices are high enough, working for yourself can actually mean more — and often better — benefits. Instead of being saddled with whatever benefit plans your employer decides are best for you, you get to pick and choose which benefit plans you really want. You pay only for the plans you need and can tailor your benefit plans to your own unique wants and desires.

For instance, is having income in the event that you're disabled — and unable to work — particularly important to you? (If your work involves physical labor or you're the primary wage earner in your household, it should be.)

If it is, focus on getting good disability coverage. Do you want to ensure that you'll be able to retire comfortably? (We can't think of anyone who doesn't want to do so.) If so, you can structure a retirement plan that meets your exact needs. Or if you simply want to have the best medical plan you can buy, go for it. It's your choice. Whichever benefits you choose to obtain, you need to do some planning and research before you settle on anything.

As a home-based businessperson, you — not someone else — get to decide what the best solution is for you and your loved ones. Having the ability to decide such important issues yourself is one of the things that makes working for yourself such an attractive option.

ASK PAUL & SARAH

Working benefits into the mix

Q: This is my fourth year as a freelance translator, and it's been a good experience so far. My problem is not being able to secure individual health insurance thanks to past health conditions. Another concern is how to set aside funds for retirement. My income is good at times, but some months are typically low. Taking a vacation also seems impossible because I can't afford to have no income while I'm away. Plus, I may lose clients when they discover I'm not available when they need me. Any advice?

A: You're definitely not alone in worrying about how to provide for benefits like vacations, healthcare, and retirement. These three concerns are among the most critical issues facing people who are or want to be self-employed. The hurdles in lining up such benefits keep too many people working in less-than-rewarding salaried jobs instead of pursuing their dreams to be their own bosses.

Although lining up these benefits is more difficult than it should be, doing so needs to be one of your top priorities if you want to become your own employer. Try to develop a new attitude toward these responsibilities: Keep in mind that the cost of benefits, such as vacation time, retirement funds, and health insurance, are part of the cost of doing business, and you must build them into your fee structure and set aside the funds needed to cover them. If you can't afford to take vacations, for example, you're either not charging enough or you need to develop a marketing campaign to bring in more business during the slow times you mention.

That said, here are some options for getting past the difficulties involved in lining up these benefits:

- **Health insurance:** Obtaining affordable health insurance is a national crisis, especially for the self-employed. One option is to go through a professional association, which may be able to negotiate coverage for its members. In addition, some states — such as California, Colorado, Connecticut, Maryland, and Texas — have a mandatory small business insurance provision. If you have two people working in your company (which can include your spouse!), you can get health insurance. To find out the situation in your state, check with your state insurance commissioner, visit `www.healthinsurecoverage.com`, or contact an insurance agent.
- **Retirement:** Open a SEP-IRA account and put 10 percent (or as high a percentage as you can afford) of everything you earn into it or some other retirement account. Make this a habit.

Choosing Your Healthcare Coverage

Of all the benefits available to most workers today, one in particular creates the most concern for people considering a move to starting their own home-based businesses, and that's health insurance. Unfortunately, health insurance has a (much-deserved) reputation for being hard to obtain for individuals, it's often expensive, and the consequences of not having sufficient coverage can be financially catastrophic — particularly in the event of a major or prolonged illness.

In fact, the fear of having inadequate health insurance — or, even worse, no coverage at all — keeps many people from making the move to starting their own businesses. Instead, they remain stuck in jobs they don't like, getting paid less than they feel they should, to ensure that their health needs are met.

The simple fact is that you, as a home-based business owner today, have more options available to you than ever before. You have more options both in the kinds of coverage available to you and in the different approaches you can take to get the coverage you need. In some cases, the healthcare plan you select as a home-based business owner may even provide better coverage for you and your family for a lower premium than you ever paid in your regular job. Not only that, but as a self-employed individual it's highly likely that you'll be able to deduct as a business expense 100 percent of your medical and dental insurance costs. Be sure to consult with a CPA or qualified tax professional to see whether your plan qualifies for this deduction, and check out Chapter 9 for more on taxes and deductions.

Exploring the spectrum of healthcare coverage

When starting your own home-based business, you have a number of healthcare choices, all of which boil down to either obtaining health insurance or going at it on your own.

At one end of the spectrum, *fee-for-service* care is the traditional form of medicine that many people grew up with (some people today call it old-fashioned). Under a fee-for-service healthcare plan, you decide which doctor you want to see, schedule your own exam, get diagnosed and treated, and make your payment directly to the doctor on the way out the door.

At the other end of the spectrum is a particular kind of health insurance, the *health maintenance organization* — also commonly known as an HMO. In an HMO, you agree to have all your healthcare needs taken care of by the HMO and its administrators and physicians. The HMO hires and pays the doctors, nurses, and physician's assistants who diagnose your illnesses; the HMO builds or leases the facilities where you go for medical examinations; and the HMO decides whether or not to authorize and pay for your treatment. In many cases, you never even see a bill or invoice, although most HMOs today require at least a nominal payment, known as a *co-payment,* at the time of service. (Today HMOs are also increasing their co-payments.)

Each of these extremes on the healthcare spectrum — and all the variations in between — has its good and bad points. By going on your own, you have maximum control and flexibility over your healthcare, but, unless you're well off financially, a catastrophic injury or illness has the power not only to put you out of business, but also to potentially bankrupt you. At the other end of the spectrum, in exchange for the peace of mind that HMOs offer, you give up a large amount of control over the management of your healthcare, as well as much of the flexibility to use whatever doctor you like, whenever you want. You go to the HMO's facilities, select a doctor from a limited list the HMO puts together for you, and generally follow that doctor's treatment options.

When seeking health insurance for your home-based business, you have a number of options available to you. For example:

- If you start up your home-based business while you're still working your regular job, you can simply keep your current healthcare plan as it is. This option is likely to be relatively inexpensive for you and your business — particularly if your employer covers some or all of the cost of your healthcare plan.
- If your spouse has health insurance at work, you can decide to use his or her plan to meet your healthcare needs as you establish your own home-based business. This option, too, can be a relatively inexpensive one for you and your business.
- If you decide to leave your regular job to start your own home-based business and you live in the United States, COBRA — the Consolidated Omnibus Budget Reconciliation Act — requires your employer to extend healthcare benefits to you for a minimum of 18 months (and in some cases, even longer) at the same rate offered to all other company employees (a piece of which most companies pay as an employee benefit) for comparable coverage. After the 18-month period elapses, you can generally convert to an individual plan with little muss or fuss, but usually at a significantly higher cost. (When Peter's COBRA plan expired a number of years ago, the cost to cover his family of five jumped from $750 a month to more than $1,350 a month. He shopped around for and found a new, less expensive plan within minutes after he got that particular bit of news.)

- If you want to find your own coverage as you begin your home-based business, you can conduct your own search for health coverage. (A growing number of Internet sites, such as `www.eHealthInsurance.com`, are dedicated to helping small business owners select and apply for health insurance.) You can start by doing a keyword search on a search engine. Alternatively, a good insurance agent or broker can find the best coverage for you while saving you precious time in the process. In comparing policies, check *deductibles* (the amount you pay before your insurance pays), co-payments, *co-insurance* (the percentage of a doctor or hospital bill you must pay beyond the co-payment), out-of-pocket limits (particularly important with co-insurance), lifetime maximum coverage, and limitations and restrictions on what is covered.

As a home-based businessperson, you have the luxury (and the burden) of almost unlimited choices when dealing with your healthcare. From fee-for-service to HMO, the choice is up to you. The right decision depends on what's best for you, your family, and your business.

Looking at fee-for-service and indemnity healthcare plans

Under traditional fee-for-service medical care, what's good for the patient is also generally good for the doctor because their goals are aligned. As we mention earlier, *fee-for-service* care is when doctors are paid directly for their medical services — whether by the patient or by an insurance company or other entity. With this kind of care, you're free to go to any doctor or hospital you choose — assuming you have enough money for the procedure. Although this method of payment is fine for simple, relatively low-cost procedures, it leaves the patient at tremendous financial risk if he becomes seriously ill or injured and requires extensive testing, hospitalization, or treatment.

With the traditional fee-for-service, on-your-own payment method, patients have the greatest freedom to choose their doctors and hospitals. They can get their healthcare directly — at any point in the system — without externally imposed limits. However, they often pay a lot of money for this privilege. Fee-for-service is the least regulated form of healthcare, and fees can be unpredictable. Its unpredictability and generally high cost are driving fee-for-service care toward extinction — despite the nostalgia that many people have for it. Today this form of healthcare is sometimes called *going bare* — that is, without insurance.

A desire to limit patient financial risk within the traditional fee-for-service approach has led to the emergence of *indemnity insurance plans.* Under indemnity plans, insurance companies agree to reimburse — or indemnify — policyholders for a fixed percentage of their medical bills after payment of a pre-established deductible. For example, patients with this form of medical insurance may pay 20 percent of a medical expense, while their insurance company picks up the remaining 80 percent. Although indemnity plans still leave patients with some amount of financial risk, many people like these plans because they allow patients to select most any doctor or hospital they desire.

Many home-based business owners find that it makes sense to take advantage of a fairly recent wrinkle in the tax laws: *health savings accounts* (HSAs). HSAs — established by Congress in 2003 — allow you to set aside pretax dollars to pay for routine (and relatively low-cost) medical procedures, such as annual physicals, eye exams, dental checkups, and the like, while reserving insurance coverage for high-cost, catastrophic health events, such as major surgeries or cancer treatments. More than 5 million Americans have enrolled in HSAs. You may be able to supplement your HSA with a primary care doctor practicing "boutique" medicine, who will, for about a hundred dollars a month, provide a level of care that includes house calls and access by cellphone.

Checking out managed care plans

Managed care is the overall term applied to a system of healthcare in which an individual pays a fixed premium for a guarantee of all-encompassing, preventive, and therapeutic healthcare with minimal additional out-of-pocket expenses. The entire universe of managed care systems covers an incredibly diverse range of programs — from managed indemnity insurance to HMOs. Although separating one form of managed care from another is sometimes difficult, all managed care programs implement formal policies and procedures that control three common characteristics:

- Access
- Cost
- Quality

By placing strict limits and controls on these three areas, managed care providers are able to provide complete, quality medical care to their members at lower costs than other forms of healthcare. For example, one way that certain kinds of managed care providers control costs is by hiring their own doctors and nurses. Another way to control costs is by making concerted efforts to provide preventive care to patients. Preventing a serious illness is generally far less expensive than curing it.

In the next sections, we distinguish between two types of managed care: health maintenance organizations (HMOs) and preferred provider organizations (PPOs).

Health maintenance organizations (HMOs)

An *HMO* is a form of managed care that either operates its own healthcare facilities or contracts with hospitals and doctors to provide healthcare services at predetermined rates. The membership fees go into a pool of money that pays for doctors, nurses, equipment, facilities, and the other costs of providing healthcare services to members. Any money left over is profit. After the membership fee has been paid, the greatest risk to the HMO is providing too much care or care that's too expensive.

All HMOs rely on the primary care physician to control costs by controlling access to the services of the HMO. A *primary care physician* is a doctor whose job is to assess a patient's medical condition and determine which services are required to bring her back to a state of good health at the minimum necessary cost. Primary care physicians are often under considerable pressure to keep costs down, so their jobs sometimes appear to be to find ways to deny care rather than provide it. Because of this perception, primary care physicians are often known as *gatekeepers*.

Comparison shopping among different HMOs can be frustratingly difficult. Sophisticated, often confusing issues require your consideration, including a wide array of different co-payments (both for services and for prescribed drugs), coverage limitations and exclusions, waiting periods, and more. At times, even the information sources you use may not permit easy comparison of one HMO to another. Consider the following as you try to find the right HMO for you:

- **Your healthcare needs:** You and your family want high quality, low costs, and easy access to your healthcare provider and a broad range of covered services. But you have to consider the limits in terms of the amount of dollars you're willing and able to put into your quest for quality healthcare and the choice of plans that are available to you. Further, it's unlikely that you'll find a plan that meets all your needs at a price you can afford. Your final selection will, therefore, involve some compromise.

  Unless you have unlimited resources to pour into purchasing your healthcare, selecting an HMO also forces you to face some limits. Finding the best HMO for you and your family involves striking a balance between your healthcare needs and wishes and the resources you have available to purchase them.

- **Other deciding factors:** Although you have your own unique medical needs, every healthcare consumer should consider several factors when shopping for an HMO. Depending on your personal situation, you may have several health plans to choose from, or you may have only one or two. Whatever the options available to you, you need to carefully weigh the advantages and disadvantages of each before you make your final decision.

TIP

After you enroll in a plan, switching plans may not be easy to do if you discover you made the wrong choice, so take your time to review each plan carefully and consider the following in your decision:

- **Basic needs versus extras:** With medical care, keep in mind the difference between what you need and what you want. Does the HMO you've chosen provide all the basic health services you need to maintain your health or return you from illness? Does it also provide the extras — such as a pleasant and relaxing environment, clean and modern hospitals, or free car seats for newborns — that you consider important to your healthcare experience?
- **Access:** Does the HMO you're considering provide you with access to the full range of physicians and medical facilities that are required to maintain your good health? Does the HMO offer specialists who are trained and competent in orthopedics, pediatrics, surgery, and so on? Are appointments readily available, or will you be required to wait long periods of time to see a doctor? Will you have access to 24-hour-a-day emergency-room care at a reasonable price?
- **Choice:** A hot button for many healthcare consumers is the right to see the doctor of their choice. Although some HMOs are restrictive and offer few care options, others offer a wide variety of doctors, clinics, and hospitals to choose from. When considering an HMO, be sure to find out how flexible your plan will be. Will the HMO assign you to a primary care doctor, or will you be able to make your own choice? If you don't like your doctor, can you easily switch to another? Will you have to go to a specific clinic or hospital, or will you have the option to select which one you want to go to? Ask an insurance agent what would happen under different hypothetical situations.
- **Cost:** The price of healthcare is always a major issue for healthcare consumers. Is the plan affordable? Will you receive a full range of services for an amount you can afford? If you're comparing plans, what do you get in the higher-priced plan that the lower-priced plan doesn't offer? Should you consider add-ons to the plan, such as point-of-service options?
- **Coverage:** Every HMO is different — some provide more extensive coverage than others. What does the plan cover? Does it include office visits and hospital stays? How about eye and dental care? Are certain procedures excluded from the plan? Do you understand how your HMO defines *experimental* or *unproven* cures? What about pre-existing conditions? If you have asthma when you join the plan, for example, will your new HMO cover it? If you're outside the plan area, will the plan pay for emergency care at another hospital?
- **Ease of use:** Every form of healthcare involves a certain amount of red tape and bureaucracy — HMOs are no exception. Are office hours convenient, and are facilities, clinics, and hospitals within a

reasonable distance from your home or work? Does the plan offer evening or weekend appointments? Are special phone lines available to make appointments or ask questions that don't require a physician's intervention? What kinds of paperwork (and how much) will you be required to fill out?

- **Quality:** The old adage that you get what you pay for is often true when it comes to healthcare. Are the doctors and nurses in the plan top-notch, or are they something less? Are the facilities modern, clean, and large enough to handle the needs of the plan's members? What's the overall quality of care dispensed by the HMO — is it excellent, good, or just adequate? How does the plan score on member satisfaction? Does the HMO have a history of extensive member complaints and grievances? Is the HMO National Committee on Quality Assurance (NCQA) or federally qualified?

As you research your healthcare options, you quickly find significant differences among plans. It's your job to determine whether a specific plan meets your needs. While the HMO's glossy brochures and glowing advertisements may seem attractive, try to get beyond its sugar-coated exteriors to the real story. Ask your insurance broker pointed questions. Which plan did he pick, and why? Is he happy with his choice? Why or why not? Is he planning to switch to another plan when he gets the opportunity?

Ultimately, you're faced with a choice that balances your healthcare needs with the resources you have available to pay for those needs. The best choice for you is the choice that closely balances these two competing demands.

San Diego cares about its businesses

In most cities in the United States, small businesses are left to fend for themselves when it comes to finding affordable healthcare solutions, but the city of San Diego, California, has decided to change all that. Specifically designed for local small businesses with two or more employees, the City Care Benefits Plan — sponsored by the Business Improvement District Council — offers comprehensive group health, dental, and vision plans at the kind of rates usually available only to very large businesses. A variety of procedures and services are fully covered under these plans, with small co-payments of $10 to $20 for office visits and drug prescriptions. With this progressive benefits plan, San Diego has addressed a very important need in the community. Scott Kessler, CEO of the Business Improvement District Council, said, "Many small business owners forgo health insurance due to cost, quality, and administrative obstacles. The City Care Benefits Plan is designed to meet the unique needs of small businesses." Considering that 85 percent of the uninsured population of San Diego work for small businesses, the City Care Benefits Plan may have a major impact on many thousands of employees and their families. For more information, visit the San Diego Business Improvement District Council Web site at `www.bidcouncil.org/city-care-benefits`.

Preferred provider organizations (PPOs)

Some years ago, in an effort to contain spiraling costs, indemnity insurers introduced a new form of healthcare — the *preferred provider organization* (PPO). In a PPO, the insurer strikes deals with selected physicians to provide care on a discounted fee-for-service basis. Patients are then given financial incentives to use physicians on a list provided to them by their insurance company. PPOs can be thought of as a transitional arrangement between fee-for-service and HMOs because they exhibit some elements of a loosely organized managed care network while maintaining a degree of physician choice and/or service locations for the patient. They're also like fee-for-service plans in the sense that the more doctors do for you, the more they get paid.

Typical PPOs provide some expense predictability for their enrollees by having maximum out-of-pocket limits, but they often have exclusions and waiting periods for pre-existing conditions, which could include pregnancy. Within a PPO, preventive services are minimal, but most have disease screening and usually provide smoking-cessation programs. If you go out of the network for your care, your out-of-pocket costs increase.

Investigating other healthcare coverage

A number of other health-related benefits, besides your main healthcare plan, are available to you. Depending on your situation, they may or may not make sense for you and your business, so be sure to study your options carefully before committing to a plan. The following are just a few of the additional health-related benefits you may want to consider:

- **Dental:** You can find a variety of dental insurance plans to choose from. Although many dental plans have high deductibles and rigid guidelines for what they pay for — and how much — a dental plan can be a godsend in the event of a catastrophic dental problem, accident, or illness.
- **Vision care:** Vision care plans generally pay for eye examinations and sometimes for glasses or contact lenses, as well. Elective procedures, such as surgery to permanently correct nearsightedness, usually aren't covered.
- **Gyms and health clubs:** Many large companies have their own on-site gyms and health clubs. Although you may not have the room (or the money) to set up your own on-site gym, don't let this stop you from joining a local gym and working out regularly.

Because many healthcare plans don't include dental, vision, or access to gyms or health clubs, you need to decide whether they're important enough for you to purchase using the proceeds of your business.

TIP

Ways to cut your healthcare costs

Although healthcare plans are becoming more flexible and easier to obtain for their users, the cost of healthcare continues to rise because of increased competitive pressures within the industry. In his book *Human Resources Kit For Dummies,* 2nd Edition (Wiley), Harold Messmer offers the following advice for cutting your healthcare costs:

- **Affiliate with the largest group possible.** Although you can find exceptions, the larger the group that's insured, the more competitive the rates tend to be. Instead of seeking coverage as a one-person, home-based business, check into healthcare plans offered by local chambers of commerce, industry associations, alumni associations, and professional organizations. Many of these groups offer healthcare plans with competitive rates. Other plans to check are those offered by national organizations like the National Federation of Independent Businesses (`www.nfib.org`) and the Freelancers Union (`www.freelancersunion.org`) or regional or state organizations like Support Services Alliance (`www.ssamembers.com`), which serves New Yorkers.
- **Increase the deductible (co-payment).** You can save anywhere from 10 to 50 percent on your premiums simply by increasing your deductibles or, in the case of HMOs, your co-payments. Increasing your deductible can be particularly effective if you aren't a big user of your healthcare plan. Check with your health plan provider to see what your options are.
- **Consider working with a benefits consultant.** Unless you're fully dedicated to studying all the different healthcare coverage options available, it's nearly impossible to know whether you're getting the plan that's best for you and your business. A benefits consultant is fully dedicated to that task and can be a genuine asset — both in locating the right plan for you and in negotiating the best rates possible. Ask friends and business associates for a referral to a qualified consultant, or check the Yellow Pages.

In addition to following this advice, as a self-employed individual, you likely can deduct 100 percent of what you pay for medical and dental insurance from your earnings. Fortunately for you is the fact that you can deduct "above the line" from adjusted gross income. In addition, you can deduct a qualified, long-term care insurance contract for you, your spouse, or your dependents.

Just make sure you check IRS Publication 535 or consult with a tax professional to verify that you're purchasing insurance that qualifies for this favorable treatment.

Considering the Need for Other Benefits

If you currently work — or have worked in the past — in a regular business, you know that you may want to provide yourself some other benefits besides health insurance. While insuring yourself against a catastrophic loss in the event of a serious or protracted illness is critically important for most people, other less critical benefits can help you protect your income, save for the future, and provide financial and psychic benefits.

In this section, we discuss the most common benefits besides healthcare.

Income protection

Imagine that you're a professional writer, as is Peter, one of the authors of this book. And imagine that you depend on your physical ability to use your computer keyboard to do your writing. Now imagine that you're diagnosed with carpal tunnel syndrome or a repetitive-motion injury that prevents you from using your computer for weeks or even months or years. What can you do, and how can you and your family survive the loss of income that such an injury causes?

Benefits in the income protection category protect workers and owners from potentially disastrous financial events like Peter's carpel tunnel and include the following:

- **Disability insurance:** This form of insurance pays a percentage of income — generally less than 100 percent — in the event that injury or illness prevents a worker or owner from performing his or her job. Disability insurance is available to home-based businesses in either short- or long-term versions, but both can be very expensive.
- **Workers' compensation:** This kind of insurance provides a fixed amount of income to workers who are injured on the job and is required of companies with three or more employees or when non-owner employees are hired. Each state has different workers' compensation insurance rules, so be sure to research your own situation before taking action.
- **Unemployment insurance:** This type of insurance provides a fixed amount of income to workers who lose their jobs through no fault of their own and is required by federal and state law of employers with one or more employees for at least 20 weeks in a calendar year.

For most home-based businesses, long-term disability insurance is the only form of income protection benefit you need to seriously consider. If you eventually hire employees, workers' compensation and unemployment insurance may be a requirement for your home-based business.

Life insurance

Of course, no one likes to think about dying and leaving loved ones without a source of income. But if you die without having established some sort of retirement fund or a life insurance policy, that's exactly what you'll do. Life insurance pays whomever you designate as your beneficiary a lump sum of money if you die, thus providing some peace of mind that that person's financial needs will be taken care of in the event of your death. The following are two types of life insurance:

- **Life insurance policies:** General life insurance policies are widely available, affordable, and easy to get. Find a good broker and have him explain the advantages and disadvantages of the different kinds of life insurance available to you, including term, universal, and whole life.
- **Dependent life insurance:** This type of life insurance provides coverage for the spouse of a home-based business owner and is often available for a small additional charge beyond your own policy.

Life insurance is an essential part of the benefits package of many home-based businesses. Although the money paid out in the event of your death doesn't do you any good personally (remember: you can't take it with you!), the peace of mind it provides knowing that your loved ones will have the financial wherewithal to continue without you is often well worth the price.

Retirement and savings plans

Retirement and savings plans are a regular part of most businesses, and they can and should be part of your home-based business. As we discuss in Chapter 7, the prices you charge for your products and services should be high enough to provide you with a decent income and benefits.

You probably already know that Social Security alone simply can't fill the bill for ensuring a comfortable and worry-free retirement. Unless you have a retirement plan or pension from your previous employer, the only way you're going to have any sort of retirement plan for your home-based business is if you create one yourself. If you want to provide yourself a reliable source of income after you leave the world of work behind once and for all, you must start and grow a retirement fund.

Here are a few different options available to you:

- **Simplified Employee Pension (SEP-IRA):** Any home-based businessperson with at least some self-employment income can set up a tax-deferred SEP-IRA account to provide steady income in retirement. SEP-IRAs are easy to open and can be maintained with minimal paperwork or red tape. The beauty of the SEP-IRA is that you're allowed to contribute up to $49,000 or 25 percent of your business's adjusted earned income per year, whichever is less. (Note that the flat dollar limit increases each year.) This amount may be ten times higher than you can contribute to plain old IRAs.

- **Keogh plans:** Keogh plans offer the highest limits for tax-deferred contributions, but they're complicated to set up and maintain. They come in two types:
  - **Defined contribution plan:** This plan fixes the amount and the source of the contributions (contributions are limited to $49,000 or 20 percent of your gross self-employment income for the year, whichever is less).
  - **Defined benefit plan:** This plan attempts to pay out a particular sum of money each month in retirement (contributions are limited to the amount needed to eventually produce an annual pension payment of the lesser of $160,000 or 100 percent of your average compensation for your three highest years).
- **SIMPLE:** The Savings Incentive Match Plan for Employees (SIMPLE) allows employees to make elective contributions of up to $11,500 per year and requires employers to make matching contributions of up to 3 percent of each employee's pay. Alternatively, you can decide to make a blanket contribution of 2 percent of each participating employee's pay regardless of whether she makes any elective contributions.

Each of these options has its pluses and minuses, and one may be better for your business than another. Consult an accountant or professional tax expert before you decide on a particular plan. After you set up your plan, you're pretty much stuck with it. Changing plan types is generally not encouraged by the tax code, and Congress has built in a variety of disincentives to ensure that you get the message.

Time off

Most regular businesses provide a wide variety of different forms of time off, including holidays and vacations. As the owner of your own home-based business, you get to decide which days you take off. In a home-based business, however, time off works a bit differently than it does in a regular job. In a regular job, you usually get paid for holidays and vacation leave — even though you don't actually work while you're on leave. In a home-based business, if you don't work, you don't get paid.

Even though you don't get paid, however, be sure to set aside some time off to get out of the office and recharge your batteries with family and friends. The two main forms of time off you need to consider as a home-based business owner are

- **Holidays:** A number of standardized holidays are available for you to choose from, including Memorial Day, Independence Day, Labor Day, Thanksgiving, and Christmas. You decide whether you're open for business on those days.
- **Vacations:** Many small business owners find themselves working far harder than they ever did in a regular job, which makes setting aside vacation time away from the business even more important.

Make taking time off a regular part of your benefits package and an established part of the way you do business — your attitude, as well as your relationships with friends and family, will benefit.

Child care

Working at home offers you a unique advantage that working outside the home doesn't — you can be at home with your young children every day of the week if you want to. For parents who want to work but who don't want to sacrifice their family lives to do so, working at home is truly the best of both worlds. However, if you work at home and have young children, you need to figure out how to keep them out of your way (and out of the way of your clients and customers) during your normal working hours. To do so, you generally need to obtain some sort of child care or else you'll face ongoing challenges of meeting deadlines.

When it comes to child care, you basically have two options:

- **On-site child care:** Hire a babysitter or nanny to take care of your children in your home on a regular schedule. If you have in-town relatives — perhaps your children's grandparents, aunts, or uncles — even better! In-your-home care is often an ideal situation because you're nearby if needed, but you're still able to close your office door and leave your family life behind while you work.
- **Off-site child care:** Numerous off-site child care facilities are available to the home-based businessperson. From individual day-care providers to programs at schools and churches to neighborhood centers, you have plenty of options for ensuring quality care for your children.

Flip to Chapter 14 for information on developing your own thriving home-based business while maintaining the contact and relationship with your children that you desire.

Chapter 9

Getting a Grip on Taxes and Deductions

In This Chapter

- Knowing what and when you need to pay
- Investigating the home-office deduction
- Figuring out what else you can deduct
- Reducing your tax burden
- Collecting sales taxes

According to the General Accounting Office, small business owners (including most home-based businesses) have more than 200 different Internal Revenue Service (IRS) forms and schedules to choose from in any given tax year. These forms and schedules — with more than 8,000 lines, boxes, and blanks to fill in with your business's unique set of numbers — are accompanied by more than 700 pages of instructions. And although no one business would ever have to use anything approaching all 200 of these forms and schedules, the paperwork problem is so overwhelming that it can easily threaten to bury the unwary home-based business owner.

If you fail to pay all the taxes you owe, pleading that you were confused by all the forms and schedules won't earn you any sympathy with your friendly, local IRS agent. In addition to being billed for all the taxes you failed to pay, you can expect to pay interest and penalties on top of them. In some cases, the interest and penalties alone can amount to thousands of dollars.

Is it any wonder that the first thing many savvy home-based businesspeople do when they start their businesses is hire a tax lawyer, certified public accountant (CPA), or both to help them plan and file their taxes? For many home-based business owners, the investment in a good tax planner can pay off many times over as the business grows and evolves.

This chapter is all about taxes: who pays them, when to pay them, and how much to pay. And although our intent isn't to make you an expert on the subject of taxes (we don't want to put any accountants out of business), we do want to provide you with a basic understanding of the topic — enough to help you get your business started and talk intelligently with any tax professionals.

Knowing Which Taxes to Pay — and When to Pay Them

Just like any other business, home-based businesses are required to pay income tax to the federal, state, and — in some cases — city government in which the business is located. The forms you use to calculate and file your taxes and the kinds of expenses you're able to deduct depend on the form of business you select: sole proprietorship, partnership, limited liability company, subchapter S corporation, or regular corporation (see Chapter 10 for details about each of these business forms). And although home-based businesses are granted some special tax breaks by the government — unless you have some amazing tax deductions or you're not making any money — you're still going to have to pay at least some tax.

Who has to pay what?

Within the United States, all businesses are required to file an annual income tax return. Whether you make money or lose money, you still need to file a return.

Of course, we're assuming that your business is really a business and not just a hobby. Suppose, for example, that you're an avid collector of *Star Wars* figures, and you buy and sell them on a regular basis. Not only that, but you also take a home-office deduction and write off other business expenses — but you don't conduct this activity on a businesslike basis (that is, to make a profit). In this case, the IRS doesn't allow you to deduct all your expenses as business expenses — including the all-important home-office deduction (more about this deduction in the "Taking a Look at the Home-Office Deduction" section). If you've been taking these deductions for years, get audited by the IRS, and find out that these deductions aren't allowed, the financial impact on you and your "business" can be more than simply inconvenient — it can be devastating.

Web sites that can make your job less taxing

While Congress continues to mystify the tax codes, the Internet does just the opposite. In response to popular taxpayer demand, a number of Web sites have sprung up to dispense help and assistance. These sites work hard to take the mystery out of preparing your income taxes. Here are some of the best ones:

- **OPEN: American Express Small Business Network:** This site contains articles addressing a variety of income tax issues of particular interest to small and home-based businesses at `www.americanexpress.com/smallbusiness`.
- **Business Owner's Toolkit:** This comprehensive guide to starting and building a successful business has an extensive tax section at `www.toolkit.com`.
- **IRS Online:** For home office startup information and online publications and forms, go to `www.irs.ustreas.gov/businesses`.
- **State tax forms:** Too bushed to mount a search for your state income tax forms this year? Try `www.1040.com`.

Adhering to the hobby loss rule

Aside from the freedom that having one's own home business can provide, one of the main reasons for starting a home-based business is for the financial benefits — including taxes. If you want to benefit from the tax deductions and other advantages that having your own home-based business affords you (which can be considerable), it's in your interest for the IRS to agree that indeed you're operating a business and not a hobby.

And believe us, the IRS is on the lookout for businesses — home based and otherwise — that are incorrectly applying the rules. According to a Treasury Inspector General for Tax Administration audit report (titled "Significant Challenges Exist in Determining Whether Taxpayers with Schedule C Losses Are Engaged in Tax Abuse"):

> About 1.5 million taxpayers, many with significant income from other sources, filed Form 1040 Schedule C showing no profits, only losses, over consecutive Tax Years 2002–2005 (4 years); 73 percent of these taxpayers were assisted by tax practitioners. By claiming these losses to reduce their taxable incomes, about 1.2 million of the 1.5 million taxpayers potentially avoided paying $2.8 billion in taxes in Tax Year 2005. Changes are needed to prevent taxpayers from continually deducting losses in potentially not-for-profit activities to reduce their tax liabilities.

According to research studies, if you work for yourself, the odds are four times greater that you will be audited than if you work for someone else. And if you gross more than $100,000 a year, the chances you will be audited go up even more.

So how do you know whether your enterprise is a business or a hobby? The place to start is a law established by Congress called the *hobby loss rule.* In essence, the hobby loss rule says that to be considered a business rather than a hobby, your activity must have made a profit in at least three of the preceding five years. If your business is a new one — without an established track record of profit — or if it's truly an unprofitable business, it may still qualify as a business instead of a hobby. It just has to meet a few requirements first.

To help you decide which side of the fence your business is on, the IRS has established nine factors, which are contained within Internal Revenue Code Section 183. According to the IRS, no single factor is more important than any of the others, and you don't necessarily have to satisfy all these criteria to be considered a business. But you can bet that the more you satisfy, the better position you'll be in if an IRS agent comes knocking on your door. The nine factors are

- **The manner in which the taxpayer carries on the activity:** If your business is really a business, it should conduct itself like a business, not a hobby. For example, a business establishes accounting records and develops business plans and strategies. It obtains a business license and adheres to any zoning or other legal requirements. It establishes financial goals, abandons strategies that don't help it achieve its goals, and constantly seeks out and executes new strategies that help it achieve its goals. It strives to make a profit and avoids financial losses. The owner establishes systems and resources dedicated to the business, such as dedicated computers and phone lines, Internet connections, an office, office equipment and supplies, a business logo or trademark, stationery, and business cards.
- **The expertise of the taxpayer or his or her advisers:** The knowledge and expertise that a home-based businessperson has in running his or her particular line of business can be a significant factor in deciding whether a particular activity is a business or a hobby. In fact, a person's knowledge or effort in managing a successful enterprise has been considered by the courts in several cases. Similarly, a home-based businessperson who retains an accountant, a lawyer, and other experts to provide business advice tends to indicate that the activity is indeed a business and not a hobby.
- **The time and effort expended by the taxpayer in carrying on the activity:** Although the IRS doesn't expect you to spend every waking hour working in your home-based business, it does expect you to show some sort of serious personal commitment of your own time and effort on

behalf of the business. If, for example, you develop, create, and deliver all your business's products or services, and doing so takes an average of 20 hours a week to accomplish, you clearly have a major commitment of time and effort. On the other hand, devoting two minutes a week to these activities likely wouldn't qualify in the eyes of the IRS. If you quit another job or go to part-time status so that you can devote even more energy to your new venture, you're clearly making a serious investment of time and effort in your activity.

- **The expectation that the assets used in the activity may appreciate in value:** Every business has assets, some more valuable than others. And although some business assets — such as computers, printers, and vehicles — tend to decrease in value over time, other assets — such as real estate and intellectual property — tend to increase over time. Most businesses start out in a loss position, so even if the activity isn't making a profit at the time, a new home-based business owner can demonstrate that he or she expects the company's key assets to appreciate, indicating that the activity is a business, not a hobby.
- **The success of the taxpayer in carrying on other similar or dissimilar activities:** A home-based businessperson may have a personal history of establishing a number of businesses that are initially unprofitable, but which he or she then shepherds into operations that are both profitable and successful. A track record like this can go a long way to convincing an outside observer that a particular activity is truly a business even if it isn't profitable yet.
- **The taxpayer's history of income or loss with respect to the activity:** If your activity is generating a profit, it's clearly a profit making activity. The fact that an activity doesn't generate profits, however, doesn't necessarily mean it isn't engaged in for-profit activities. The first years of a business can be a time of building and securing assets that the business needs to operate effectively. After these expenses are paid and revenues begin to climb, the activity should begin to show a profit. In some cases, extraordinary situations, such as the loss of a major client or the death of a principal in the business, may push the business into unprofitability for a period of time. Such explanations may help show that the activity is a business. Years and years of activity with no profit to show for it, however, may indicate that the activity is indeed a hobby and not a business for tax purposes.
- **The amount of occasional profits, if any, that are earned:** It's not enough to simply make a dollar or two profit in three years out of five. The amount of the profit made has to be reasonably significant. So, for example, a home-based business that shows a profit of $10,000 in each of three years out of five will likely have no problem whatsoever establishing itself as a business. A home-based business that shows only $10 profit in each of three years out of five may have a serious problem defending its status as a business rather than a hobby.

- **The financial status of the taxpayer:** Are you earning most of your money from your home-based business or are you earning most of your money from another source, perhaps a regular full-time job? If most of your income comes from your home-based activity, you greatly enhance your case that the activity is a business. If, however, most of your income comes from another source, you'll have a harder time proving that your home-based activity is actually a real, live business and not just a hobby.
- **Elements of personal pleasure or recreation:** Do you carry out the activity purely for recreation or personal pleasure, or is it intended to generate a profit? Peter, for example, loves to write. As much as Peter loves to write, however, his overriding concern (aside from doing the best job of writing that he possibly can) is to make a good living doing it. So in Peter's case, making a profit overrides Peter's joy of writing. The IRS says that it's okay to enjoy what you're doing for a living, as long as your primary focus is on making a profit doing it.

So if you're absolutely sure your home-based business is really a business, take a close look at your business — and at your personal motivations in creating your business — to see what you need to change to make it more a business and less a hobby in the eyes of the IRS.

Different tax forms for different business forms

The forms you need to submit when you file your taxes are different depending on what form of business your home-based business takes (and how many people you employ). It's easy to get lost in the many different forms and schedules available for you to use when calculating and filing your taxes (which is another reason why you should seriously consider hiring an accountant or CPA to help you with your company's finances).

Table 9-1 gives you a summary of the kinds of taxes you may have to pay and the forms you need to use to pay them.

Table 9-1 Taxes to Pay and Forms to File

Taxes to Pay	*Forms to File*
Sole Proprietor	
Income tax	Form 1040 and Schedule C or C-EZ
Self-employment tax	Schedule SE
Estimated tax	1040-ES
Employment taxes, Social Security, Medicare taxes, and income tax withholding	Form 941 (943 for farm employees)
Federal unemployment (FUTA) tax	Form 940 or 940-EZ
Depositing employment taxes	Form 8109

Taxes to Pay	*Forms to File*
Partnership	
Annual return of income	Form 1065
Employment taxes	Same as sole proprietor
Partner in a Partnership (Individual)	
Income tax	Form 1040 and Schedule E
Self-employment tax	Schedule SE
Estimated tax	Form 1040-ES
Corporation or S Corporation	
Income tax	Form 1120 (corporation); Form 1120S (S corporation)
Estimated tax	Form 1120-W (corporation only) and Form 8109
Employment taxes	Same as sole proprietor
S Corporation Shareholder	
Income tax	Form 1040 and Schedule E
Estimated tax	Form 1040-ES

The one form of business that isn't listed in Table 9-1 that you need to be aware of is the limited liability company (LLC). LLCs are created under state law. For tax purposes, LLCs default to general partnerships, and the rules and taxes for partnerships apply. However, you can also elect to file as a C corporation, S corporation, or a sole proprietor; whichever form you choose to file as, file all the tax forms that apply to that particular business form. Remember that each state has its own rules for limited liability companies — be sure to check out your state's unique tax rules before filing your state income taxes.

When do you have to pay?

As the IRS loves to remind the self-employed, the federal income tax is a *pay-as-you-go* system — in other words, you should be paying your taxes at roughly the same time you're making your income.

When you're an employee working in a regular job, the process is relatively painless. Your employer deducts a fixed amount of money from your pay-checks — before you even get them. When you start your own home-based business, however, you need to plan to pay estimated taxes four times a year, on April 15, June 15, September 15, and January 15. (Corporate estimated taxes are due on the 15th day of the 4th, 6th, 9th, and 12th months during the company's fiscal year.) If you mail your payments, be sure your envelope is postmarked no later than these dates. After you start making your estimated payments — and writing the big checks to the federal government that go along with them — you'll surely long for the time when your employer took a little out of each paycheck.

The rules for paying estimated taxes are different for the different forms of business. Here's a brief summary of the differences:

- **Sole proprietors, partners, and S corporation shareholders:** If you expect to owe taxes of $1,000 or more when you file your income tax return, you probably need to make estimated payments to the federal government. Use Form 1040-ES — Estimated Tax for Individuals — to determine how much to pay and then to submit your payment.
- **Corporations:** If you expect to owe taxes of $500 or more when you file your tax return, you probably need to make estimated payments to the federal government. Use Form 1120-W — Estimated Tax for Corporations — to determine how much to pay and then to submit your payment.

Of course, the day of reckoning for most home-based businesses comes each year on the same day that it does for individual taxpayers: April 15. (Corporations have a slightly different arrangement; corporate federal tax returns are due on the 15th day of the 3rd month after the close of the company's fiscal year, or March 15 for a fiscal year that ends on December 31.) This due date is the day that you submit your tax return for the preceding year and the day that you write out one more check to pay the IRS for tax shortfalls that weren't already covered in your estimated payments (and the day you celebrate if you have money coming back because you overpaid your estimated payments).

How much do you have to pay?

How much you have to pay in taxes is the $64 question (or, perhaps, more like the $6,400 or the $64,000 question, depending on your situation). Every business is different, and every business has its own unique tax situation. One thing is for certain, though: The kind of business entity your business is has a definite bearing on the amount of taxes you pay.

If your home-based business is a sole proprietorship, a partnership, or a subchapter S corporation, your taxable business income will be combined with any other source of income and taxed at the individual level on your Form 1040. At the time of this writing, the current individual tax rates range from 10 percent to 35 percent. C corporation tax rates range from 15 percent to 39 percent. The tax on the first $75,000 of taxable income is in the same neighborhood for both individuals and corporations. Generally speaking, however, corporate tax far exceeds individual tax after income is above the $75,000 mark.

A corporation is a separate tax-paying entity unless it elects to take advantage of subchapter S of the tax code. C corporations pay taxes at corporate rates. Choosing to use subchapter S enables you to not pay separate (federal) taxes, which means that you show the corporation's income on your 1040. However, in doing so, some tax deductions available to corporations are lost. Corporations can be started as S and changed to a C later or can have their S status revoked. A corporation is considered a C corporation unless subchapter S is elected.

C corporations aren't allowed to take a home-office deduction because a corporation can't have a home; it can have only a business location. Ten-percent shareholders can't rent their homes to the corporation, either. However, an employee and/or shareholder can submit a reimbursement request for use of their home. You need to consider many ramifications in choosing the proper business entity and how it relates to deductible home offices and reimbursements to the owner. We strongly suggest you seek out the services of a professional tax advisor before you make your final decision. (See Chapter 10 for more details about the different business forms.)

What if you can't afford to pay right now?

When your business gets into full swing — and you start bringing in a lot more income — you may be surprised just how much extra income tax you'll owe on April 15. You may be especially shocked if you're not using a CPA to keep an eye on your finances and to warn you that you should start putting aside some cash for just such an outcome.

So what should you do if you can't afford to pay the income taxes you owe? One option is to submit a request for an automatic six-month extension of the date to file your taxes to October 15 by using the government's e-file system (`www.irs.gov/efile`) or by mailing Form 4868.

TIP

If you can't raise the money you need by tapping your savings or other resources, you can apply to the IRS for an installment agreement using Form 9465. According to the rules, the IRS must accept installment payments if you owe less than $10,000, you've paid your taxes on time for the past five years, and you propose to pay off your balance within three years. You will, of course, be charged interest on the unpaid balance. However, setting up this arrangement may mean the difference between sinking and swimming.

Hiring yourself out

Q: I'm a computer contractor working within a niche in a specific software package. Few people in this locale are qualified to work with this application and even fewer have experience with this package. So my competition is essentially the manufacturer of the software. The company knows who I am and wants to subcontract with me, if not hire me. Because of its business practices, however, I'd prefer not to represent this company, even though I'd actually make more money subbing out to it. My problem is finding potential clients and key contacts without this company's help. Do you have any suggestions?

A: You're wise not to become encumbered with a company with poor business practices. Life is too short and litigation too costly. Can you work out something other than a subcontracting relationship with this company — for example, a referral relationship through which you pay a referral fee? You can make clear to your clients that your relationship with the company is limited to its referring clients to you. Alternatively, can you rent the company's mailing list? From this, you can do mailings (snail or e-mail), create a newsletter, embellish a Web site, and so on. If a publication already exists for these users, can you contribute articles, a column, or letters to the editor? If the company is a poor one to work with, customers will gladly want to know about you as an alternative. Just be sure not to bad-mouth the company.

When is an independent contractor not an independent contractor?

Imagine that you've started your own home-based business and you're starting to deliver services — say, interior design — to a client. Chances are you consider yourself to be a business separate from your client's business — in other words, an *independent contractor.* But what if we told you there's a possibility that the IRS may not agree with your particular view of your business and that the IRS may instead decide that you're performing your services as an employee? "Okay, that's interesting," you may say to yourself, "but what's the big deal?"

You may be in for an unpleasant surprise if you think you're a home-based business — and take advantage of all the deductions for business expenses that you're entitled to — if the IRS decides that you're really an employee of your client. This unpleasant surprise includes disallowing all the deductions you've been taking for your home-based business and recalculating your taxes without them — possibly resulting in a substantial amount of money (plus penalties and interest) now owed to the IRS. Believe us, this is one surprise everyone could do without. The good news is that you can take a few steps right now to ensure that you're not surprised come tax day.

In its ongoing quest to be helpful, the IRS has developed guidelines to help you determine whether you're an independent contractor or an employee. These guidelines are categorized by how much behavioral and financial control a business has over the person doing the work and the exact nature of the relationship. Here are the IRS's independent contractor guidelines, presented as they currently appear in *Publication 15-A: Employer's Supplemental Tax Guide*:

- **Behavioral control:** Facts that show whether the business has a right to direct and control how the worker does the task for which the worker is hired include the type and degree of the following:
  - **Instructions that the business gives to the worker:** An employee is generally subject to the business's instructions about when, where, and how to work. All the following are examples of types of instructions about how to do work:

    When and where to do the work

    What tools or equipment to use

    What workers to hire or assist with the work

    Where to purchase supplies and services

    What work must be performed by a specified individual

    What order or sequence to follow

    The amount of instruction needed varies among different jobs. Even if no instructions are given, sufficient behavioral control may exist if the employer has the right to control how the work results are achieved. A business may lack the knowledge to instruct some highly specialized professionals; in other cases, the task may require little or no instruction. The key consideration is whether the business has retained the right to control the details of a worker's performance or instead has given up that right.
  - **Training that the business gives to the worker:** An employee may be trained to perform services in a particular manner. Independent contractors ordinarily use their own methods.
- **Financial control:** Facts that show whether the business has a right to control the business aspects of the worker's job include:
  - **The extent to which the worker has unreimbursed business expenses:** Independent contractors are more likely to have unreimbursed expenses than are employees. Fixed, ongoing costs that are incurred regardless of whether work is currently being performed are especially important. However, employees may also incur unreimbursed expenses in connection with the services that they perform for their business.

- **The extent of the worker's investment:** An independent contractor often has a significant investment in the facilities he or she uses to perform services for someone else. However, a significant investment isn't necessary for independent contractor status.
- **The extent to which the worker makes his or her services available to the relevant market:** An independent contractor is generally free to seek out business opportunities. Independent contractors often advertise, maintain a visible business location, and are available to work in the relevant market.
- **How the business pays the worker:** An employee is generally guaranteed a regular wage amount for an hourly, weekly, or other period of time. This guaranteed wage usually indicates that a worker is an employee, even when the wage or salary is supplemented by a commission. An independent contractor is usually paid a flat fee for the job. However, it's common in some professions, such as law, to pay independent contractors hourly.
- **The extent to which the worker can realize a profit or incur a loss:** An independent contractor can make a profit or loss. An employee can't.

✔ **Type of relationship:** Facts that show the parties' type of relationship include:

- **Written contracts describing the relationship the parties intended to create:** Independent contractors typically use contracts to create business relationships with clients; employees, on the other hand, don't typically use contracts to create business relationships with their employers.
- **The extent to which benefits are involved:** If the business provides the worker with employee-type benefits, such as insurance, a pension plan, vacation pay, or sick pay, it's most likely an employer-employee relationship. If no such benefits are involved, it's most likely an independent contractor-client relationship. While employees are often provided with benefits by their employer, independent contractors generally have to provide their own.
- **The permanency of the relationship:** Engaging a worker with the expectation that the relationship will continue indefinitely, instead of for a specific project or period, is generally considered evidence that you intended to create an employer-employee relationship.
- **The extent to which services performed by the worker are a key aspect of the regular business of the company:** If a worker provides services that are a key aspect of your regular business activity, you're more likely to have the right to direct and control

his or her activities. For example, if a law firm hires an attorney, it will likely present the attorney's work as its own and have the right to control or direct that work. This arrangement indicates an employer-employee relationship.

The lines that separate independent contractors from employees can be blurry. Here are a couple of examples that the IRS itself uses to illustrate the problem. Review the following examples, and see who you think is an employee and who is an independent contractor:

- Steve Smith, a computer programmer, is laid off when Megabyte, Inc., downsizes. Megabyte agrees to pay Steve a flat amount to complete a one-time project to create a certain product. It isn't clear how long it will take to complete the project, and Steve isn't guaranteed any minimum payment for the hours spent on the program. Megabyte provides Steve with no instructions beyond the specifications for the product itself. Steve and Megabyte have a written contract, which provides that Steve is considered to be an independent contractor, is required to pay federal and state taxes, and receives no benefits from Megabyte. Megabyte will file a Form 1099-MISC. Steve does the work on a new high-end computer that cost him $7,000. Steve works at home and isn't expected or allowed to attend meetings of the software development group. Employee or independent contractor?
- Jerry Jones has an agreement with Wilma White to supervise the remodeling of her house. She didn't advance funds to help him carry on the work. She makes direct payments to the suppliers for all necessary materials. She carries liability and workers' compensation insurance covering Jerry and others that he engaged to assist him. She pays them an hourly rate and exercises almost constant supervision over the work. Jerry isn't free to transfer his assistants to other jobs. He may not work on other jobs while working for Wilma. He assumes no responsibility to complete the work and will incur no contractual liability if he fails to do so. He and his assistants perform personal services for hourly wages. Employee or independent contractor?

What did you guess? According to the IRS, Steve Smith is an independent contractor, and Jerry Jones and his assistants are employees.

TIP

Be constantly aware of how you do business, and guard against conducting business in a way that would cause the IRS to believe that you're actually an employee instead of an independent contractor. The differences are often subtle, and the line between them is easy to cross. With a bit of forethought and planning, however, you can always make sure that you're on the right side of that line.

Taking a Look at the Home-Office Deduction

For many home-based businesspeople, taking the home-office deduction is a major financial incentive to start their businesses in the first place, and it can have a significant and positive effect on a home-based business's financial position (as well as the personal financial situation of the owner). In more than a few cases, the ability to take the home-office deduction literally means the difference between success and failure.

The beauty of the home-office deduction is that it allows you to deduct the costs of operating and maintaining the part of your home that you use for business. And it doesn't matter what kind of home you live in. Whether you live in a single-family home, a condominium, a commercial building, or even a houseboat, if you meet the IRS's criteria for the home-office deduction, you're eligible to take it.

To qualify to deduct expenses for the business use of your home, you must use part of your home in one of the following ways:

- Exclusively and regularly as your principal place of business
- Exclusively and regularly as a place where you meet or deal with patients, clients, or customers in the normal course of your trade or business
- In connection with your trade or business in the case of a separate structure that isn't attached to your home
- For rental use
- As a daycare facility

Note: Two exceptions to the exclusive-use test are (1) if you use part of your home for the storage of inventory or product samples and (2) if you use part of your home as a daycare facility. In other words, the part of your home you devote (and deduct) for your rental or daycare home business doesn't have to be *exclusively* used for those purposes to qualify for the home-office deduction.

So assuming you meet these criteria, you can take the home-office deduction. The benefits of doing so are immediate and extensive. Not only are you allowed to deduct your normal business expenses (paper, pencils, phone calls, and so on), but you're also able to deduct a portion of the indirect expenses related to your entire home! Here are some of the most common indirect expenses that you may be able to at least partially deduct under the IRS's home-office rules:

- Rent
- Mortgage interest
- Security system
- Housekeeping
- Household supplies
- Condominium association fees
- Trash collection
- Utilities (gas, electric, and so on)

To determine the total amount of indirect expenses that you can deduct under the home-office deduction, you first have to calculate the percentage of your home devoted to your home office. So, for example, suppose you have a 240-square-foot spare bedroom (12 x 20 feet) that you've set aside as a home office and that the total square footage of your home is 1,200 square feet. Here's how to determine the portion of your indirect expenses that you can deduct with your home-office deduction:

240 sq. ft. office ÷ 1,200 sq. ft. home = Percent of expenses deductible

240 ÷ 1,200 = 20 percent

You can, therefore, deduct 20 percent of your home's indirect expenses — an amount that, depending on your situation, may be quite substantial. Keep in mind, though, that the tax rules don't allow you to deduct an amount greater than the amount of gross income that you earn in your home-based business. The government doesn't mind if you make money from individuals and other companies, but it doesn't want you to make money off the IRS.

Be aware that if you take the home-office deduction, you're required to depreciate the home-office square footage of your home. When you sell your home, you have to reduce your cost basis by the amount of depreciation deducted. When you sell a home that you lived in for more than two years, you can exclude $250,000 (or $500,000 on a joint return) of your gain. The gain is a capital gain eligible for reduced preferential rates, which are taxed at a maximum rate of 15 percent. However, as a home-office deductor, you have to do one more calculation: You have to subtract from the capital gain the amount of depreciation taken and pay tax at a maximum rate of 25 percent. This calculation is known as *depreciation recapture.*

It's widely believed that taking the home-office deduction waves a red flag that can gain you extra scrutiny by the IRS — and perhaps an audit. Although we don't know whether this belief is really true, we do know that you should consult with an accountant, tax planner, or other tax professional before you take the home-office deduction. The rules are complicated, and the penalties for abusing the deduction can be significant. For more information on the allowability of deductions for your home-based business, check out *IRS Publication 587: Business Use of Your Home* at the IRS Web site (`www.irs.gov/pub/irs-pdf/p587.pdf`).

Reviewing Other Important Tax Deductions

Aside from the important home-office deduction, home-based businesses are allowed to deduct a wide variety of other business expenses from their taxes. To be deductible, the Internal Revenue Code specifies that expenses must be *ordinary and necessary* for the operation of your business. So although the purchase of a vintage 1959 sunburst Gibson Les Paul electric guitar for $250,000 may be ordinary and necessary (and thus an allowable deduction) for a professional musician, it likely wouldn't fly for a home-based software designer — in fact, it would surely sink like a lead balloon.

As you may imagine, you can legally deduct many different expenses from your taxes as a home-based business owner. Here are just a few examples of legal deductions:

- Phones
- Utilities
- Postage
- Health insurance
- Auto expenses
- Internet access
- Business travel
- Business meals and entertainment
- Professional services and consultants
- Business cards and stationery
- Retirement plans
- Interest payments on business credit cards
- Education
- Office supplies
- Office furniture

As you may also imagine, the federal government has determined plenty of expenses that aren't deductible. Too bad! Here are a number of deductions that the IRS doesn't consider legal:

- Anticipated liabilities
- Bribes and kickbacks
- Demolition expenses
- Personal expenses
- Social or recreational clubs
- Lobbying expenses
- Political contributions
- Federal income taxes
- Penalties and fines

When in doubt, consult with an accountant or tax advisor to see which expenses you're allowed to deduct and which ones you aren't. It's far better to be sure about your allowable deductions *before* you take them instead of years later when your business expenses are disallowed by the IRS.

Be sure when setting up your business that you apply for and obtain a business license. If you're doing a DBA ("doing business as"), you need to register your name with the city — which is part of the business license application. Failure to obtain a business license can be a very costly mistake. For more information on business licenses, be sure to take a look at Chapter 10.

Discovering Often Overlooked Ways to Save On Your Taxes

As you're probably well aware, the rules that govern income taxes and the deductions you're allowed to take are complex. But despite appearances to the contrary, you're not required to pay any more tax than is necessary. In fact, you shouldn't pay any more tax than you're legally required to pay.

Because of the complexity of the tax rules and the fact that they change — sometimes substantially — every year, hiring a professional tax lawyer or accountant can really pay off, and it's deductible, too.

However, we understand if you'd prefer not to spend a lot of money paying for a tax lawyer or accountant just yet. You can still employ a variety of strategies to reduce your tax burden. Consider the following ways to save on your taxes that sometimes get overlooked:

- **Maximize your vehicle deduction.** You can choose between the standard mileage deduction (55 cents per mile in 2009) or the actual costs of operating your vehicle, which includes fuel, maintenance, taxes, and license fees. Where you live can determine whether choosing to use the standard deduction will save you more money than reporting actual costs. Runzheimer International (`www.runzheimer.com`), which analyzes the cost of owning and operating a vehicle in cities across the United States, found that it costs almost twice as much to operate a mid-size vehicle in Detroit than it does in Portland, Oregon. So taking the standard deduction may make more sense in Detroit, Los Angeles, and other higher cost places than it does in Portland and other lower-cost places. Note, however, that if you use the actual cost method in the first year you use a vehicle, you must stick with this method ever after. And unless you use a vehicle 100 percent for business, you need to keep a log of your business use, including dates, mileage, and the purpose of your business travels.
- **Make the most of hiring employees.** If you need an employee, consider hiring a family member. A child in a lower tax bracket enables you to keep income in the family. Depending on how much the child earns, no tax at all may be owed on his or her earnings. Sometimes tax credits are available for hiring designated workers, such as Native Americans, or if you live in an economic empowerment zone.
- **Reduce your taxes with a retirement plan.** Putting money into a retirement fund reduces your Adjusted Gross Income, which is what you use to calculate other deductions, such as a casualty loss, medical, and miscellaneous itemized deductions. The self-employed are able to invest more money using a Keogh, SEP, or SIMPLE plan than with an IRA. To find out more about retirement plans for the self-employed, obtain IRS Publication 560 (`www.irs.gov/pub/irs-pdf/p560.pdf`) and be sure to check out Chapter 8.
- **Make the most of a bad year.** Because it's possible to carry business losses both back as well as forward, consult a tax professional to determine whether you would be better off getting an immediate tax refund or carrying your loss into your next business year. Keep in mind that the tax law on handling losses changes frequently.

REMEMBER

Of course, it's against the law to evade paying your taxes, but it's your duty to avoid paying more taxes than you're legally obligated to. The IRS isn't going to give you any gold stars or special privileges for paying more taxes than you have to — you're throwing away your money if you do. And that's the last thing any home-based businessperson should ever do.

Tax software to the rescue

When home-based businesspeople prepare their taxes, they have two key options: pay someone to do them or do the taxes themselves. If you decide to do your own taxes, you may find that tax software makes the process much easier and far more accurate than filling out forms the old-fashioned way. Here are a couple of reliable tax software packages to consider:

- **TaxCut:** `www.taxcut.com`
- **TurboTax:** `www.turbotax.com`

The Ins and Outs of Sales Tax

According to the people who keep track of such things as sales tax, there are more than 10,000 different sales tax rates nationwide, and these rates are in a constant state of change as voters approve rate changes to fund local improvements or scale down sales taxes to save the consumer a bit of money. But although sales taxes are in a constant state of change, one thing's for sure: If you sell products or provide certain kinds of services to people within your state (the exact services taxed differ from state to state — check with your local tax authorities to find out whether or not the services you offer are subject to sales tax), you better be sure to collect sales tax while you're at it.

As of this writing, only five states — Alaska, Delaware, Montana, New Hampshire, and Oregon — don't have sales taxes. All other states do, and they expect you to collect each and every dollar and cent owed and then to submit them to the appropriate tax authorities regularly.

Here's how the sales tax setup and collection process generally works:

1. **File an application with your state sales tax authority to obtain a *reseller's permit*, also known as a *certificate of authority, sales tax permit, resale permit*, or *sales tax number*, depending on the state in which you reside.**
2. **File appropriate sales tax forms with your state or local tax authorities, with estimated collections for quarter or year (or whatever period of time is requested).**
3. **Receive instructions from state or local tax authorities with information on how often to submit tax collections and where to send them.**
4. **Submit taxes at the time and place directed by the state or local tax authorities.**

Although the collection of sales taxes is a fairly routine and straightforward process (perhaps even boring), one thing that has brought a lot of excitement to the topic is the ongoing debate over collecting sales taxes for products sold over the Internet. Congress has temporarily exempted Internet sales from the payment of sales taxes, much to the delight of e-commerce firms, such as Amazon.com and others, but much to the consternation of the states that can't collect the sales tax revenue that's increasingly being lost to online sales. Although online companies still have to collect sales taxes for sales made within their home states, just as mail-order companies do, they don't have to collect sales taxes for sales made to people or companies outside their states.

Part III
Avoiding Problems

The 5th Wave By Rich Tennant

"We've run the business out of the kitchen for years, but things got tight, so we bought the office equipment and just lease the pots and pans."

In this part . . .

Starting a business is far more than just hanging an "Open" sign on your door. You have to create a foundation that will last for years. In this part, we review the most common legal do's and don'ts and explore how to leverage outside resources to your advantage. Finally, we take an in-depth look at the many different kinds of home-based business rip-offs and scams — and explain how to defend yourself against them.

Chapter 10

Knowing Your Legal Do's and Don'ts

In This Chapter

- Choosing the right form (or legal structure) for your business
- Selecting and registering your business's name
- Dealing with trademarks, copyrights, and patents
- Complying with zoning requirements, licensing, and permits
- Considering your tax situation

If you think you have enough laws, statutes, and regulations to worry about now, just wait until you start your own business — you haven't seen anything, yet! Actually, it's not quite that bad, but depending on what kind of home-based business you plan to start, you may be surprised to see how many city and local agencies and departments want to play some role in your life and how many rules and regulations you have to comply with.

And the government isn't the only player you have to take into account. Your own neighborhood or housing development may have restrictive covenants (that you agreed to honor when you bought your house, whether or not you noticed them in the fine print of your purchase agreement) that determine whether you can run a business out of your home. You're wise to pay attention to all these covenants and regulations: The consequences of not doing so include fines, penalties, and even closure of your precious home-based business.

REMEMBER

Laws and regulations determine where you can locate your home-based business and during what hours you can operate it. They also require you to get permits if your business prepares and sells food or if you have an alarm to protect your premises. And if you're a private investigator, hairdresser, masseuse, building contractor, plumber, or any of hundreds more occupations, you need a license (and you need to pay a licensing fee) before you can operate your business.

To some degree, the government determines which kind of business form or legal structure (sole proprietorship, partnership, limited liability company, or corporation) you're eligible to use; plus, it decides the financial and tax implications on your business as a result of which form you use.

In this chapter, we discuss a wide variety of legal issues that every home-based business owner faces, including how to choose the legal structure that's right for your business, how to select and register a company name, and how to consider the potential impact of zoning, licensing, and permits on your business. We also take a look at trademarks, copyrights, and patents and how they may affect your business. Finally, we briefly visit the potential impact of tax considerations on your home-based business (see Chapter 9 for the complete lowdown on taxes).

Our aim isn't to turn you into a lawyer or an accountant (not that we have anything against lawyers or accountants) but to arm you with enough knowledge to take care of the basics and to know where to turn when you need more information.

Understanding the Major Business Forms

One of the first decisions you have to make after you decide to start your own home-based business is what *form* of business — that is, what *legal structure* — it will take.

You may have noticed a few interesting words or initials after the names of some of your favorite companies. Global fast-food giant McDonald's, for example, isn't simply named *McDonald's* — it's *McDonald's Corporation* — which means that McDonald's is organized as a *corporation form* of business. Quiznos Master LLC — the number-two sub sandwich chain in the United States after Subway — is organized as a *limited liability company.*

Each of the different forms of business (and its accompanying alphabet soup of letters) comes with a wide variety of legal implications for many facets of your business, including legal liability in case of lawsuit, taxes, and more. It's important, therefore, that you take time to understand all these implications upfront — as you make and implement your business plans.

Which form of business is right for you? This section gives you some basic guidelines to consider as you weigh the different options available to you. Although these guidelines are certainly sufficient to help you get your business off the ground and to help you become an informed home-business owner, our advice is to first contact an attorney or accountant to discern the specific advantages and legal requirements of each form of business and then to decide which is best for you. The money you save over the years will probably pay for this advice many times over.

Consider the following issues when you're deciding which form of business to use for your home-based business:

- The impact on your business's image
- The impact of planned business growth
- The cost to start up your business
- The cost to maintain your business
- Your tax goals
- The impact of government regulation
- Your financing needs
- The amount of personal legal risk you're willing to take for your business

In the sections that follow, we consider the four major forms of business, discussing the pros and cons of each one for home-based businesses. As you review each form, think about the kind of business you want to run — not just today, but years into the future.

We know it may be difficult to picture what your business will be like a couple of weeks into the future, much less a couple of months or a couple of years. The good news is that you can change the form of your business almost any time you want with a minimum of muss or fuss (corporations are the exception here because they require the filing of special forms with your state government). But try to picture where your business may go, anyway; settling now on a form that will carry your business for many years into the future may be easier in the long run.

Surveying sole proprietorships

By far, the vast majority of home-based businesses are *sole proprietorships,* which means they have only one business owner — in your case, that one owner is you. You're the boss, the leader, the one to congratulate when the business does well and the one to blame when the business does badly.

In a sole proprietorship, you report the income you derive from your business on your Form 1040 along with any other personal income you make during the course of the year — in other words, you don't need to file a separate tax return for your business. Similarly, any debts you incur as a sole proprietor are the same as your personal debts.

Why are so many home-based businesses organized as sole proprietorships? Perhaps one reason is that by default your business is considered a sole proprietorship if you do nothing to formally organize your business. In other words, by doing nothing, you automatically make the decision to become a sole proprietorship. Another reason may be that creating a partnership or corporation is more difficult because doing so requires creating partnership agreements or filing incorporation forms with the government.

Fortunately, the sole proprietorship isn't a bad form for many home-based businesses to take. After all, it's the simplest and least regulated form of business organization, startup costs are minimal or nil, and one person owns the business and wields full control over it. The sole proprietor is responsible for securing financing, and he or she receives all company profits. Business income under the sole-proprietorship form of business is taxed as personal income, which works out just fine for most home-business owners.

On the other hand, a sole proprietorship offers major disadvantages in the areas of legal liability for the owner (who can be personally sued for any and all business-related issues) and potential dissolution of the business upon the owner's death. Table 10-1 summarizes the pros and cons of a sole proprietorship.

Table 10-1 Sole Proprietorship

Pros	*Cons*
The owner has complete control over all aspects of the business.	The sole proprietorship is considered less prestigious than some other forms of business.
Starting a sole proprietorship is inexpensive.	Creating and maintaining secure outside financing can be particularly difficult.
A sole proprietorship is easy to start and easy to close.	The business dies when the owner does.
The owner gets to keep all profits.	The owner is personally liable in the event of a lawsuit (as a result of malpractice, product failure, and so on).

Perusing partnerships

If you have two or more owners of your home-based business — perhaps you and a close friend or relative — consider choosing the partnership form of business. In a *partnership,* each partner commits to provide specific skills, expertise, and effort — and to share the partnership's expenses — in return for an agreed-on portion of the company's profits. The agreement spelling out these terms is called (not surprisingly) a *partnership agreement.*

Partnerships take advantage of the different skills, expertise, and resources — including cash — that the different partners bring to an organization. And they're fairly easy to put together and administer; all you really need is a simple written agreement, which you can make more complicated if the stakes are high.

Be sure, however, to have a lawyer take a look at your partnership agreement before you sign it. Because partners have a legally recognized ownership stake in the business, each is an agent for the partnership and can hire employees, borrow money, and operate the business.

On the plus side, a partnership's profits are taxed as personal income, with each partner taxed on his or her portion of the profits. On the minus side of the ledger, however, partners are personally liable for debts and taxes. And personal assets can be confiscated if the partnership can't satisfy creditors' claims. If you have a nice home or a car or two, keep this point in mind before you enter into a partnership. Table 10-2 shows the advantages and disadvantages in detail.

In the event that partners want to avoid personal liability, they can form a special legal arrangement called a *limited partnership*. Limited partnerships must be registered and must also pay a *franchise fee* charged by the state to file a certificate of limited partnership. Don't forget: Although it's legally possible to create a partnership with only a handshake and sometimes less, in the event of disagreement or when it's time to dissolve the partnership, you'll wish you had a written agreement. Consider having a lawyer either draft or review your partnership agreement. Remember: The money you pay now for a lawyer's help will save you many headaches and, potentially, big stacks of cash down the road.

Table 10-2 Partnership

Pros	*Cons*
A partnership incorporates the skills, expertise, and efforts of two or more people.	Partners don't always agree on every course of action, a situation that may eventually harm the business.
Business risks are diffused across one or more partners.	Each partner is legally liable for actions of the other partners, including hiring employees, borrowing money, and operating the business.
Partners support one another and provide a stimulating social environment.	Some partners may think they deserve more of the business's profits than the other partners.
Government exerts little direct control over partnerships.	Like divorces, when partnerships break up, things can get messy fast.
All partners share the expenses.	All partners share the profits.

Looking at limited liability companies

The *limited liability company* (LLC) is a fairly recent innovation, providing flexibility in management the way a general partnership does while offering the limited liability of a corporation. On one hand, LLCs are treated as partnerships for U.S. income tax purposes, but, on the other hand, they receive the protection from personal liability that corporations enjoy. LLCs are now legally recognized in all 50 states, in the District of Columbia, and in many foreign countries.

Owners of LLCs are known as *members* — comparable to stockholders in a corporation or limited partners in a limited partnership. If you decide to create an LLC, you have to file articles of organization with your secretary of state. Each LLC member must also execute an operating agreement that defines the relationship between the company and its members. Check your state's procedures to find out the requirements that apply to you.

The LLC form of business may be the preferred choice for certain new operations and joint ventures. The pluses and minuses of LLCs are similar to those of partnerships, with the exception of the limitation of liability that corporations enjoy. Table 10-3 gives you some other pros and cons.

Table 10-3 Limited Liability Company

Pros	*Cons*
LLCs offer limited liability for the company's principals (owners).	Many states require that the business include more than one person.
Federal taxes treat LLCs as partnerships, though some states, including California, treat them as corporations.	LLCs dissolve on the death of an owner.
LLCs cost less to form and maintain than do corporations and require less paperwork.	LLCs cost more to set up and maintain than do sole proprietorships.

Checking out corporations

Without a doubt, the *corporation* is the most complex form of business. Corporations are unique because they're legal entities that exist separately from their owners, which is why corporations limit the personal liability of their owners. Although they limit the owners from personal liability, however, a *double taxation on earnings* (corporate tax and personal tax) may result, putting corporations at a tax disadvantage in certain circumstances. Corporations are identified by having the words *Incorporated (Inc.)* or *Corporation (Corp.)* in or after their names.

On the positive side of things, the corporation form may help you finance your company because it allows you to raise capital easily through the sale of corporate stocks or bonds. And because a corporation exists apart from its owners, it can function even without key individuals. The corporation form of business also enables employees to participate in various types of insurance and profit-sharing plans that may not be available to sole proprietorships, partnerships, or LLCs.

On the minus side, corporations can be expensive to start and maintain, and the required paperwork may be a nightmare for people who dislike red tape. Costs and procedures for incorporating vary from state to state, and you have to be careful to do it right the first time. Contact your secretary of state for more information (find out more info on your state's Web site). Table 10-4 shares more of the advantages and disadvantages of corporations.

A special type of corporation — an *S corporation* — allows owners to overcome the double tax problem of regular corporations (called *C corporations*) by allowing shareholders to offset business losses with personal income. However, as if the government (in this case, state government) didn't already charge enough to incorporate, S corporations are subject to an additional annual surcharge from the federal government. Everyone, it seems, wants a piece of the action.

Table 10-4 Corporation

Pros	*Cons*
A corporation has the best overall business image.	A corporation is expensive to start and operate.
Personal liability of owners and stockholders is limited.	Starting and maintaining a corporation involves mountains of paperwork.
A corporation can (and generally does) survive its owners.	Tax benefits may be little or nil compared with the other forms of business.
A corporation is easier to sell, although a majority of voting stock-holders is required to do so.	All the paperwork required to form a cor-poration require quite a bit of effort to make changes to.
A corporation can sell stock and bonds, making raising capital easier than with other forms of business.	A corporation is double taxed in some states, and insurance may be more expensive than for other forms of business.

The Web has taken a lot of the hassle and cost out of incorporating. Sites that provide incorporating services include Intuit's MyCorporation (`mycorporation.intuit.com`), LegalZoom (`www.legalzoom.com`), and BizFilings (`www.bizfilings.com`). Their services and costs vary.

Despite all the options available to home-based businesses, most start out as either sole proprietorships or partnerships. Forming sole proprietorships or partnerships is the easiest way to go, and it costs little or no money.

Eventually, though, many home-based businesses consider the other major available forms of business — LLCs and corporations — because each one offers unique advantages and disadvantages to home-based businesses, especially when it comes to liability and taxes.

Figuring Out What to Call Your Business: Name Registration

Choosing the name of your company is one of the most critical decisions you make as you set up your business. We're not exaggerating when we say that the right name can help pave the way to sales and success, and the wrong name can lead to all kinds of problems for you and your business — success not being one of them.

According to global corporate image expert Naseem Javed, quoted in the *San Diego Union Tribune* newspaper, "If you don't have a good name, you'll be throwing away advertising money and profit potential."

REMEMBER

Here's an interesting bit of information: An average of 4,000 to 5,000 commercial messages are aimed at every person each day. Think about it for a minute — television and radio ads, newspapers, magazines, Internet pop-up and click-through ads, ads on the sides of buses, company names on sports stadiums, junk mail, junk faxes, junk e-mail . . . the list goes on and on. How will your home-based business cut through all that noise and capture the interest and attention of your prospective customers? A good name can make all the difference.

The best business names

- Describe the service or product that the business offers
- Are protected by trademark or service mark
- Are novel

Naming your business isn't something to do with friends over a few beers while you're grilling burgers in the backyard — it requires careful thought and planning. Your business name should give people some idea of the exact nature of your business (*The Pink Poodle* would be much better for a pet grooming business than for a tree-trimming business, for example), and it should also project the image you want your business to have. Names can be simple, sophisticated, or even silly (not too silly, though).

Think several years into the future; try to pick a name that will grow with your business over time instead of limiting it. The Pleasant Hawaiian Holidays travel agency, for example, decided it would be a good idea to change its name to Pleasant Holidays when its trip offerings expanded beyond the Hawaiian Islands.

Here are some tips on selecting a name:

- Use your own name — if you have a reputation or plan to grow one. Peter's home-based business, for example, is titled Peter Economy Incorporated. Although it doesn't tell potential customers what the company does, it does tell them who's going to do it.
- Use your name with a tag line or motto (Sara's Place: Where Cookies Are Number 1).
- Use a super-catchy Web site name (`freecash4u.com`, `no-homework.com`).
- Use a name that communicates a primary benefit (No Mess Chimney Sweep).
- Use a name that describes your specialty (Fantastic Fabric Creations).
- Use a made-up name that suggests what you do or how you do it (Springfield Hand-Built Log Homes).

Of course, just as you can find general guidelines about what kinds of names you should use, think about the kinds of names you should avoid. Here are five key qualities to avoid when choosing your name, according to corporate image expert Naseem Javed:

- Overused ("There are 53,573 U.S. businesses or products with the name *King* in them and 5,730 with *Mr.*," said Javed.)
- Politically incorrect (Aunt Jemima)
- Sound-alike (General, International, Dynamic, U.S.)
- Neutral (Gold Seal, Lucky, Micro, Data)
- Confusing (Ben Gay)

Along with a name, many businesses develop a logo — the graphic symbol of the business. As they say, a picture is worth a thousand words. As with your name, you should carefully design your logo to project the exact image you want for your business. See Chapter 14 for more on creating a logo.

After you've decided on a name, the next step is to make sure it isn't already in use by another company. If the name you use is trademarked or otherwise legally protected by another business, not only can you be sued to stop using the name, but you can also lose the thousands of dollars for advertising and promotion you spent developing and promoting your brand and products.

Here are a few resources you can use to find out whether your proposed business name is already in use:

- **Local phone books:** Call directory assistance for the most recent listings, but understand that many home-based businesses don't list business phone numbers.
- **Local Web sites:** Check out your county's Web site for fictitious name registrations, also referred to as *DBAs* ("doing business as").
- **Domain name registrars:** You can use sites like `easywhois.com` or `whois.net`; plus, most domain name registrars provide access to the WhoIs database.
- **Online directories:** Use online directories, such as `www.anywho.com` and `www.infospace.com`, and search engines, such as `www.google.com`, `www.alltheweb.com`, `www.bing.com`, and `www.yahoo.com`.
- **Trademark specialists:** Search using a database, such as the U.S. Patent and Trademark Office (`www.uspto.gov/main/trademarks.htm`) or Corporation Service Company (`www.cscprotectsbrands.com`), or, better yet, an attorney specializing in trademarks and patents.

If all that searching sounds like a pain in the neck (and it does to us), hire someone to do a search for you.

When you've finally settled on a name, it may be worth your time and money to obtain a trademark from the U.S. Patent and Trademark Office to protect your business name and logo. If you don't, someone else may take them away from you — along with all the customer goodwill you worked so hard to build.

If the name you choose isn't your name, you'll have to file a fictitious-business-name statement (also called a *doing business as, DBA,* or *d/b/a*). Filing a DBA is also necessary if the business name implies greater ownership with such words as *and Company*, *and Associates*, or *& Son/Daughter.*

TIP Although regulations vary from state to state (check with your local authorities to make sure you know exactly what you have to do), fictitious-business-name statements are generally filed with the county clerk and may also have to be published in a newspaper of general circulation once a week for four successive weeks in the county where the principal place of business is located. Because the cost of publishing legal notices, such as fictitious-business-name statements, varies widely from newspaper to newspaper, it pays to shop around.

After your legal notice has been published for the required period of time, you have to file an affidavit of publication with the county clerk or requisite local or state agency within 30 days after publication. Again, check the requirements in your locale to be sure you have a complete understanding of the filing requirements so you don't miss anything.

Differentiating between Trademarks, Copyrights, and Patents

When you think of the word *asset,* the first thing that comes to your mind may be cash, a computer, a company car, or perhaps the equipment you use to make the items you sell to customers. However, one of the most important assets for many businesses today isn't any of those things — it's *intellectual property,* the unique ideas and knowledge that give a business a competitive advantage in the marketplace.

Intellectual property can range from a unique product design or the ingredients in your award-winning chili recipe to your company's name, a song or photograph, or the exact words you wrote in a newspaper or magazine article.

The value of your intellectual property depends on the nature of the ideas and their demand in the marketplace. But one thing is for sure: The value of your intellectual property is in jeopardy if you don't take steps to protect it from theft, which is where trademarks, copyrights, and patents come in.

Trademarks

A *trademark* (™) is a distinctive word, name, symbol, or device — or any combination of the four — used to distinguish a product or service from those of competitors. A *service mark* (℠) is simply a trademark for services.

The word, name, symbol, or device you select to trademark must be sufficiently unique to separate your products from their generic source. You can't, for example, trademark the generic word *cola,* but you can trademark a trade name for your unique brand of cola known as *Coca-Cola* (or, that is, you could've if someone hadn't beaten you to it 125 years or so ago).

You can apply the trademark or service-mark symbols to your distinctive word, name, or symbol at any time; you don't have to get anyone's permission to do so. If, however, you want to legally protect the trademark to ensure that someone else doesn't steal it away from you (not a bad idea, in our humble opinions), consider registering it.

You can register trademarks and service marks through some state governments if you want protection only within the state in which your business is located or through the U.S. Patent and Trademark Office (USPTO) if you want nationwide protection. When your trademark is registered on a nationwide basis, you can use the familiar ® symbol on your products and product information.

TIP

If you're wondering whether someone has already registered a trademark or service mark, you can look it up in the USPTO trademark database online at `www.uspto.gov`.

REMEMBER

A trademark may not prevent someone from stealing (or mistakenly using) your unique word, name, or symbol, but it does provide you with legal recourse in court in case someone does. In the long run, that provision may be worth its weight in gold to you and your business.

Copyrights

Copyright is a form of protection provided to the authors of "original works of authorship," including literary, dramatic, musical, artistic, and certain other intellectual works, both published and unpublished. This book is copyrighted, for example. The script for the latest *Harry Potter* movie is copyrighted. That song you were humming in the shower this morning is probably copyrighted.

U.S. copyright laws generally give the owner of copyright the exclusive right to reproduce the copyrighted work, prepare *derivative works* (works taken from the copyrighted work that owe their existence to the original work), distribute copies or phonograph records (those big, round, black things people bought before the invention of compact discs) of the copyrighted work, perform the copyrighted work publicly, or display the copyrighted work publicly.

TIP

A copyright is automatically created when the work itself is created — no need to file any forms or pay someone a bunch of money to copyright your work for you.

As is the case with trademarks and service marks, you can apply a copyright symbol (©) to your work at any time without getting anyone's approval to do so. If, however, you want to be able to legally protect your work (again, a smart move, in our humble opinions), make sure you register your copyright and apply the © to it. Here are just some of the advantages of registering your copyright:

- Registration establishes a public record of the copyright claim — extremely valuable evidence that you have a right to your copyright.
- Registering your copyright gives you, as the creator of the work, protection for your entire lifetime plus 70 years (ideally, that should be long enough to cover you).
- Registration is necessary for works of U.S. origin before you can file an infringement suit in court.
- If made before or within five years of publication, registration establishes that the facts stated in the certificate of copyright are presumed to be true unless proven otherwise.
- If registration is made within three months after publication of the work or prior to an infringement of the work, damages specified by statute (or law) and attorney's fees will be available to the copyright owner in court actions. Otherwise, only an award of actual damages and profits is available to the copyright owner.
- Registration allows the owner of the copyright to record the registration with the U.S. Customs Service for protection against copies being imported that infringe on your copyright.

Registering your copyright is simple. To register basic claims for literary works, visual art works, performing arts works — including motion pictures, sound recordings, and single serials — the preferred method is online registration through the electronic Copyright Office (eCO). To register through the eCO, visit `www.copyright.gov` and click on the link to the electronic Copyright Office.

A basic copyright claim includes:

- A single work
- Multiple unpublished works if they're all by the same author(s) and owned by the same claimant
- Multiple published works if they're all first published together in the same publication on the same date and owned by the same claimant

Filing a copyright electronically currently costs just $35 for a basic claim. If you don't want to file electronically, you can choose to mail in your copyright registration. Certain kinds of filings — copyrighting the design of a ship's hull or preregistration of certain unpublished works, for example — can't be filed electronically. The fees for nonelectronic filing are higher, however, and the process takes longer to complete. For complete details and forms, visit the Web site for the Copyright Office at `www.copyright.gov`.

Patents

A *patent* for an invention is the grant of a property right to the inventor, issued by the USPTO. The term of a new patent is 20 years from the date on which the application for the patent was filed in the United States and, in special circumstances, from a filing outside the United States at an earlier date. U.S. patent grants are effective only within the United States and its territories and possessions.

The idea of patents is to allow the inventor or patent holder an exclusive right to obtain the full financial benefits of his or her invention — allowing the inventor to recover his or her investment of time and money — before others are allowed to help themselves to a piece of the financial pie.

Imagine that you spent ten years of your life designing a new kind of mousetrap — far superior and more cost-effective than any currently on the market — and began selling it, only to have someone immediately copy it and undercut your price, putting you out of business in the process. In such a case, a patent is essential to protect you and your business.

What can and can't be patented has been subject to much debate over the years — witness the recent furor over the patenting of genetically modified seeds for corn and other crops and unique software programs, such as Amazon.com's 1-Click ordering process. According to U.S. patent law, any person who "invents or discovers any new and useful process, machine, manufacture, or composition of matter, or any new and useful improvement thereof, may obtain a patent," subject to the conditions and requirements of the law.

If you think you have an item that can and should be patented, we suggest that you run — don't walk — to a competent patent attorney. The patent application process requires considerable research, and the appropriate forms have to be filed the right way and at the right time and place. When you're talking about something that may turn out to be your major source of income for many years into the future — and may very well make you rich — don't try doing it yourself — seek professional help fast. Although filing a patent isn't inexpensive, a competent patent attorney can save you lots of time, money, and heartache.

Getting information about trademarks, copyrights, and patents

If you need more specific information about trademarks, copyrights, and patents, help is on the way. Simply surf your way over to the following Web sites or call the following phone numbers for more information:

- **Trademarks and patents:** U.S. Patent and Trademark Office; phone 800-786-9199 or 571-272-1000; Web site `www.uspto.gov`
- **Copyrights:** Copyright Office, Library of Congress; phone 202-707-3000; Web site `www.copyright.gov`

Determining the Need for Zoning, Licensing, and Permits

Zoning, licensing, and permits — this is where the red tape really gets sticky . . . and thick. No matter which governments — federal, state, or local — have jurisdiction in your particular place of business, you can bet they all have something to say about how, when, and where you can and can't run your business.

Although you may have an easier time sticking your head in the sand and ignoring all the rules and regulations that the different government organizations want you to follow, you do so at your own risk. When sufficiently motivated (as they will be if your neighbors complain to elected officials about cars that suddenly start parking in front of your house), most government agencies and departments aren't the slightest bit shy about issuing fines, imposing penalties, and — if compliance isn't forthcoming in a reasonable amount of time — closing down offending businesses.

Working your way through the maze of government regulations can certainly be one of the most confusing aspects of doing business, but it's also critical for your success in the long run. Yes, the process can be intimidating, and, yes, you'd much rather be selling your products and services than messing with all this red tape and paperwork, but it's definitely worth your while to dig in.

Instead of ignoring government regulations and requirements, consider this step as one that will enhance the professionalism of your business. In order for people to take you and your business seriously, you need to establish your business in a professional way (in other words, according to government rules and regulations). And for many home-based businesses, being taken seriously is one of the key steps to finding long-term success.

Zoning

For some reason, many homeowners — particularly ones who live in quiet residential areas — don't like the idea of having a busy (loud, junky, or otherwise obnoxious) business move in next door. Just the thought of a constant parade of customer cars coming and going at all hours of the day or night, the clatter and noise coming from a makeshift appliance-repair shop out in your garage, or the vision of partly assembled cars littering the driveway is enough to send many homeowners into a fit of concern or even anger. And indeed, when people buy their homes, they (surprise!) generally expect to get some measure of peace and quiet along with them.

Peter remembers the time a few years ago when one of his next-door neighbors decided to open an automobile-restoration business in his backyard. It wouldn't have been so bad in itself except for the loud air compressor that the neighbor found necessary to run 12 hours a day to drive his sandblasting equipment — waking Peter's 1-year-old daughter and making writing his books and articles a difficult proposition during daylight hours. It took Peter six months — from the day he first complained to his neighbor about the noise (and being told to jump in a lake) to the day the city zoning department finally shut down the operation — to get relief. But he did eventually get relief.

Zoning laws are, among other things, the government's favorite way of trying to keep residential areas residential and business areas business — making everyone (well, almost everyone) happy in the process. An estimated 90 percent of all U.S. cities place restrictions on home-based work.

In general, zoning laws do work. After a citizen makes a complaint, most jurisdictions follow an established procedure to determine whether a business owner is breaking the rules or not — and take action only when necessary. Unfortunately, the very zoning laws that attempt to ensure that someone doesn't decide to build a coal-fired power generation plant across the street from your house are also the same laws that may restrict (and in some cases prevent) you from starting a business in your own home.

Here are some of the categories of rules that zoning laws may impose in your particular city or county:

- Advertising signage
- Parking and vehicle traffic

- The percentage of your home devoted to business
- The number of people you employ and the jobs you employ them to perform
- The use of hazardous materials and chemicals
- Noise, smoke, and odor

If you're wondering what zoning laws, rules, and regulations may impact your home-based business, visit your city or county planning, zoning, or building code compliance department, or spend some time in a local law library. Your local chamber of commerce or small business administration office may also be a good source of information.

REMEMBER

One more thing: Although your local zoning laws may permit you to run your home-based business as you intend, your particular neighborhood, development, condominium project, or rental property may have rules, covenants, or other deeded restrictions on those very same activities. Check your real estate purchase or leasing documents to see whether such rules, covenants, or restrictions apply to you.

So what can you do if zoning regulations make your home-based business illegal or are so restrictive that you can't operate your business effectively? You can certainly ignore the regulations and hope you don't get caught, but that's not really the best long-term solution, and we don't recommend it.

You're apt to discover that at least one of your neighbors isn't going to be happy about some aspect of your business and will file a complaint. Not only that, but also, keep in mind the fact that if you operate an illegal business, you're breaking the law. And if you break the law, you'd better be ready to pay the consequences (we'll keep an eye on the Court TV listings just in case you make an appearance).

A better idea is to try one of the following approaches:

- **Get permission.** If you're living in a rental property and your lease restricts the kinds of business activities you can undertake, ask your landlord for permission to do what you need to do. So long as you're not creating a nuisance or causing damage to your property, you may find that your landlord will work with you.
- **Request a variance.** Government agencies and departments routinely grant variances to rules and regulations for property owners who request them. Often, you only have to fill out a short form. In other cases, your request may have to be publicly heard before your city council, zoning board, or other body (in the case of conflicts with neighborhood covenants, you may need to appeal to your neighborhood association). Check with your zoning or planning department to find out what options are available for you.

- **Fight city hall.** In some cases, you may have no other choice but to take action to change the rules or regulations that restrict your ability to start and operate a home-based business. A variety of approaches are available to you, from buttonholing your district's council member, to circulating a petition, to lobbying for legislative change, to filing a lawsuit. The exact action you take depends on your community's political environment. If you have any friends, relatives, or business acquaintances who have taken on city hall, ask what worked for them.

Although zoning regulations can get in the way of your home-business plans, they don't have to be the end of your dream. If the rules aren't in your favor, you have legally viable options for either living with them, bending them, or changing them.

Licensing and permits

There really is a business license or permit for most any occasion. Which ones does your home-based business need? It really depends on which city, county, and state your business is located in.

Ask questions, starting with your city and/or county government. Describe the kind of business you have in mind to find out which forms and requirements are appropriate for you. Your local government may even have a special booklet or package of forms specifically for new or home-based businesses. After you check with your local government, contact the state and federal agencies that apply to your business.

Some of the most common licenses and permits include the following:

- **Business license:** The standard permit to operate a business locally, it's required of most every business, no matter how large or small. Check with your local business agency for details.
- **Home occupation permit:** If your community restricts home-based businesses, you need one of these permits.
- **Miscellaneous local permits:** Contact your local business agency to see whether any other business permits are required.
- **Police permit:** Some businesses need police clearance or a police permit. You may also need a police permit if your business has an alarm that generates a police response when it goes off.
- **Food permit:** Businesses that make or sell food need this permit.

- **Seller's permit:** Businesses that sell taxable products in states with sales tax need one of these permits. (Note that only a few states don't have sales tax.)

  The definition of *taxable products* varies from state to state. Graphic design services, for example, may be considered a nontaxable service in one state but taxable in another.

- **Building permits, fire certificates, and zoning permits:** Check with your local planning department for restrictions on the kinds of business activities you can conduct in your home. Some localities, for example, restrict home-based businesses that operate in residentially zoned communities from having customers come to the place of business.
- **State occupational licenses:** Certain occupations (for example, doctors, lawyers, general contractors, day-care providers, and so on) require a special license. Check with the state agency regulating consumer affairs.
- **Federal export licenses:** If you want to export goods to another country, your business will be subject to all kinds of federal regulation. Get more information from the U.S. Department of Commerce at `www.doc.gov`. A number of optional certifications can help in some situations: You may want to look into being certified as a small business, minority-owned, woman-owned, or disabled-veteran-owned enterprise.

Starting a collections agency

Q: I'm interested in starting my own collections agency, but I'm unclear about the rules and regulations I have to follow in doing this business, as well as the types of software and other materials I need.

A: The major piece of legislation you need to become familiar with is The Fair Debt Collection Practices Act. You can learn about the key legislation and about operating a collections business in a course titled "Debt Collectors Collection Training System." Check out the Web site `www.MichelleDunn.com` for more information.

Collections software programs you may want to check out include

- Debtmaster from Comtronic Systems; phone 509-674-7000; Web site `www.comtronic.com`
- Collect!; phone 250-391-0466; Web site `www.collect.org`
- Collection Resource System; phone 703-934-9060; Web site `www.crsoftwareinc.com`
- EZCollector; phone 888-439-7638 or 561-997-9003; Web site `www.CollectionAgencySoftware.com`

Don't get discouraged by all this paperwork and red tape. Owning and operating your own business is the light at the end tunnel created by all these blasted forms. Remember that people are ready, willing, and able to help if you feel overwhelmed. Contact your local small business development center, chamber of commerce, or other local economic development organization for guidance on these local, state, and federal issues; you'll be glad you did.

Scrutinizing Your Tax Requirements

You can be sure that your business is going to owe taxes to somebody, somewhere, particularly if your business is making a profit. Depending on the state where you're located, the kind of business you conduct, and the form of business you select, you may owe taxes to many different people in many different places.

Take a look at the following list for a hint of the kinds of taxes you can look forward to paying when you own your own home-based business:

- Income tax
- Self-employment tax
- Estimated tax
- Social Security tax
- Unemployment tax
- Sales tax
- Excise tax
- Use tax
- Business tax

Now you know why good accountants and tax advisors are so popular with all kinds of businesspeople, including owners of home-based businesses. For much more information about taxes — including what taxes you need to pay and ways to reduce your income tax burden — take a look at Chapter 9.

Chapter 11

Using Outside Resources and Experts

In This Chapter

- Creating trade accounts and increasing your cash flow at the same time
- Taking advantage of support services
- Looking to outside professionals for help
- Bartering safely and effectively

Okay, so you're the boss, owner, and chief bottle-washer of your home-based business. Now what? In theory, you could probably do each and every job on your own — from reviewing contracts to picking the best insurance coverage to representing your business in court to designing and printing your own letterhead stationery — but you really should think twice before doing so. Specialists — lawyers, certified public accountants, insurance brokers, and others — are much more knowledgeable and up-to-date about certain topics than you can ever be, and using their services allows you to focus on doing the things that you do best — namely, running your business.

Beyond these outside professionals, you should (and likely will have to) consider using a variety of outside resources when the opportunities present themselves. Establishing trade accounts with the outside vendors you rely on to sell you the products and services you need to do business is just one example.

In this chapter, we look at why, when, and how to take advantage of outside resources. Doing so can give you a real edge against your competition and help you provide your customers with the best products and services possible.

Establishing Trade Accounts

A *trade account* is an informal agreement between you and a supplier or vendor — such as an office supply store, printing company, or warehouse superstore — that allows you to purchase goods or services on credit and be billed by the supplier on a regular, usually monthly, basis. A trade account is a win-win situation for both parties — you can purchase whatever you want whenever you want, and your supplier gains a steady customer.

REMEMBER

The care and maintenance of trade accounts is essential for almost any business, because these accounts speed the purchasing process and often provide customers with special discounts unavailable to regular customers or with premiums such as free overnight delivery. Companies that don't have trade accounts miss out on these and other benefits. Another important benefit of trade accounts is that when a company agrees to establish a trade account with you, its management is essentially agreeing to extend a short-term, interest-free loan to your company — allowing you to pay your bill anywhere from a few days to a month or more after you complete your purchase and receive your goods or services. This free loan is a good deal for your company and one worth actively pursuing and maintaining. The longer you hold on to your money, the more positive the impact on your company's cash flow.

As you continue to grow your business, you may find that some of the following trade accounts are beneficial for you to establish:

- **Product vendors:** If you sell products on a retail basis, you have to buy them from vendors or purchase the raw materials from suppliers. Establishing trade accounts with such vendors makes your life much easier; you can place orders now and pay for your purchases later — usually up to 30 days after you receive your invoice.
- **Office supply stores:** If you regularly purchase large quantities of office supplies, consider building a relationship (by establishing a trade account) with one office supply vendor that can meet your needs quickly and accurately. The big office supply chains like Staples and Office Depot offer their own business customer credit programs. Simply fill out an online application and submit it for approval. If your credit record is good, you should have no problem gaining approval.
- **Warehouse superstores:** Warehouse superstores, such as Costco and Sam's Club, offer everything most home offices need — from appliances to office supplies to groceries and baked goods — at great prices, so setting up a trade account with one of these superstores is a good idea for many businesses.
- **Copying/reproduction centers:** If you constantly find yourself sending jobs out for printing or copying, you may want to establish a trade account with your printer so that you receive a monthly bill instead of having to pay every time you run a job. Copy centers such as FedEx

Office offer their own charge cards to business customers, which they bill on a monthly basis. The monthly invoices, which present detailed information about each order, are also a great way to keep track of your copying and reproduction jobs.

- **Office equipment repair companies:** Has your computer's hard drive ever crashed? If so, you know just how scary life can be — and how dependent you are on office machines and equipment. Having an established relationship with a good computer/office equipment repair person *before* — not after — your equipment goes down can really pay off. In all honesty, the question isn't whether your office equipment will break, but when. Even if you don't go through the trouble of establishing a relationship with an office equipment repair company before you need it, take some time to become familiar with who's good and who's not so good. That way, when the inevitable emergency does occur, you know where to take your sick machine.
- **Support services:** Numerous support services are available to you, depending on the nature of your business. From typists and architects to paralegals and consulting engineers, you can establish relationships and trade accounts with just about anyone. (In the next section, we address how to decide which support services you need and then how to identify and hire them.)
- **Courier/messenger services:** Although more and more transactions are being handled over the Internet, some items, such as products and signed documents, must be physically sent and received. When you establish an account with an overnight courier service, such as FedEx or UPS, or with a local messenger service, you receive preprinted, multipart shipping documents or air bills. Even better, most of these companies now allow you to set up your shipments online, printing out shipping documents on your computer and making it easy to track your package's progress — from your home office to your customer's front door.

Trade accounts are a good thing, and you should try to establish them with all your regular vendors, suppliers, and service providers. Not only do they streamline your business dealings, but because you hold on to your money for a longer period of time, they also help you improve your cash flow. And because a trade account is basically a short-term loan, the fact that you have trade accounts in good standing shows that your business is creditworthy, making it easier for you to obtain other trade accounts and business credit.

TIP

Trade accounts also work the other way — other businesses may want to establish trade accounts with you. Allowing them to do so may make a lot of sense because it encourages repeat business and the development of long-term business relationships. You must, however, protect yourself from customers who don't pay their bills. Check credit references scrupulously. Don't just take a business's word for it — especially when you have a lot of money on the line. Do a Google search for *credit application form,* and you'll find plenty of sample forms that you can easily adapt for your own purposes.

Using Support Services

With just 24 hours in a day, if you're the sole proprietor and only employee of your home-based business, you may find that you have difficulty doing day-to-day support and administrative tasks while still doing the work that your customers pay you to do — which is where using support services comes in.

Support services include everything from short-term employees to temporary employment firms to professionals, such as lawyers, accountants, and consultants — in fact, support services potentially include any business service you can imagine.

Consider using support services for the following three reasons:

- **You can take advantage of people who have more experience than you do in certain areas.** Do you know how to file a patent application? Or the best way to set up a computerized accounting system? Or which healthcare plans offer the best deal for home-based businesses in your state? If not, providers of support services — many of whom are owners of home-based businesses themselves — do. People who provide support services are specialists at what they do, just as you're a specialist at what you do. One of the great things about using support services is that you can take advantage of as much or as little of their experience as you like — usually for a reasonable hourly fee.
- **You can leverage your experience.** Using certain support services, such as hiring a temporary employee as an assistant, can allow you to leverage your own experience — greatly increasing your effectiveness in the process. After you teach another person to perform a high-dollar-return task that you're an expert at, that other person can do the same thing you do, instantly multiplying the effort spent on that task and substantially increasing the financial return. For example, why not consider hiring someone to make cold calls to prospective customers or to create and distribute flyers advertising your business? While you're busy working, your new employee can be drumming up new customers.
- **You can focus your efforts.** Instead of getting caught up in all the details of producing 500 copies of a 12-page brochure (finding the right kind of paper, using the right machine, dealing with jams and equipment breakdowns, collating, and folding), why not just drop it off at FedEx Office or another copy center, and let them worry about it? Doing so lets you focus your efforts on the things that bring money into your firm — such as selling products and writing proposals.

Leasing employees

Q: I have a home-based medical-billing business, and I'm ready to hire employees. Because I didn't want to hassle with payroll, workman's comp, and so on, I called several employee-leasing companies. To my surprise, none would provide me with employees because I'm home based. What should I do?

A: We're surprised and appalled to discover that some employee-leasing companies are discriminating against home-based businesses! Like many home-based companies, we use employee leasing ourselves. We've worked with two different companies for more than five years, and the results have been more than satisfactory. So we recommend that you keep looking to find more-enlightened companies.

Be sure that you're actually contacting employee-leasing companies — not temp agencies. *Professional employer organizations,* as employee-leasing companies are called, carry out the administrative functions of having employees. You recruit the personnel, interview them, and select them. When you're ready to put them to work, you contact the leasing company, which puts them on the payroll and handles all aspects of their employment for you. *Temporary-help agencies,* on the other hand, recruit, interview, and train employees, whom they then send to work with companies on a short- or long-term basis.

For many years, we've been aware that some temporary agencies won't place their temps in home offices. However, some temp agencies do. Consider working with an employee-leasing company if you have an employee in mind or want to find someone yourself. If you want an agency to find and place someone to work in your business, contact a temporary-help agency.

To locate such companies, you can contact the following:

- National Association of Professional Employer Organizations, 707 N. Saint Asaph St., Alexandria, VA 22314; phone 703-836-0466; Web site `www.napeo.org`
- American Staffing Association, 277 S. Washington St., Suite 200, Alexandria, VA 22314; phone 703-253-2020; Web site `www.americanstaffing.net`

So what kinds of support services should you consider using for your home-based business? Here's a partial list (but keep in mind that many more are available to home-business owners):

- Copying, printing, and graphics design
- Public relations
- Packaging and shipping
- Professional services, such as accounting, legal, banking, and so on
- Temporary help
- Advertising
- Cleaning

Although you may have plenty of time to do these tasks when your company is new and has little business, after it starts to grow, you'll want to devote more time to selling and fulfilling customer needs and less time to doing the kinds of tasks that don't directly generate cash for the business.

Finding Good Lawyers, Accountants, and Other Professionals

When you own a home-based business, you're responsible for just about everything. Whether you're selling your products, paying the bills, or taking out the trash, the business begins and ends with you — without you, you have no business.

This simple fact doesn't mean, however, that you have to go at it alone. Any number of outside professionals are ready, willing, and able to help you build and expand your business and help you make sure you're on a firm footing — legally and financially. By leveraging the services of key professionals, such as lawyers, accountants, bankers, insurance agents, and others, a small business can be just as effective as a much larger organization — perhaps even more so.

REMEMBER

No matter what kinds of professionals you decide to affiliate with, check them out thoroughly before you commit to doing business with them. Don't forget: Your goal is to find someone who is not only talented and affordable, but who also can grow with you and your company and become a long-term partner and trusted associate. (Peter, for example, has been working with the same accountant since 1986 and the same lawyer since 1992.) Take your time when you're selecting the professionals you want to work with; believe us, the time you invest in the process now will pay off many times over in the years to come. Consider the following during the selection process:

- **Qualifications:** Hire professionals who are as qualified and experienced as possible; you don't want your business to be the place where they learn the ropes. Don't hire someone who merely dabbles in an area of professional expertise or who does it as a hobby. You need someone who's a pro and who's fully committed to your success.
- **Accessibility:** You may have a difficult time getting some professionals' attention when you really need them. Make sure the professionals you hire aren't already so overcommitted with other clients that they can't meet your needs quickly, when you need them the most.

- **Price:** Although you should never select a professional based on price alone, price certainly does enter into the equation. With some big-city lawyers charging more than $400 an hour, every dollar really does count. Don't be afraid to shop around for the best combination of skill, experience, and price.
- **Ethics:** Hire professionals who have ethical standards that are just as high as the standards you uphold. Choosing someone with flexible ethics is asking for trouble.
- **Compatibility:** The preceding characteristics don't mean much if you aren't compatible with your chosen professional. Conversely, you may be willing to give up some experience or price in exchange for someone you really get along with. The ideal situation is to find someone who meets all your criteria and is also compatible with you and any business partners and associates you may have.

In the following sections, we take a close look at some of the kinds of professionals that home-based business owners most often turn to for help and support.

Hiring the right lawyers

Question: How many lawyers does it take to change a light bulb? Answer: How many can you afford? Actually, most lawyers really are nice people to work with, and they do have other things on their minds besides emptying your bank accounts. In fact, an attorney's services are an important part of any business's — including any home-based business's — support team.

What exactly can attorneys do for your business? Here are some of the most common tasks attorneys take on for small-business clients like you:

- Choosing a business form (legal structure) for your business
- Writing, reviewing, and negotiating business contracts
- Dealing with employee issues
- Helping with credit problems and bankruptcy
- Addressing consumer issues and complaints
- Working with rental or leasing agreements
- Outlining workers' compensation and Social Security benefits
- Advising you on your legal rights and obligations
- Representing you in court

TIP

Be sure to seek out an attorney who specializes in working with small businesses and startups. Any other attorney may not have the exact skill set you need. If you have a family attorney, start there. If he or she isn't the best person for the job, chances are you'll get a good referral to someone who is. One more thing: Make a point of asking your attorney how much a particular task costs — *before* you engage his or her services. There's nothing worse than getting a bill that's in the thousands of dollars when you expected to pay far less. For those of you who are understandably wary about working with a lawyer who charges by the hour, there's a move afoot to get lawyers to change to *project billing* — that is, a flat rate for a specific task, such as incorporating your business or filing a trademark application. Ask your lawyer to give you a flat price for the work you need done. Doing so helps you avoid nasty financial surprises and keeps your relationship on good terms.

Picking good accountants

If you're not an expert in accounting — and even if you *are* but would rather devote your precious time to taking care of your customers' needs — getting a good accountant is a definite must. As the owner of your business, you need to know exactly how much money is going in and out of your business and for what purposes it's being used. This knowledge allows you to assess the financial health of your company and helps you make plans for the future. Plus, the information contained in your accounting system provides the basis for determining how much you owe the government in taxes and other fees.

REMEMBER

Inadequate recordkeeping is a principal contributor to the failure of many small businesses. A good accountant can be a tremendous help in setting up a useful financial recordkeeping system, as well as providing ongoing financial advice.

Here are some of the most common tasks that accountants perform for their small-business customers:

- Small-business startup, business sale, or business purchase
- Accounting system design and implementation
- Preparation, review, and audit of financial statements
- Tax planning
- Preparation of income tax returns
- Tax appeals

Keep in mind that you may not need the services of a full-blown accountant or certified public accountant (CPA). You may find that for simple tracking of money in and out of your business, a bookkeeper is just what the doctor ordered. A *bookkeeper* is someone (often a home-based businessperson) who records the accounts and transactions of a business. He or she probably doesn't have a college degree in accounting nor the license required to be a CPA. However, for many basic tasks, such as entering and keeping track of income and expense transactions in an accounting system, a bookkeeper is a more affordable option. And if you just need someone to represent you with the Internal Revenue Service for tax audits, collections, and appeals, consider using the services of an enrolled agent. *Enrolled agents* are federally authorized tax practitioners who are trained experts in the field of taxation. They specialize in advising, representing, and preparing tax returns for individuals, partnerships, corporations, estates, and trusts, and may have more experience in taxes than a typical accountant or bookkeeper.

Find and choose an accountant the same way you select any other professional adviser. Check with friends and business associates for recommendations. Interview at least three candidates to be sure that your personalities are compatible.

When you interview your prospective candidates (either in person or over the phone), make sure you get answers to the following questions:

- Does your candidate have specific experience working with home-based businesses?
- Does your candidate show an active interest in the financial aspects of your business operations (cash flow, inventory, and so on)?
- Does your candidate have specific experience with income tax, and does he or she keep abreast of the latest changes in the tax law as it pertains to your industry?
- What do the candidate's references say about his or her performance and reliability?
- What is the candidate's fee structure?
- Does your candidate have a network of other potentially beneficial financial contacts within your community (loan officers at local banks, for example)?
- Are you comfortable with the candidate, and are your financial philosophies compatible?

One thing you'll notice as you search for the right accountant for your business is that some have the initials *CPA* following their names. A *certified public accountant* (CPA) is an accountant who has met his or her state's minimum educational requirements and passed a rigorous examination covering accounting, business law, auditing, and taxes. CPAs are required to have a college degree (which, in some cases, can be offset by extensive work experience) and must meet an annual continuing-education requirement. So, basically, when you choose to affiliate with a CPA, you're getting someone who's at the top of the profession. A CPA may be more expensive than a regular accountant, but depending on your specific needs, the extra cost may be well worth your money.

Any skilled accountant — whether or not she has *CPA* after her name — may be just right for you and your business. It all depends on the experience and expertise she brings to the table, as well as her willingness to be available to help you when you really need it. Don't exclude good candidates merely because they lack the letters *CPA*.

Be sure you have at least a basic understanding of accounting and the particular bookkeeping system you're using. Even if you decide to hire an accountant to take care of the details, as the owner of your own business you have to understand how the financial side of your business works. Take advantage of the financial reporting functions of your system, and know how to read and interpret your company's financial reports. For more information on doing just that, be sure to check out Chapter 6.

Banking on the best bankers

You want to have a relationship with your bank already in place when you need it; after all, you never know when you may need financing. It may be when you're in the startup phase of your business or when you get a huge order from a customer and need to pay your suppliers before you receive payment. Or it may be when your business starts to grow, and you need to finance your expansion. Even if you don't plan to expand any time soon and have no need for a loan or financing, having a relationship with your bank can still be helpful. For example, depending on the size of the checks you deposit, you may not have immediate access to your funds. Whether your bank puts a hold on the checks you deposit often depends on your banking relationship, how long your account has been open, and your average balance. These ongoing financial needs make finding and establishing a relationship with a good local banker a must.

Soon after Peter established a business account for his new corporation at a large local bank, he was shocked to find out that any checks for more than $500 would be put on hold for a week or more while the bank waited for them to clear. Such an unexpected outcome can really put the hurt on your fledgling business if you're not ready to deal with it. In Peter's case, a combination of lots of begging, sweet-talking, and threats to move his account to another bank helped keep his cash flowing.

Establish a relationship with your banker (which is most often the branch manager) *before* you apply for a loan and *before* you deposit a $10,000 check that may take ten days to clear. The relationship you have with a banker at the time you apply for a loan can make the difference between getting approved and getting turned down.

The big question is: What kind of financial institution is right for your kind of home-based business? Several different kinds of financial institutions are available to you, and each one has a unique spin on the world of money and banking. Here are the main financial institutions you have to choose from:

- **Banks:** The first choice of many home-based businesses, banks include savings banks, savings and loans, and commercial banks. Banks traditionally make a wide variety of loans, both commercial and consumer, and they're the place to go for special small-business loans offered in conjunction with the Small Business Administration (SBA). Most banks also offer special accounts designed specifically for businesses, along with a wide array of business-oriented products and services, which makes them the logical first choice for most businesses.
- **Credit unions:** Although credit unions are similar to banks in some ways, they're owned by their members rather than public shareholders. This member ownership results in lower costs of operation, which are passed on to members in the form of lower interest rates on loans, higher savings interest rates, and free checking accounts. Most credit unions specialize in consumer loans rather than commercial loans. Credit unions are less likely than regular banks to offer special accounts and products and services for businesses, and in some cases (for example, if your home-based business is a corporation that issues stock), they may not be able to accept your business as a customer.
- **Credit card companies:** As you probably already know, credit card companies offer interest rates that are often significantly higher than the rates you'd get on the same amount of money from a bank or credit union, yet thousands of companies regularly use credit cards to finance purchases. Why? Because using credit cards is usually far more convenient than applying for a loan every time you want to make a major purchase or make some other financial move. Keep in mind that even if the credit card has your company name on it, you're likely personally responsible for the charges. If your business fails, the credit card company will look for you when the monthly payment is due.
- **Commercial finance companies:** These companies specialize in working with businesses, usually in financing equipment leasing or purchases or in acquiring inventory. The deals that commercial finance companies offer — particularly in leasing — may offer attractive tax advantages and are worth checking out.

- **Consumer finance companies:** These businesses specialize in making loans to borrowers who have a hard time obtaining loans from their banks or credit unions, perhaps because they have defaulted on loans in the past or because their credit is already overextended. Because those borrowers are considered higher risks for defaulting on loans, consumer finance companies generally charge significantly higher interest rates than banks and credit unions do. Therefore, most businesses should consider consumer finance companies a funding source of last resort.

REMEMBER

Be sure that you anticipate your financing needs well in advance. Waiting until the last minute to develop a relationship with your banker or to apply for a critically needed loan is a recipe for financial disaster.

Consulting business consultants

Everyone has talents in many areas, but even you can't be the master of everything. Don't worry, though: *Consultants* are available to assist you in the areas in which you need expert help. You can hire business, management, and marketing consultants; promotion experts; financial planners; and a host of other specialists who can help make your business more successful.

Regardless of exactly which kind of consultant you decide to hire, follow these nine steps to select the right one:

1. **Clearly define your objectives.**

   Describe the job you want done, and specify the things you expect from the assignment. Understand precisely how you expect your business to benefit from the work. Decide on the time frame, scope, and any constraints on the assignment. Clarify your own role and explain how the consultant's time will be made available.

2. **Research a variety of consultants, select the three best, and ask for written proposals.**

   Make sure you ask for proposals only from consultants qualified to carry out your objectives. Good consultants will be more than happy to send you basic information about them and talk with you about your needs, without charge. Invite your best prospects to submit written proposals, which should include the following:

   - Their understanding of the problem
   - Their approach to solving the problem
   - Names and résumés of the consultant(s) who will do the work
   - Experience of the firm

- References
- Other support provided by the firm
- Work plan
- Reports and/or systems that will be supplied to you
- Fees, expenses, and schedules of payment
- Any inputs required from you

3. **Clearly explain your desired outcomes.**

   Prepare a concise brief that clearly defines the objectives, scope, time frame, reporting procedure, and constraints of the project and provide this brief to your top three consultant prospects to use as they prepare their proposals. Remember that the cheapest price won't necessarily give you the best value for your money and that consultant fees may be negotiable.

4. **Interview your top consultant candidates.**

   Successful consulting requires goodwill in human communications. Meet the consultant who will do the job, and brief him or her well, using a written brief and any background information you think is necessary. Talk through each proposal with the consultant who submitted it before making a final decision to make sure the consultant has addressed all your concerns. If you're not happy with any aspects of the proposal, don't feel pressured to accept it. Continue discussions with the consultants until you reach a full agreement on the proposal. Select the firm or individual that you feel has the best qualifications and experience and that you feel you can work with comfortably.

5. **Ask for references — and follow up on them.**

   After you make your selection, ask the chosen consulting firm or individual for names or written references from former clients to verify the consultant's suitability for the assignment.

6. **Sign a written contract and start the assignment.**

   This step almost goes without saying, but we're including it anyway: Have your lawyer take a look at the contract before you sign on the dotted line.

7. **Keep in touch with your consultant as the project progresses.**

   Using consultants effectively demands a commitment of time as well as money from clients. Remember that you must keep in touch with the progress of the assignment if you want to get the most from it. Consultants are likely to be most cost-effective when working on an agreed program and time frame. Make sure that you hold regular progress meetings and that the consultant keeps you fully briefed on progress against the program.

8. **Be sure you don't find any surprises in the final report.**

   The consultant's report is often his or her most tangible *deliverable* (what he or she provides in fulfillment of a contract), but it must be in a format that's beneficial to you. If necessary, ask the consultant to produce a draft report so you can review the findings and recommendations before the final report is produced. The final report should contain no surprises.

9. **Implement the recommendations, and involve yourself as well as the consultant.**

   You may need to make arrangements for the consultant to help with the implementation. You can do so cost-effectively by involving the consultant in regular progress meetings. Get a written fee quotation and proposal for any implementation work, even if it follows directly from an assignment.

Hiring the right consultant for your business at the right time can mean the difference between just getting by and achieving tremendous success.

Working with insurance agents and brokers

Not only can you find a dizzying array of different insurance policies and programs available to businesses, but you also certainly notice the hundreds of insurance companies that offer them. Which company and policy offers the best coverage for you? To get an inkling of the answer, you have to extensively research insurance policies and companies — definitely not the best use of your time.

A better way to find out what insurance is available (and necessary) for your business, and which deals are the best for you, is to use insurance agents and brokers. Insurance professionals can save you precious time and money — sometimes thousands of dollars — while providing you with the peace of mind that comes from knowing your insurance needs are being met.

Not only can a good insurance agent or broker advise you about the type and amount of coverage that's best for your business, but he or she can probably also tailor a package that meets your specific needs at reasonable rates. All these services are worth their weight in gold to busy home-based business owners who have neither an extensive knowledge of insurance and risk management nor the time to mess with them.

TIP

When choosing an insurance agent for your business, we suggest that you do the following:

- Solicit bids from two or three established agents to see who can deliver the lowest price for a specified level of coverage.
- Evaluate the professional experience and qualifications of prospective agents as though you were choosing a new attorney or accountant.
- Interview prospective agents with an eye toward the same qualities you seek in a key employee.

The following steps can help you find the agent or broker who best meets your business's needs:

1. **Look for an agent who's knowledgeable about your industry and who regularly works with home-based businesses.**

   Different companies have different needs. A wildlife photographer, for example, has very different insurance needs than does a home inspector. And what's good for a high-tech company may not necessarily be right for an online operation or retail outlet. One thing is for sure: No one agent can effectively keep up with every different kind of insurance for every different type of business.

2. **Ask your friends and business associates for referrals to good agents or brokers, check with professional and trade associations, or use an online service** like **4freequotes.com** (`www.4freequotes.com`), **einsurance.com** (`www.einsurance.com`), **or Insure.com** (`www.insure.com`).

   Be sure to look for someone who regularly handles accounts of your size (many agents and brokers consider one-person businesses too small to be worth the "trouble" to service). Expect your agent to add value to your enterprise, just as an attorney or accountant does.

3. **Choose an agent who's knowledgeable, dependable, loyal, and effective at communicating.**

   You want the agent to work well for you and know how to expedite claims when necessary. Check out the agent's support structure to make sure it's adequate to handle your account. Visit the agent's office, and meet the people who handle day-to-day operations. Confidence in them will increase your confidence in the agent or broker.

Insurance is an important part of every business, and it'll pay off for you to get the best advice possible. Although most home-based businesses never have to use their insurance, if you need it — because of an auto accident, fire, product-liability lawsuit, or other covered risk — you'll be glad you have it.

Cashing In on Barter

Bartering means trading goods or services without exchanging money. Even though it doesn't involve a direct money transaction, bartering still has implications for your cash flow. You may be wondering how home-based businesses can benefit from bartering. Well, we're here to tell you!

Taking advantage of bartering

Short on cash but long on time? Then bartering your products and services in exchange for the products and services of another business may be just the ticket for you and your home-based business. After all, bartering allows you to keep more cash in the bank — cash you can use to help grow your own business instead of someone else's. For example, if you need a bookkeeper to keep track of your lawn-care business's financials but don't want to pay the $50-an-hour fee, give bartering a try. Find a bookkeeper who needs lawn care on an ongoing basis, and barter your services for the bookkeeper's.

Here are six tips to keep in mind when you want to take advantage of bartering in your business:

- **Work with a bartering exchange or club as you begin to barter your products or services for someone else's.** A *bartering exchange* or *club* is a company that serves as a clearinghouse for getting barterers together. Another way to think of a bartering exchange is as a bank for keeping track of barters in terms of barter points, credits, or "dollars," rather than direct barter, in which you swap your service or product for the service or product of someone else.
- **Find out as much as you can about your local bartering clubs before joining them.** Membership in a bartering exchange costs money. Besides the initial registration fee, exchanges charge a 12- to 15-percent fee per transaction, due in cash. Some exchanges also charge monthly fees. You can find local bartering exchanges through one of two bartering organizations: the International Reciprocal Trade Association (IRTA) and the National Association of Trade Exchanges. Both have online directories that list their member exchanges (`www.irta.com` and `www.nate.org`). IRTA offers a checklist of things to consider before joining a bartering exchange. Another way to find out about local bartering clubs is through *BarterNews* magazine (`www.barternews.com`).
- **Try to find barter partners on craigslist (`www.craiglist.org`) — for which you don't have to pay any charge — if you don't want to join a bartering exchange.** Some Web sites also post a notice that they'll barter.
- **Take into account that *barter is considered a form of income and has tax consequences.*** Whether or not you join a bartering exchange,

you must report the fair market value of all the goods and services you exchange as income in the year you receive them, but you may deduct costs incurred to perform the bartered work. Barter exchanges must comply with their own reporting requirements on Form 1099-B for all transactions.

- **Beware of scams on the Web, and check out local exchanges as you would any other business, using organizations like the Better Business Bureau (`www.bbb.org`).** And be sure your barter exchange files the proper tax reports. Existing members can tell you whether they've been getting 1099s.
- **Be selective about what and how much you barter.** Read barter contracts in detail to be sure you have legal recourse if something goes amiss.

Bartering in action

"Barely surviving" is how Gilles Tessier of Moncton, Nova Scotia, described himself when he needed to come up with $400 to print flyers for his lawn-care and landscaping business. He was beginning the spring with only 14 customers and a broken-down truck, and he needed more to make a living. During this low point, he saw a television news story about a man who had put his son through flight school by bartering. Tessier, who had a college degree in small-business management, immediately contacted Maritime Barter Associates, a local barter exchange, which had grown out of the reorganization of a franchised barter operation.

After paying a membership fee of $375, Tessier immediately bartered his lawn-care services in exchange for printing and a van to replace his truck. Tessier, whose work at North of Eden Landscaping is seasonal, now hires up to four employees to help him. During the long Canadian winter, he uses his van to pick up and deliver goods for business customers in Canada and down the eastern seaboard of the United States. Bartering plays a role in his winter work, too: He has gotten his van repaired on the road and hasn't paid for a hotel room in five years.

His barter exchange works as many do. In addition to joining and annual membership fees, he pays the exchange 10 percent of the value of what he receives in barter — in cash. When his services are used, he provides the equivalent of 3 percent of his services to the barter exchange. So when Tessier receives barter goods or services worth $10,000, he pays the exchange $1,000. If he provides $1,000 worth of services to an exchange member, the exchange credits itself with an additional $30 worth of his lawn care.

About bartering and home-based businesses, Tessier observed, "When you first start a business, you have little cash flow. You must depend on your customers to pay you on time, and if someone doesn't, you have to phone to ask for payment. In effect, by bartering, I can keep cash in my business by borrowing from other businesses."

Chapter 12

Eluding Scams, Rip-Offs, and Other Headaches

In This Chapter

- Understanding the psychology of scams
- Uncovering scams and rip-offs
- Researching bogus opportunities
- Knowing what to do if you've been scammed

When you compare statistics from the Federal Trade Commission (FTC) and the Small Business Administration (SBA), you find that the number of people who actually start new businesses nearly equals the number of people who are victims of business opportunity scams each year. According to the FTC, the average business opportunity scam runs for 12 to 18 months, cheats from 100 to 150 people, and takes in a total of $3 million.

Unfortunately, very few business opportunity scammers are caught, prosecuted, and punished for their actions — no wonder home-business scams are a dime a dozen. And although the media and the government heavily publicize those scams that are caught, more than half a million people a year continue to fall victim to fraudulent business opportunities year after year. Why? This chapter takes a close look at the answer. Here we show you what you need to know to separate the real opportunities from the rip-offs.

Investigating the Psychology of Scams

Before we dive into the psychology scammers use to attract their victims, you need to understand the external factors that often lead people to buy into scams they might otherwise identify as fake. Here are just a few of the external reasons why people continue to fall for basic business scams:

- Although the business world has long been fertile ground for scams, cons, and outright fraud, the Internet has made reaching more victims even easier and cheaper for scammers. And seeing how other scammers work allows new and old scammers alike to become better at pushing the buttons of the desperation and desire so many people have.

- The recent economic downturn — and the resultant layoffs and job losses — has made an increasing number of people desperate to make money any way possible. This desperation makes them prime targets for scammers.
- Most scam victims don't complain about being victimized. Some are embarrassed; others regard collecting "business opportunities" like a crapshoot (the "maybe this one will work" mentality). And a few, despite the experience they have and the warnings they read and hear, believe that if an opportunity were really bad, the government would've closed it down.
- Despite hotlines and Web sites where potential victims can check out business opportunity vendors, many, if not most, scams never get listed — and often by the time they do, the scams' perpetrators have changed their names or moved on to new scams.

As a result of these external factors, many people find it hard to tell whether a promising opportunity is real or fake. To complicate matters even more, scammers often have a very accurate perception of what potential victims are thinking, and thus, what they can do to reel them into their scams. They're well aware of the countless people out there who will happily (and blindly) trade their hard-earned cash for big promises.

To get their victims to buy into their schemes, scammers use a variety of different methods, which we describe in detail in the "Sniffing Out Scams" section. Regardless of the method used, scammers rely on the same traits to get people to fall for scams. According to a recent report by researchers at the University of Exeter School of Psychology, these traits are:

- **Appeals to trust and authority:** People tend to obey authorities, so scammers use — and victims fall for — cues that make their offers look legitimate because they're supposedly made by reliable official institutions or established reputable businesses.
- **Visceral triggers:** Scams exploit basic human desires and needs (such as greed, fear, avoidance of physical pain, or the desire to be liked) to provoke intuitive reactions and to reduce the motivation people have to process the content of the scam messages deeply. For example, scammers use triggers that make potential victims focus on the huge prizes or benefits they offer instead of on the potential downsides of the "opportunities."
- **Scarcity cues:** Scammers often personalize their scams to create the impression that their offers are unique to their recipients. They also emphasize the urgency of a response to reduce the potential victim's motivation to process the scam content objectively — the old "this offer expires tomorrow" approach.

- **Induction of behavioral commitment:** To draw in their potential victims, scammers ask them to make small steps of compliance and, thereby, cause victims to feel committed to continue sending money. These small steps undoubtedly add up to big steps (and big scams!).
- **Disproportionate relationship between the size of the alleged reward and the cost of trying to obtain it:** Scammers often lead victims to focus on the alleged big prize or reward in comparison to the relatively small amount of money they have to send to obtain their windfall. The high-value rewards (often medically, financially, emotionally, or physically life changing) that scam victims think they'll receive by responding to the scammers' requests make the money they have to pay look rather small by comparison. In fact, victims often don't consider refusal an option.
- **Lack of emotional control:** Compared to nonvictims, scam victims report being less able to regulate and resist emotions associated with scam offers. Victims seem to be unduly open to persuasion, or perhaps unduly undiscriminating about whom they allow to persuade them. This lack of control creates an extra vulnerability in people who are socially isolated because social networks often act to induce people to regulate their emotions when they otherwise might not.

REMEMBER

As the old saying goes, "Awareness is the first step to change." Scammers are pros at pushing people's buttons and getting them to drop their defenses. However, by being aware of your own behavior and how you respond when presented with a bogus business opportunity, you can figure out how to resist it. Knowledge is power, and the more you know about yourself, the more power you have.

Sniffing Out Scams

Can you tell a scam from a legitimate business opportunity? Are you sure? The following is a sample of an ad for a business opportunity. Is it a scam, or is it real?

> It's So Simple to Earn $2,000 to $5,000 Per Week Nowadays . . .
>
> We're searching for only ten elite individuals with the work ethic necessary to generate a cash flow for themselves of $2,000 to $5,000 per week and to increase that to more than $20,000 per month in as little as four to six months. And you know what? If you really have a burning desire and commitment, we guarantee that you'll reach this explosive income!
>
> Can you read a short script to our qualified leads, and then turn the interested prospects over to our electronic sales medium? (You won't be required to do any selling.)

> Do you have the self-discipline to ignore the TV for a couple of hours a day?
>
> Are you looking for a legitimate home-based business opportunity that isn't multi-level marketing or a chain-letter scheme?
>
> If you'd like to build an amazing income that will grow lightning-fast and have you profit $1,000 every time only one prospect makes a purchase, this is for you!
>
> You can build the business under our guidance and support without having to attend meetings or sell people things they don't need.
>
> Call NOW our TOLL-FREE, PRE-RECORDED Message: 1-888-555-5555 [***Note:*** number changed].
>
> We market a real product that pays real commissions to you, $1,000 per sale, just for making the initial contacts. With our turnkey lead generation systems, you always talk to people who actually WANT to talk to you.
>
> You have nothing to lose, and there's no risk involved, nor is there any obligation whatsoever, and you may be qualified to earn thousands of extra dollars per month!
>
> So call now! The call is FREE, and there's absolutely no obligation, so what have you got to lose? Call toll free 1-888-555-5555.

So what do you think — scam or real? Not sure? Tempted by the offer?

Well, it's a scam. If you thought the ad was real, don't lose all hope, yet. We believe you can avoid becoming just another unhappy statistic if you take the following actions when you read an ad like the above example:

1. **Temper the enthusiasm with a large helping of restraint in the face of a business opportunity that sounds "too good to be true" — it probably is.** As Professor Barry Commoner once famously observed, "There is no such thing as a free lunch." Of course, the meals served by scammers aren't free; they're out to take your money. Before agreeing to anything, ask yourself if the opportunity promises high financial reward for little or no effort. If so, the opportunity deserves your very close scrutiny because it's likely a scam.
2. **Be alert to red flags.** This ad had plenty of them. In the sections that follow, you find out how to identify *red flags* — the warning signs that something isn't quite right — that should lead you to pay extra-special attention to a seemingly reputable opportunity. Then you have to take the time to thoroughly check out the red flags before you shell out your hard-earned money.

The following sections highlight some of the most common ways people lose their money to false opportunities and outright scams.

Job-at-home red flags

Yes, this book is all about self-employment, but we have to point out some warning signs for you to look for if you're tempted to seek hourly or salaried work at home based on an ad.

Here are the red flags you need to look out for as you consider any job-at-home opportunity:

- The company charges a fee for job listings or a job directory and doesn't promise a refund if you don't find work.
- The opportunity includes a *previously undisclosed* government job. All federal jobs must be advertised, and state and local governments typically have a similar requirement.
- The opportunity involves envelope stuffing or coupon clipping.
- Your gut tells you something isn't right.

For examples of other job-at-home scams, go to the Federal Trade Commission's Web site (`www.ftc.gov`), and search *job at home.*

If you're seeking fill-in work while you're developing your business or during a slack time, consider bidding for project work on such sites as `www.elance.com` and `www.guru.com` instead of falling prey to job-at-home scams.

Business opportunity red flags

Any "formula" business you buy is a business opportunity, but certain types — multi-level marketing and franchises — have special characteristics. Although many, if not most, business opportunities are indeed legitimate, the ones that *solicit* you are suspect. When you find a business opportunity that interests you, research it thoroughly to determine whether it's a legitimate opportunity — and whether it's a fit for you — before you invest your hard-earned time and money in it.

Here are the red flags you need to look out for as you consider any business opportunity:

- You're told that you won't have to sell, that the product sells itself, or that it's "easy work."
- You're pressured to make an immediate decision to buy into the business opportunity.
- The earnings claims sound too good to be true.
- You're discouraged from letting an attorney review contracts or other materials.

- For whatever reason, you can't talk to prior investors in the business opportunity.
- You never get a live person when you call the company's phone number, you get only an answering machine, and the company's address is a post-office box.
- The Web site or seller sells many different kinds of "biz ops" and isn't someone who actually does or has done this business himself.
- You live in one of the 26 states that require registration of business opportunities (Alaska, California, Connecticut, Florida, Georgia, Illinois, Indiana, Iowa, Kentucky, Louisiana, Maine, Maryland, Michigan, Minnesota, Nebraska, New Hampshire, North Carolina, Ohio, Oklahoma, South Carolina, South Dakota, Texas, Utah, Virginia, Washington, Wisconsin), and the business opportunity isn't registered. However, many states have thresholds, like $500, before a business opportunity must be registered. Some scam operators take advantage of this exception — and you guessed it — price the business op at $495 or some other number that enables them to avoid registration.
- Testimonials use only people's initials, or they use names that aren't listed in directories like `www.switchboard.com` and `www.anywho.com`. Legitimate businesses want to be listed; they aren't hiding out.
- Your gut tells you something's wrong.

Franchise red flags

Most franchises are legitimate because the amount of money and legal compliance involved in offering a franchise is substantial; however, just because they're legitimate doesn't mean they're good investments.

Even with "good" franchises, serious disputes sometimes arise between the franchisees and the franchisors. As we discuss in Chapter 2, the law requires that the franchisor give the franchisee a detailed disclosure statement, called the *Uniform Franchise Offering Circular* (UFOC). However, this documentation does you no good unless you verify everything asserted in it and have the contract reviewed by an attorney who is qualified to do franchise work.

Here are the red flags you need to look out for as you consider any franchising opportunity:

- The franchise has been around for fewer than five years. You're most apt to be successful with a franchise that was in business for five years before it was franchised — and then has been franchised for five years.

- You don't receive a copy of the disclosure documents required by law the *first time* you meet, or you're told you don't need to read them.
- A list of current franchisees doesn't exist or is curiously short.
- You're pressured into signing a franchise agreement without having it thoroughly vetted by your attorney.
- You feel that the focus of the franchisor is on selling you a franchise. A good franchisor doesn't necessarily assure that you're qualified. Instead, a good franchisor searches for the right person to add to his organization.
- The franchisor is new to the business but not new to franchising — or the franchisor is new to the business *and* new to franchising.
- Your gut tells you that something's wrong, or any of the red flags for business opportunities are present, such as claims of making big profits from a small amount of work.

Direct-selling and multi-level marketing red flags

More than 90 percent of the individuals who work in direct-selling programs do so part time, mostly because less than 2 percent of direct sellers in most organizations do well enough to produce a full-time income. Regardless, the promise of fast (and big!) riches draws a constant stream of people to direct selling.

The reality of the situation, however, is that few people make much money. As disenchanted individuals drop out of the system, established distributors feel intense pressure to find and sign up new recruits — recruits just like you!

But keep in mind that the direct-selling business has stellar performers out there, too — people like Bea Sherzer in Fern Park, Florida, who extols the benefits of the health products she sells. "They improved my health so much that everyone began asking me about them," Bea told us. "This was the best thing that ever happened to me."

REMEMBER

Unless you're thoroughly sold on the products you're trying to sell and are good at recruiting and selling, which most people aren't, don't expect significant earnings. In 2006, for example, Quixtar (since renamed Amway Global) — the Internet marketing arm of Amway's parent company, Alticor — was one of the few companies that reported distributor earnings. (It does so because of a court settlement many years ago.) The company reported that its typical distributors earned $115 a month, from which they had to pay their own overhead costs, including training, samples, and selling materials. As you can see, even for a big player in the direct-selling market such as Amway Global, the vast majority of distributors aren't exactly getting rich quick.

Sometimes we meet home-business owners who, trying to supplement their income from a principal business that isn't producing the earnings they want, take on a direct-selling company "on the side." Rarely does this attempt work unless it's a natural fit, such as a chiropractor selling supplements to his or her patients.

If you think you're being hustled or pressured to sign up for a direct-selling program before you have a chance to thoroughly check it out, including time to use the products or services, take a step back. The opportunity will be there when you feel enthusiastic and comfortable about what you'll be selling — if the company is still around (direct-selling companies have a high mortality rate).

Here are the red flags you need to look out for as you consider a particular direct-selling opportunity:

- You're told that you can achieve great success without having to actually sell anything.
- You don't receive the name of the company until after you listen to a canned sales pitch.
- You're required or pressured to buy inventory. You should be able to get started with a kit costing less than $100 and never more than $500.
- The company doesn't specifically agree to buy back any of your unsold inventory.
- The direct-selling company isn't a member of the Direct Selling Association (`www.dsa.org`). To belong to this association, companies agree to a code of ethics and have been in business for at least two years.
- Your gut tells you that something's wrong.

Keep in mind that if a direct-selling opportunity is a *legitimate* one, it won't go away overnight. (Almost nine out of ten direct-selling companies don't last five years.) And if an opportunity does disappear quickly, you're better off not having invested your time or credibility with the people you contact, so take the time to thoroughly check out any company you're considering. The time you spend now is an investment in your future that will pay for itself many times down the road.

Finally, Be Wary of . . .

Aside from the tried-and-true scams we describe in the preceding sections, plenty of new and innovative ones are popping up every day. Be extra cautious about the following new approaches to separate you from your hard-earned cash:

- **Online shills:** *Shills* are people who pose as satisfied customers to dupe others into buying a product or service. They often post messages in Internet forums and discussion groups, describing others as frauds while extolling their own companies and making false claims about their earnings.
- **Due-diligence sites:** These sites promise to differentiate honest business opportunities from frauds — either for free or for a fee — but, like shills, they actually denigrate the competition while extolling the benefits of the companies they're involved in (often on the sly).
- **Bogus escrow sites:** These third-party sites aren't always easy to identify because they may use fake logos and graphics from verification services like "VeriSign" and confusingly similar names. If you're purchasing something and you can only use a foreign payment service — not a recognized service like PayPal — or you're asked to pay in advance, beware because you're likely dealing with a bogus payment site. Use the list of places to check that we provide you in the "Places to Check" section of this chapter to help you spot the frauds.

Popular home-business scams

At the time this edition was being written, *BusinessWeek* magazine ran an article listing the ten most popular home-business scams as recently reported by the Federal Trade Commission (FTC). We mention some of these scams elsewhere in this chapter, but here's the complete list:

- **ATM machines:** Although ATM machine opportunities seem to be naturally born moneymakers on the surface, the problem is that ATM scammers either never deliver the machines after they take thousands of your hard-earned dollars or promise highly profitable locations that ultimately turn out to be anything but.
- **Envelope stuffing:** In a typical envelope-stuffing scam, the scammer sells the envelope-stuffing "opportunity" to an unsuspecting buyer for a fee. To make money, the buyer has to turn around and resell the "opportunity" to as many people as possible. In this classic pyramid scheme, you can make money only by selling the opportunity, not by actually doing any work or delivering any products or services.
- **Product assembly:** Although scammers assert that you'll make good money assembling magnets or jewelry or other items for their companies, you rarely do. You first have to pay a fee for the materials used — which often arrive in poor or unusable

condition — and then the scammers inevitably refuse to pay for the items you actually do assemble, citing their poor quality (if they respond at all).

- **Internet kiosks:** After paying thousands of dollars to buy an Internet kiosk, buyers either never receive the promised product, or, if they do, they find that their kiosk is located in a location that generates far less revenue than the scammer promised. (As you can see, this scam is very similar to the ATM scam.)
- **Internet storefronts:** In this scam, sellers promise to set you up with an affiliate marketing Web site that will generate money without actually selling any products — for a fee, of course. Unfortunately, you pay the fee, but your scam Internet storefront does nothing.
- **Medical billing:** Although not all medical-billing opportunities are scams by any means, if someone tries to sell you a list of medical-billing leads (in other words, doctors who supposedly are dying to enlist your services), think twice before you spend the money. Many such lists are actually scams.
- **Multi-level marketing:** As we mention elsewhere in this chapter, not all multi-level marketing opportunities are scams. Avon, for example, is a completely legitimate company. However, when a multi-level marketing opportunity sounds too good to be true, it probably is.
- **Pay phones:** Although you may have thought pay phones had gone the way of the dinosaur, apparently a lot of scammers make money by selling expensive pay phones and pay phone locations — and then not delivering.
- **Rack displays:** Scammers who run this scam tell you that you can make big money selling greeting cards, jewelry, or other trinkets on a display rack set up in a business in your community — say a car wash, bookstore, or bowling alley. In reality, however, you pay for the rack and not only do these community businesses not want your rack in their stores, but even if you get a business to put up your rack, the margins are so low that you never make any money.
- **Vending machines:** According to the FTC, vending-machine scams are among the most common. After paying thousands of dollars for vending machines and an inventory of items to fill them, you may or may not actually receive the promised machines and inventory. And even if you do, you'll soon discover that the opportunity isn't nearly as lucrative as the scammer promised.

Places to Check

Unfortunately, most people don't lodge complaints about being victimized by scams and rip-offs with official agencies, so you won't find an all-encompassing list containing every scam you can fall victim to. Even so, you should check out the following resources before signing up with any company you consider doing business with:

- Better Business Bureau (BBB), as well as the local BBB office in the community where the seller is located (`www.bbb.org`)

- Federal Trade Commission (www.ftccomplaintassistant.gov)
- National Consumers League's Fraud Center (www.fraud.org)
- State consumer protection agencies, often located in attorney generals' offices — sometimes called *bureaus of consumer protection* when located in a state agency other than the attorney general's office (www.consumeraction.gov/state.shtml)
- U.S. Postal Service warnings about phony job opportunities and work-at-home schemes (postalinspectors.uspis.gov)
- Web search using the company or product name and words like *scam* and *fraud*

What to Do If You've Been Scammed

If you think you've been scammed by someone who has sold you a bogus business opportunity, act quickly and assertively. Call the salesperson or the business from whom you purchased the business opportunity immediately to register your complaint and request a complete refund. Also explain that you'll pass on your experience — good or bad — to the proper government authorities. If the salesperson or business doesn't comply with your request for a refund, the Federal Trade Commission (FTC) recommends that you contact the following organizations:

- **Federal Trade Commission (FTC):** The FTC works for the consumer to prevent fraud and deception. The FTC keeps track of scams and scammers — warning the public against the latest ones — and it investigates significant scams, following up with the authorities when necessary to put the scammers out of business. Call 1-877-FTC-HELP (1-877-382-4357) or log on to www.ftc.gov.
- **The attorney general's office in your state or the state where the company is located:** The office can tell you whether you're protected by any state law that may regulate work-at-home programs.
- **Local consumer protection office:** By providing your information to such offices, you help them keep track of the latest scams. They can then inform the public and help ensure that others don't fall victim, too.
- **Local better business bureaus:** Better business bureaus are a good avenue to file a complaint against a company that has scammed you. Although they don't have the power to prosecute cases in court, they do maintain listings of businesses and customer feedback. People tend to avoid companies with a history of bad feedback.

- **Local postmaster:** The U.S. Postal Service investigates fraudulent mail practices, so contact your local postmaster if any of your correspondence with the scammer passed through the U.S. Mail. Postal inspectors will then open a case against the scammer, which could potentially lead to the arrest and prosecution of the offender.
- **Internet Crime Complaint Center (IC3):** If the scam was perpetrated via the Internet, you need to file a complaint with the federal government's IC3 at `www.ic3.gov`. Doing so provides additional data for the IC3 and — if the problem is significant — may help lead to prosecution of the scammer by a federal court.
- **The advertising manager of the publication that ran the advertisement:** The manager may be interested to find out about the problems you've had with the company. If he or she finds out about a problem, the publication may decide to no longer accept such advertising from the offending party.

Depending on the situation, you may also consider filing a police report, notifying local media (newspaper, radio, and television reporters), and taking the scammers to court. You have to decide for yourself how far to take the issue.

REMEMBER

Despite the scammers and the clever ways in which they snare unsuspecting buyers *as well as* people with experience, thousands of people find their way to successful, legitimate self-employment through formula businesses: franchises, business opportunities, and direct sales. If you find the right match, you can save yourself weeks and months of time by putting someone else's business model to work for you. You just have to check out your potential opportunities carefully *before* you hand over your cash.

ASK PAUL & SARAH

Network marketing over the Internet

Q: What do you think of direct selling or network marketing, especially over the Internet?

A: Network marketing is part of the direct-selling industry, and the Internet certainly plays a role in network marketing, though its role is small compared to that of face-to-face sales, which account for three out of four network-marketing sales. The most recent statistics from the Direct Selling Association indicate that 11.4 percent of direct sales are made over the Internet. So you can see that most network marketers still rely on the old-fashioned method of meeting face to face to make sales and recruit people into a downline.

However, you can use the Internet to help improve and increase your network marketing. For example, use social networks, particularly Facebook, to make yourself known and to reestablish relationships with people who may end up becoming customers or coming into your downline. Set up a Web site and e-mail to help support your downline, too — just know that people active on social networks seem to respond more quickly than people who use only regular e-mail. In naming your Web site, make sure your domain name doesn't duplicate or infringe on the name of the direct-selling company.

Another way to attract participants in your downline online is to actively participate in social networking groups and online forums, answering questions and offering advice that earns people's trust and interest.

Through network marketing, you can find out about the skills needed to operate a business, such as selling, managing time, and keeping yourself motivated in the face of rejection. In this sense, network marketing can be a good training experience based on the help and strength of your upline. Although such skills are primarily "offline" ones, with every passing year, more and more of what you do in life and in business involves connecting to the Web.

You can find the current research on direct selling and network marketing at `www.dsa.org`. For a comprehensive site that represents the critics of network marketing, go to `www.mlmsurvivor.com`.

Part IV
Making It Work: Moving Ahead

The 5th Wave By Rich Tennant

"It's your wife Mr. Dinker. Shall I have her take a seat in the closet, or do you want to schedule a meeting in the kitchen for later this afternoon?"

In this part . . .

Creating a successful business is more than just offering a great product or service. You must also do the kinds of things that will enable your business to grow in the future. In this part, we discuss how to leverage the power of the Internet, and we explain the importance of having the right attitude in your business. We wrap up this part with a look at how to grow your business.

Chapter 13

Making the Web Work for You

In This Chapter

- Bidding for jobs on the Internet
- Using directories to your advantage
- Networking on the Net
- Maintaining your Web site or blog
- Building an attractive online presence

Everyone has heard about the tremendous opportunities that the Internet has opened up for businesses of all sizes, shapes, and locations. Today even the smallest home-based business — located in the most remote location in the country (can anyone say Nome, Alaska?) — can sell its products and services to a worldwide base of customers via the Internet. Whether you use an established site like eBay.com or Amazon.com to reach potential customers, you reach out using social networking tools, such as Twitter or Facebook, or you create your own Web site or blog, today it's easier than ever to make the Web work for you.

But guess what? A lot of other businesses are trying to get noticed, too, and they're all trying to sell their own products and services — some of which may be exactly the same products and services *you* plan to sell. The good news is that you don't have to become a huge company to take advantage of the Internet — the costs of getting set up on the Web are quite affordable for most home-based business owners. In fact, many small, home-based businesses are doing quite well selling their products and services via the Web. And you can, too.

In this chapter, we explore how to use the Internet to bid for work and how to get listed and noticed in online directories. We explore the best approaches and places for networking with others on the Net and explain how to use social networking tools to your advantage. Finally, we consider the best ways to attract clients and customers with your Web site.

Bidding for Work Online

Something interesting has been happening on the Internet over the past several years — a number of freelance bidding sites have sprung up with the express purpose of getting independent, home-based businesspeople together with companies (including other independent, home-based businesses) that need work done. Although some of these sites may be scams (see Chapter 12 for more about those), more than a few of them offer legitimate opportunities to at-home workers.

In this section, we take a look at what you need to know to use the Internet to leverage your own business opportunities.

Taking advantage of sites that bring buyers and sellers together

So what exactly is a freelance bidding site? A *freelance bidding site* is a Web site where companies can list jobs they need done (anything from writing advertising copy to building Web sites to doing graphic design), and freelancers can bid on the work. The company needing the work selects a freelancer and assigns the work, the selected freelancer does the work and pays the bidding site a commission (usually between 5 and 10 percent), and everyone is happy.

REMEMBER

In general, follow these steps to take advantage of freelance bidding sites:

1. **Visit the bidding site of your choice and register.**
2. **Build your online résumé by adding your particular skills and experience to the site. Be specific!**
3. **Conduct a search for projects that are suited to your experience.**

   Look beyond the main categories and dig deeply into the subcategories and specialties.
4. **Bid on a project by providing an estimate of the price for the job and your time frame for completion.**
5. **Negotiate a deal with an interested company.**
6. **Do the work and get paid.**

For someone with the right skills, using a freelance bidding site can be a relatively easy way to develop an ongoing stream of work that may be quite lucrative. You have plenty of freelance bidding sites to choose from, but be sure to check out these sites first:

- `www.scriptlance.com`
- `www.smarterwork.com`
- `www.ework.com`
- `www.elance.com`
- `www.crowdspring.com`

For a very comprehensive (and up-to-date) listing of legitimate freelance bidding sites, go to `www.freelancemom.com/gigs.htm`.

Figuring out how to win bids

You may be very well qualified in whatever it is you do, and you may have tons of experience and skills out the wazoo. But guess what? You're not alone. Countless other people have just as much experience — maybe more — and you'll undoubtedly have to compete with some of them when you bid on a project, which means you have to sharpen your pencil and bid to win.

Here are ten tips on how to win your dream project:

- Become intimately familiar with how the freelance bidding site you're using works.
- Make your profile first-rate. In it, show your background in the field; your education, training, and credentials; the services you offer; and the range of your rates. If you need help writing your profile, consider posting it as a job on one of the freelance boards and hiring a writer to help you. You'll experience firsthand what it's like to receive bids and what impresses you about the bidders.
- Create an online portfolio with samples of your work. What a photographer or graphic designer uses as samples is fairly obvious, but even if you're a consultant, showing potential clients what you've done is still worthwhile. One way to do so is to post testimonials from customers declaring how great it was to work with you. To avoid cluttering up your profile, create your portfolio elsewhere — for example on your own Web site — and provide a link to it from your profile page.
- Demonstrate that you have the skills and tools needed to do the job. So if you're seeking virtual-assistant-type work and you're certified in Microsoft Office Certification, say so. Don't be shy — show the buyer everything you have to offer. You probably have only one shot, so make it the best possible.

- Don't place your bids automatically or base them on guesswork. Ask good questions of the company or person seeking bids. Often, the posted work descriptions are too sketchy or leave too many gaps. Just as you don't want to overbid and lose a good job, you don't want to underbid and win a job that you later find out requires more work than you originally anticipated.
- Do some market research; check to see what your competitors are bidding for the kind of work you want to do. Remember that you're competing against bidders from all over the world, many of whom can and will underbid the prices most North Americans can charge. But keep in mind wary buyers are apt to be just as suspicious of extremely low bids as they are turned off by high ones.
- Propose payment schedules that will show you're motivated to get the work done in a timely manner, such as asking for a relatively low initial down payment of 20 or 25 percent with progress payments based on agreed-on milestones.
- Go into more depth on your own Web site or blog than you can on your profile. Profile portfolios can be too long, taxing buyers with too much to look at. Remember: They're reviewing other bidders' profiles and portfolios, too. If you interest them on your profile, they'll want to know more about you and will dig more deeply.
- If you're using Elance, consider becoming a Select Service provider. Doing so improves the positioning of your bid and assures your prospects that your credentials have been verified.
- If at first you don't succeed . . . learn from your experience and try again!

Keeping clients and building your business with them

The best business relationships are long-term business relationships. Believe us: A bird in hand is definitely worth two or three in the bush. It's a general rule that your best clients are your current clients. Whenever possible, work to build strong relationships with your current clients and customers that will keep them coming back to you many years into the future.

TIP

Here are some tips for keeping your clients happy and building long-term business relationships:

- **Be on time and on budget.** No client likes to hire someone who delivers the products or services late or who wants more money to do the work than originally quoted.
- **Do great work.** Great work speaks for itself, and it separates you from the home-based business wannabes.

- **Be flexible.** Business today takes place faster than ever, and companies must be able to change direction at a moment's notice to keep up. So be flexible and ready to change accordingly.
- **Be dependable and reliable.** Be someone your client can rely on through thick and thin — if you are, you've already got most of your competition beat.
- **Don't surprise your client with bad news.** Keep your client informed if you anticipate problems or delays — no matter what they are.

Getting Listed in Directories

Back in the good old pre-Internet days, if you were a small business and you wanted to attract customers or clients — especially if you ran your business out of your home or some other nonstorefront location — one of the first things you had to do was run an ad in the Yellow Pages. Having a listing in the Yellow Pages was essential for many kinds of businesses, especially service businesses, such as plumbers, building contractors, tree trimmers, and many others.

Although the Yellow Pages aren't obsolete yet (Peter's copy hits the recycle bin within minutes after its arrival each year), there's a new directory on the block: the *online directory*. In this section, we explore some of the most common versions of this new business tool.

Online business directories

Online business directories — the electronic successors to the old-fashioned paper Yellow Pages — are all over the Internet today. Like anything else in life, some are better than others. Here are a few of the best:

- `directory.google.com`
- `search.yahoo.com/dir`
- `www.dmoz.org`
- `www.alibaba.com`
- `www.bizweb.com`
- `www.abusinessresource.com`
- `www.industrialquicksearch.com`
- `www.businesspatrol.com/directory/`
- `www.b2btoday.com`

You can get your site placed on any number of online directories, but our advice is to stick with the top ones — that is, the ones that get the most traffic and the ones specifically targeted to your kind of business (for example, a directory of landscape architects isn't the best place for you to list your eldercare business). Seek out the top-notch directories in your field, and apply to have your Web site listed. You may have to follow up to make sure that your site really gets listed and that the listing information is correct. After you have a correct listing in the prominent directories, don't forget to promote your listing. Be persistent if you need to be — it's your business we're talking about here.

Association memberships

Do you belong to an association? For example, if you're a graphic artist, you may belong to the Graphic Artists Guild (`www.graphicartistsguild.org`) or the Society of American Graphic Artists (`saga.monmouth.edu`). Or you may belong to your local chamber of commerce or a community-based business association. Whatever your affiliations are, one of the fringe benefits of belonging to many associations is the opportunity to be listed in their online member directories.

Go to the Graphic Artists Guild Web site, for example, and you can look at not only a listing of association members, but samples of their work as well, organized by practice: cartooning, graphic design, package design, and so forth. Many associations include such samples to showcase the work of their members — all the better for a potential client who's looking for a certain style of artwork.

If you don't yet belong to an association, consider joining one and getting listed in its online directory. If you already belong, make sure to take advantage of all the promotional and networking activities your association has to offer, including being listed in its online directory.

TIP

One more thing: If anything changes in your business, such as your phone number, Web site, or e-mail address, remember to submit updates to all your online directories to keep your listings current.

Local directories and review sites

The problem with many online search engines and directories is that they include the whole world when you just want to attract customers in your small town in Saskatchewan. In response to this issue, some search engines, directories, and business review sites are creating services that focus on local offerings. When you use a local directory to do a search for a specific kind of business — say, an aquarium or bookkeeping service — you can specify a city and state in which to search, thus providing results that are much more relevant and useful than what you'd get if the entire world were included in the search.

Here are some of the most popular local directories:

- www.yellowpages.com
- www.yelp.com
- www.citysearch.com
- www.local.yahoo.com
- www.jumptoyourcity.com
- www.insiderpages.com
- referrals.respond.com
- www.yell.com (Great Britain)

Again, follow up after you apply for your listing to make sure your business is indeed listed. As soon as your listing goes live, be sure to check the information — business name, address, phone number, e-mail address, Web site — for accuracy.

Networking the Internet Way

There's more to getting noticed online than just putting up a Web site and waiting for the crowds to arrive. You can also make a splash — while driving traffic to your own site — by personally getting noticed on *other people's* Web sites. If you have a particularly lively personality, or if you're knowledgeable and enjoy giving advice to others (in a polite way, of course) you may soon find yourself a very popular fixture on many different Web sites — not just your own. In this section, we cover the most common networking tools currently available online.

WARNING!

Truth be told, you can choose from a bazillion and one ways to use online networking to promote your home-based business. However, when using the various networking tools we describe in this section, you have to be careful not to get so caught up in sending Twitter messages or updating your Facebook page that you run out of time to take care of your current customers and clients, or to do the other kinds of marketing you need to do to keep a steady stream of new customers and clients walking through your door. Be sure to test the results of your networking efforts regularly. If you find that they aren't resulting in enough new business to be worth their while, quickly move on to something else.

The real beauty of making the Web work for you is that you can quickly, easily, and inexpensively change your approach — literally in just minutes. So, if at first you don't succeed, try, try again — with a new and different approach, of course!

Discovering the benefits of online forums

Today you can find online forums devoted to just about every conceivable hobby, business, activity, and avocation imaginable: parenting; steam trains; TiVo digital video recorders; vintage Jeeps; genealogy; politics; personal finance and investing; math; freedom; children book writing; scrapbooking; and much, much more. If you can imagine it, someone probably already has a forum on it.

Here's how one home-based business owner networks with potential customers through an online forum:

> Doug Roccaforte is the founder and owner of Roccaforte Amps (`www.roccaforteamps.com`), a Brea, California–based manufacturer of high-end electric guitar amplifiers used by professional musicians, such as Marc Ford, Ben Harper, Cesar Rosas, and many others. Sure, Doug could be content attending trade shows, developing his dealer network, and placing advertisements in guitar magazines, but he also chooses to spend time on the Amps discussion forum at `www.harmony-central.com`, which is likely the most popular guitar-amplifier forum on the Internet. Doug is a very well-known and popular regular there. Not only is he a colorful personality — with strong opinions and a wry sense of humor — but he's also respected by forum members as one of today's greatest and most knowledgeable guitar-amplifier designers and manufacturers. The fact that he spends time on the site and is willing to give his advice and opinions about topics of interest to forum members keeps his products front and center in their minds and develops a buzz that no amount of advertising alone could buy, leading to lots of additional sales — sales that wouldn't occur without Doug's presence on the forum.

What sites and forums are devoted to topics that relate to your products or services? Seek them out, become a member, and begin contributing. For a relatively small investment of your time, you'll definitely see a positive impact on your bottom line.

You can find lists of forums and newsgroups on Google's Group directory site (`groups.google.com`) and the Yahoo! Groups site (`groups.yahoo.com`). Joining forums is easy, but remember to honor the unique etiquette for each group you join (see the "Making winning relationships the right way" section for more on the etiquette of networking online).

Many trade and professional associations have forums; some associations open them up to nonmembers. You can find listings of many of these associations at the ASAE (American Society of Association Executives) and the Center for Association Leadership Web site (`www.asaecenter.org`), where the group provides its "Gateway to Associations" searchable directory as a service to the public.

Souping up your social networking

Social networking sites — Web sites devoted to creating networks and communities of new friends and acquaintances — are a relatively recent phenomenon. As members continue to join these sites, they bring along their own networks of family and friends, quickly creating large online social networks, some linked by common interests (such as business) and some linked by who knows what.

In recent years, social networking has become all the rage as businesses of all shapes and sizes scramble to establish a meaningful presence on social Web sites dedicated to this purpose. Here are the current top ten social networking sites:

- `www.facebook.com`
- `www.myspace.com`
- `www.twitter.com`
- `www.flixster.com`
- `www.linkedin.com`
- `www.tagged.com`
- `www.classmates.com`
- `www.myyearbook.com`
- `www.livejournal.com`
- `www.imeem.com`

Although the chances of developing serious business by participating in social networking sites are more remote than by participating in forums specific to your expertise or business, giving them a try may be worth your time to make your presence known.

Bankrate.com (`www.bankrate.com`) offers the following five best ways for small businesses (including home-based businesses) to use social networking sites to their advantage:

- **Use free sites.** Use free online services, such as Twitter and popular networking sites like Facebook and LinkedIn, to post significant news, specials, or events.
- **Shift marketing costs to social media.** After figuring out how social networking operates, use social media to free up traditional marketing dollars for your small business by putting it online. You can quickly determine which of your Facebook or MySpace "friends" or online "group" members received and responded to your message.
- **Do your own social-media optimization project.** Find out about the competitors in your industry and geographic region that are tapping in to social networking. Start by researching the competition in the major search engines — Yahoo! and Google.
- **Take social-network marketing to the next level.** Create and post richer content about what your customers would expect from someone in your business. Don't view social media sites as a place to simply hype your wares — make them a place for conversation.
- **Use blogging to drive search results and help new customers find you.** The more mentions you and your home-based business get on the Web, the more often the search engines will find you. By blogging regularly, you create lots of content for the search engines to find when people search using terms related to your business.

TIP

If you belong to multiple social networking sites, check out Ping (`ping.fm`) and Snag (`www.dapper.net/dapplications/Snag`), which enable you to make one entry that's then transmitted to multiple social networks. These sites save you the time of having to make multiple logons.

Making winning relationships the right way

Just like you have rules of etiquette for behaving in your offline life, you have rules and norms for behaving in online forums and networks. Here are some basic rules to follow so that you find yourself a welcome participant rather than someone to be avoided (or worse, talked negatively about).

- **Stay on topic.** Make a point of posting only messages that are relevant to the subject of the forum or network in which you're participating.

- **Include the necessary information.** If you're asking a question of forum members, be sure to give them a complete description of what your problem or issue is. Doing so helps other readers of the forum determine a resolution to your issue.
- **Indicate whether you've asked your question elsewhere.** If you pose your question through other channels, such as third-party mailing lists and so forth, indicate in your message all the places where you're posting the question so your question gets answered only once. Doing so saves effort and enables forum members to answer your question and other people's questions faster.
- **Be nice.** If you want the welcome mat to be out for you, refrain from inappropriate language and personal attacks. Remember the first rule of karma: What goes around comes around.
- **Choose a descriptive title.** A descriptive title helps subsequent visitors to the forum successfully identify your topic.
- **Don't cross-post.** Posting a message to more than one forum is unnecessary and creates extra traffic for you and others to read through.
- **Don't quote previous messages.** Quote only when absolutely necessary. Readers can easily view previous messages in their newsreader when needed, so you're just wasting space — and risking the ire of your forum mates — by quoting previous messages.
- **Don't spam the site!** Although most forums and online social networks tolerate a small amount of plugging your business, blatant and ongoing plugs will incur the wrath of your forum mates. Your best bet is to put a brief plug about your business (along with a link to your Web site) in your *signature,* the identifying line or lines tacked to the bottom of your messages.
- **Don't include graphics or other files in the forum posts.** Don't post attachments. Most users don't want to download a file when reading your post, for time and security reasons. Just explain your point in writing and include the URL of the file in your post so others can view it *if* they want to.
- **Don't duplicate threads.** Before posting messages, be sure to familiarize yourself with the forum. If possible, check to make sure your topic hasn't already been addressed in a recent thread — after all, you won't get far by duplicating another recent post.
- **Don't get too personal.** Remember, all messages are public and will be viewed by others.
- **Don't perpetuate off-topic threads.** If someone makes an inappropriate or *spam* post, don't add more noise by replying to the forum. Criticize via private message (PM) or e-mail if you must.

Be polite, helpful, and friendly — you'll attract far more business with honey than vinegar.

Building and Maintaining a Blog or Web Site

Okay, so you've decided to start your own Web site — congratulations! Now what? Well, the first step is to build it. You can either hire someone to do it for you or do it yourself. (Peter built his Web site at `www.petereconomy.com` years ago using Microsoft FrontPage. He has since switched to Macromedia Dreamweaver and maintains his site himself to this day.)

Each approach, of course, has its pluses and minuses. Hiring someone to create and maintain your Web site will likely get you the most professional-looking site, but it may cost a lot of money, and you may have to wait for your Webmaster to make site updates for you. A busy Webmaster can take weeks to get around to executing your requested updates. If you build your own site, on the other hand, you have ultimate control over the site and you'll likely pay less than hiring someone to do it for you. However, the results may look amateurish at best, and, while you're playing with the software and troubleshooting the inevitable issues that arise during the site-building process, you may get distracted from doing the things you normally do to make money — you know, fulfilling customer orders and providing services.

Hiring someone to create and maintain your blog or Web site

If you have no interest in creating and maintaining your own Web site or blog, plenty of Web site design companies (many of them home-based businesses, by the way) would love to design it for you. It probably won't be cheap — anywhere from a couple of hundred dollars for a simple site to thousands for a much more complex one — but if you have no interest in learning the ins and outs of Web sites yourself (and we can't blame you if you don't), hiring an expert is clearly the best option.

Don't hire just *anyone*. Remember: Your site will be the first (and perhaps the last) thing that many potential customers and clients see regarding your business. Make sure their first impression is a good one.

TIP

Here are a few tips for finding a great Web site designer:

- Interview Web site designers just as you would a new employee. Get references, do interviews, check them out — the whole enchilada.
- Ask your business acquaintances if they know of anyone who's good at designing Web sites.
- After you locate some candidates, ask each of them for a list of active Web sites that they've developed and actively maintain — and then visit them on your computer. How do they look? Are they attractive and well produced, or are they a turnoff? Are they current and up-to-date, or do they look like they haven't been touched for months?
- Compare the work of several different designers before deciding. Only after you have a chance to fully explore your candidates' work and compare it with the work of others should you select a Web site designer.
- Ask how soon your site will be up and running and how much it will cost — not just to set it up, but also to periodically maintain it and troubleshoot problems.
- If you see a Web site that knocks your socks off, find out who designed it. Sometimes the designer's name is posted on the site, often at the bottom of the home page, but sometimes you need to ask the site owner. It's a good idea to talk with prior clients anyway.

The price to hire someone to build a blog or Web site for you has been steadily decreasing as more people learn the skills involved. Now it's relatively easy to find and engage an affordable (and, probably, home-based) Web site designer. Although some prefabricated designs look decent, you may find that you can hire a talented Web designer to establish a unique and professional-looking Web presence for your business at a price that definitely doesn't break the bank.

Creating a blog or Web site yourself

If you have a basic knowledge of the Internet and how it works, you may be able to create your own Web site and have a lot of fun in the process. Although building your own site can be a lot of fun, make sure you don't have so much fun that you forget to sell your products and services, too.

Follow these steps to create a working blog or Web site:

1. **Select a Web-hosting service.**

   A *Web-hosting service* sets up your Web site address (or *URL*), something like yourname.com, and then hosts your site on its computers where anyone with access to the Web can access it. You have countless Web-hosting services to choose from, and they vary considerably in price and level of service. Thus, it pays to shop around. Most home-based businesses can get by with a bare-bones level of service, and you can figure on paying around $15 to $25 a month. Before you select a Web-hosting service, ask around for references, and be sure to visit some of the hosted sites to see how well they work. Peter's personal favorite is Dotster (www.dotster.com), but another option is the original Internet registrar: Network Solutions (www.networksolutions.com). If you're planning to set up a blog, consider such sites as Blogger (www.blogger.com) or TypePad (www.typepad.com).

2. **Build your Web site or blog.**

   Some hosting services offer simple, built-in software for creating Web sites and blogs as part of their hosting packages. This kind of package may be all you need to create the site you want, and it's probably the best option if you're new to all this Internet stuff. However, if your needs go beyond what your host provides, consider buying software specifically designed for creating Web sites. Microsoft Expression Web, Macromedia Dreamweaver, and NetObjects Fusion are powerful and simple to use. If you're building a blog, popular programs include Wordpress, Movable Type, and Joomla. In essence, if you can use a basic word-processing program, such as Microsoft Word, you can create your own Web site or blog. And here's a news flash: Microsoft Word even allows you to save regular text pages as HTML (Hypertext Markup Language; the language of the Web) documents. Woo hoo!

   Get free templates for Web sites at freesitetemplates.com, and find out more about design standards at www.webstyleguide.com.

3. **Maintain your Web site or blog.**

   The great thing about creating and maintaining your own Web site or blog is that you have full control over the content, as well as when and how you update or modify it. Need to add a new product to your listings? In five minutes, you're done. If you had to go through a hired third party, it could take days or even weeks for him or her to make the minor update. Google offers a terrific tool — the Google Web site Optimizer — which can help you test and improve your site. You'll find the Optimizer at www.google.com/websiteoptimizer. As the site's administrator, you also have direct access to your Web site's or blog's statistics: how many visitors your site has, who they are, and where they're coming from. Using these statistics, you can find out which of your pages are the most and least popular and adjust accordingly.

For more information on creating your own Web site to meet your business's marketing needs, be sure to take a look at *Web Marketing For Dummies,* 2nd Edition, by Jan Zimmerman (Wiley).

Skipping the blog or Web site and creating an e-commerce site

You can create an effective store on the Internet without having a Web site at all. How? An increasing number of established Web sites, including Yahoo! and Amazon.com, have gotten into the business of hosting e-commerce sites for other businesses.

Of the current e-commerce providers, one of the best is Yahoo! Merchant Solutions (`smallbusiness.yahoo.com/ecommerce`). For only $40 a month for a basic plan (plus a one-time setup fee of $50 and a nominal fee — currently 1.5 percent — for each transaction), you can get your own online storefront up and running in minutes. Your customers can view photos of your products, put them into a shopping cart, and pay for their purchases by credit card. You have access to an amazingly comprehensive statistics package (telling you what products are selling best, how much revenue you make by item, what sites shoppers are coming from, and much more); plus, you're in good company: Ben & Jerry's, the Oakland Raiders football team, the Lance Armstrong Foundation, American Pearl, and many more all use Yahoo! e-commerce sites.

Making your site good regardless of who creates it

The following tips can help you create a Web site or blog that attracts and holds your clients' interests and encourages them to send their money your way:

- **Be easy to find.** Don't make it difficult for your clients to find you. Your URL (`www.yourname.com`) should be intuitively obvious. If, for example, your company's name is Acme Computer, your URL should be something like `www.acmecomputer.com`. That way, clients (and clients-to-be) who don't have your address at their fingertips can easily guess it. Also, take the time to register your Web site or blog with the four or five most-visited Internet search engines and directories. Referrals from these sites — including Yahoo!, Bing, and Google — are a critical link in helping people find you. Check out a site called The Art of Business Web Site Promotion (`www.deadlock.com/promote`) for free advice on how to work the search engines to your advantage.

Of course, many domains are already taken, so you may have to settle for one that's longer and a little less direct (like `AcmeofSacramento.com`). Or, because many domain names are minimally used, you may be able to purchase a domain name you want from its current owner. If the domain name you want isn't being actively used and you're willing to wait for it to expire, you can back-order the name from a domain registration service. Another approach is to come up with a name that's catchy (and readily available), but that says nothing at all about what products or services your business sells, such as `google.com`, `joomla.com`, and `squidoo.com`. Whatever your approach, put on your thinking cap and be creative!

- **Advertise your new address like crazy.** Get your address out everywhere, all the time. Include it on your business cards, letterhead stationery, invoices, marketing brochures, and any other place you can possibly fit all those letters and dots.

You may be approached by firms that promise to increase the traffic to your Web site. Maybe they will, and maybe they won't. If you do decide to hire a firm to increase traffic, be sure to ask exactly what it plans to do to reach the people most likely to buy your products and services and what sort of guarantee it offers. Chances are you can do the same things on your own and save a lot of money in the process.

- **Give your visitors a reason to visit — and to come back again and again.** The attention span of the average Web surfer can be measured in seconds. If your site is boring, or if it takes too long to load, your client or prospect will click out of the site just as quickly as he or she clicked in. Take a look at your competitors' sites to get an idea of what works and what doesn't. Use graphics, photographs, and attractive backgrounds to make your site look more appealing, but be careful that these byte-intensive files don't dramatically slow the speed at which your Web pages load. Above all, provide lots of fresh, value-added content in the form of news, reports, articles, surveys, industry trends, networking forums, and the like that will keep your clients and prospects coming back for more. (See the next section for more tips on how to attract customers and clients to your site.)
- **Capture contact information.** When people visit your site, they're probably not there by accident — they're there because they're interested in what you have to sell. Take advantage of this opportunity by encouraging your visitors to give you contact information you can use in your organization's marketing and promotional efforts. For example, you can set up a guestbook where visitors can leave comments about your site, along with their name, title, address, and phone number. Or you can offer to mail a complementary copy of your client newsletter to prospects who are willing to give you their contact information. Contests, special offers, and surveys are all great ways to encourage your visitors to give you their contact information.

- **Check Web stats.** A good hosting service gives you access to vital statistics related to your Web site: the number of visitors each day; where they're from; how long they stayed; which pages they viewed; which search engine (if any) referred them to your site; and much, much more. By analyzing these statistics, you can quickly identify which parts of your site attract the most (and the least) visitors and test visitor response to site changes on a real-time basis. (Hint: Do more of what your visitors like and less of what they don't.)

  If your service provider doesn't offer a decent statistics package, check out Google Analytics (`www.google.com/analytics`). This free Google service is extremely powerful and comprehensive. As Google says, "With Google Analytics, you're more prepared to write better-targeted ads, strengthen your marketing initiatives, and create higher converting Web sites." Can't beat that, can you?

- **Regularly visit your Web site or blog.** Make sure it's working the way it's supposed to. Perhaps you won't be surprised to hear that some hosting services are better than others, and it's in your best interest to make sure your site is on more often than it's off. The easiest way to make a habit of visiting your site is to set it as your browser's home page. That way, it pops up every time you log on to the Internet. And ask your friends and family to check it frequently and let you know if they run into any problems. If you're not sure how to change your browser's home page settings, click the Help button.

Using a Blog or Web Site to Attract Customers and Clients

Well, you've created a Web site or blog; now what? Now you have to figure out how to attract attention in the vast, open space that is the Internet. As of this writing, more than 111 million *domain names* (Web site names such as `dummies.com` and `pathwaystotransition.com`) are currently in use, many of which have their own functioning business, special-interest, personal, and other Web sites attached to them. That's a lot of competition for customer eyeballs.

In the sections that follow, we take a look at how to attract potential customers to your Web site or blog and how to get them to buy once they find their way there.

Knowing what it takes to get traffic

Traffic — that is, visitors to your Web site — is perhaps the key element that can make or break your online business. Generally, the more traffic, the better, assuming that the traffic consists of people who may be interested in buying what you have for sale.

Just because you have a Web site or blog doesn't mean anyone is going to show up for your party. You may think *if I build it, they will come,* but although that mantra may work in a Hollywood baseball fantasy, it probably won't work for your new Web site or blog. If you hope to be successful, you need to get more — and the right kind of — traffic to your site. Here are a few of the most effective ideas for doing so:

- **Register with the most-visited search engines.** There are hundreds of search engines available, but, in our humble opinion, you shouldn't waste your time with 99.9 percent of them. Our advice is to stick with the following top five search engines (based on the number of visits they get):
  - Google (`www.google.com`)
  - Yahoo! (`www.yahoo.com`)
  - Bing (`www.bing.com`)
  - Ask.com (`www.ask.com`)
  - America Online (`www.aolsearch.com`)
- **Register with pay-per-click search engines.** The Google and Yahoo! search engines offer an additional service, where you can pay to have your company's site show up in a prominent location when someone searches a specific keyword or phrase (Google's service is called Google AdWords: `www.adwords.google.com`; Yahoo!'s is called Yahoo! Sponsored Search: `sem.smallbusiness.yahoo.com/searchenginemarketing`). Imagine that your home-based business is wedding consulting. Using Google AdWords for a price, you can have a small ad with a link show up any time someone searches the keywords *wedding consultant.* You pay only when someone does a search using your keywords, and the amount you pay depends on how popular the keywords are — more keyword competition means higher prices.
- **Create unique content.** Don't make your Web site just a place to buy things; make it a place people want to visit to find out something new or participate in a unique experience. Take time to create unique content for your site that will attract busy Web surfers and then make them want to stick around awhile. For example, if you're a dog breeder specializing in French bulldogs, why not create a Web site that is *the* best source of information on that breed? By doing so, you're sure to drive all kinds of traffic to your site.

- **Start an affiliate program.** Offer other Web site owners a commission on sales they send your way. The big sites, like Amazon, make affiliate programs a central part of their selling model — driving more traffic to their sites and increasing their sales. You can, too. Check out a variety of affiliate programs using an affiliate directory, such as `www.affiliatescout.com` or `www.affiliateseeking.com`, to see how commissions are structured and to get ideas for how to set up your own program.
- **Exchange links.** Have you found some sites out there that are somehow related to what you do but aren't in direct competition? If so, ask the site's Webmaster to place a link to your site on that site in exchange for putting a link to that site on yours. For example, if you provide fishing-guide services in the Yellowstone area, why not exchange links with fishing Web sites or Web sites devoted to Yellowstone National Park?

Making it easy for visitors to become customers

The two main reasons for having a Web site or blog for your home-based business are to (1) attract potential customers to your offer and then (2) to make it easy for them to buy. Although many Web sites do a fine job getting people to visit, they drop the ball when it comes to converting visits to sales, often simply because they're too confusing, too slow, or just too much trouble to use.

TIP: So your job is to make it easy for customers to buy what they want directly through your Web site, assuming you've got a product or service that lends itself to buying online. Here are some tips for doing just that:

- **Have a well-organized, professional-looking site.** Nothing's worse than trying to buy something from an amateurish, disorganized site.
- **If you're selling products, put up lots of high-quality photos and detailed descriptions.** Many people want to see what they're getting before they order it.
- **Make sure your hosting service has ample bandwidth to load your pages quickly.** Slow servers mean your visitors will quickly get bored and leave.
- **Give your customers plenty of payment options.** Use a prepackaged e-commerce site, such as Yahoo! Small Business Merchant Solutions, that allows customers to use charge cards. Or consider signing up for a payment service, such as PayPal, that also allows customers to use their charge cards to pay.

- **Provide ample contact information for customers who have questions.** If you can quickly address questions — via phone, Internet audio or video links (for example, Skype at `www.skype.com`), or e-mail — you greatly increase your chances of converting the contact into a sale.

Not sure whether your site is welcoming or not? Give it a try yourself. Is it easy to get around? Does it load quickly? Is it easy to place an order? Have friends and family try it out, too. Use their feedback to fine-tune your site and make it as user-friendly as possible.

The ten best ways to promote your Web site or blog

A Web site or blog won't do you or your business much good if no one knows about it or visits it. So what can you do to make sure people find your site and visit it? Here are just a few ideas to get you started:

- Send announcements for your Web site or blog (including a picture of your home page) to all your customers and clients, as well as to the media and targeted mailing lists of potential clients.
- Include your Web site or blog address on all external materials, including letterheads, business cards, catalogs, invoices, newsletters, packaging, and so on.
- Incorporate your Web site or blog address into your standard fax cover sheet.
- Include your Web site or blog address in your voice-mail system and in your on-hold message.
- Include your Web site or blog address in all advertising.
- Visit Internet newsgroups and message boards, leave messages, and participate in relevant discussions.
- Seek out busy Web sites where you can volunteer to host online chats and conferences. Large sites, such as America Online and iVillage, are always looking for knowledgeable hosts who are willing to share their expertise with others.
- Register your site with the five most popular Internet search engines (Google, Yahoo!, Bing, Ask, and America Online), and be sure you optimize your site to rank high in the search results (by incorporating metatags and other tricks of the trade). Check out *Search Engine Optimization For Dummies,* 3rd Edition, by Peter Kent (Wiley), for a lot more information about these tags and tricks.
- Trade links with your customers and clients and with other relevant Web sites or blogs.
- Create an e-mail signature for yourself and your employees that includes your Web site or blog address. A *signature* is a short paragraph that's automatically included at the bottom of every e-mail message you send. It usually contains a plug for your business, along with your address, phone or fax number, and a Web site or blog address.

Chapter 14

Balancing Your Business and Your Life

In This Chapter

- Having a serious business attitude
- Keeping your work life and personal life separate
- Dodging interruptions and distractions at home
- Managing your time
- Teaming up with a friend or family member

Many people dream about starting and running their own businesses, but relatively few actually do it — and even fewer start businesses that turn out to be successful for the long haul. What makes the difference between those who succeed and those who don't? In many cases, it's all about attitude — and not just any attitude, a serious business attitude.

In this chapter, we examine exactly what having a serious business attitude is all about — and why it's so important. We also discuss how to keep your work life and personal life separate, at least enough to get some work done! We assess two of the most common problems facing home-based business-people — interruptions and distractions — and provide you with a variety of tips to help you beat them. Finally, we consider the importance of developing regular work routines, as well as the whys and hows of getting organized.

Starting with a Serious Business Attitude

Most successful businesses are successful in part because the people who own and run them are serious about doing business. But why is being serious about your business so incredibly important? Well, we offer you two main reasons, both of which involve perception and both of which have a way of becoming self-fulfilling prophecies:

- **If you're not serious about your business, you probably won't put your all into making it a success.** You won't be able to imagine that your modest little enterprise will ever have the potential to provide you and your family with a livable wage or that it will ever provide you with an alternative to a regular 9-to-5 job.
- **If you're not serious about your business, no one else will be either.** Why should your potential clients and customers take your business seriously if you don't? The answer to that question is easy: They shouldn't. And if your potential clients and customers don't take your business seriously, you have no business at all.

The first step to developing your serious business attitude is realizing that your home-based business is no different from any other business. You may have decided to start your home-based business because doing so gives you something that working for someone else simply can't provide. Maybe it's freedom, autonomy, control, flexibility, money, or any number of other reasons.

Regardless of why you started your own business, realize that your home-based business is a business first and foremost. If you hope to be successful (and we're sure you do), you have to treat it like a serious business, which means recognizing that your business is *not* any of the following:

- A hobby
- Something you do every once in a while
- Merely a tax shelter
- A get-rich-quick scheme
- A lark

Having fun in your business is fine — in fact, you should — but don't forget that your home-based business can be your ticket for leaving the rat race behind once and for all. Many successful home-based business owners have done just that, and you can, too.

Building success from the inside

Starting your own business can cause nervousness and trepidation. If you've always worked for someone else, the thought of working for yourself can truly feel like a step into the great unknown. And in many ways, it is an unknown world for you: Will customers buy your products? Will you be able to make enough money to support your family? Will you be able to get health insurance? What will you do if a much larger competitor tries to steal all your ideas?

TIP

Having a serious business attitude starts on the inside. It starts with being knowledgeable about your services and products and having the confidence that comes with that knowledge. Above all, it starts with a conscious decision to make the dream of starting your own home-based business a reality. Here are some of the ways you can start to build a successful home-based business from the inside out:

- **Have confidence.** Confidence — or the lack thereof — can make all the difference in the world when you're starting and growing your own business. When you're confident, you feel like you can overcome any hurdle you come up against. And you know what? You probably can!
- **Keep a positive attitude.** Most successful entrepreneurs tend to be optimistic about themselves, their businesses, and the future. They see the glass as half full rather than half empty. A positive attitude can take you far in this world, both in business and in your personal life.
- **Expect the best from yourself and others.** Set your standards high, and refuse to settle for less. The quality of your products and services begins — and ends — with you.
- **Care about your customers.** Would you rather do business with someone who really cares about you and who takes the time to show it or someone who doesn't? If you take care of your customers and clients, they'll take care of you.
- **Make the decision.** Plant your foot firmly on the other side of the fence, and make the decision once and for all to turn your home-based business dream into a reality. Quit talking about it; just do it!

Take the time to build your serious business attitude from the inside out. If you already have all the self-confidence and positive attitude in the world, that's great — you have a big head start toward business success!

TIP

If you still have some way to go to build the serious business attitude you need, don't be afraid to work into your business slowly, one step at a time. Instead of leaving your regular job to start your own business, consider starting your home-based business while still working your regular job. Not only will this approach take much of the pressure off you to create an immediately successful enterprise — boosting your self-confidence in the process — but it will also give you the time you need to really get to know your products and services and to network with potential customers and clients.

TIP

Creating an identity

One of the first things most home-based businesspeople do is order business cards and stationery for their new home-based businesses, which raises a question: Should you develop a logo design to represent your business while you're at it?

If you're serious about building your business and committing to it for the long haul, you need to create an identity that will help your business stand out in the crowded marketplace. Although you may be able to create a logo yourself, hiring a professional graphic artist to develop a logo for your business is probably a better idea. You'll use your logo for a variety of purposes, including business cards, stationery, your Web site, advertising and promotional materials, brochures, reports, and more.

Although your graphic artist may present you with a wide variety of options and alternatives, remember that the logo design you select for your home-based business should be:

- **Simple:** A logo design should never be so complex that it becomes confusing. In the case of logos, simpler usually means better. Think McDonald's golden arches, AT&T's globe, or Nike's swoosh.
- **Unique and recognizable:** Take a look at the cover of this book. What do you see? The Dummies Man — the mascot of the *For Dummies* brand — is at once unique and recognizable. After you see him on one *For Dummies* book, you associate his face with this brand, no matter which book it is.
- **Compatible with your business's image:** Is your business conservative, such as a management consulting or investment firm? Then you want to have a conservative logo that reflects the rock-solid image you want your firm to project. But if your firm is dynamic, exciting, and takes chances, your logo should, too!

Keep in mind that other elements of your business besides your logo help create an identity for your business. For instance, the way you answer your phone, the color and type of paper you use in customer correspondence, the design of your Web site, the friendliness with which you handle customer problems, and even the message you leave on your answering machine or voice mail all build the image that people have of your business and, therefore, its identity in the marketplace.

Take the time to step outside your business from time to time to experience what your customers and clients experience. Are you happy with what you see? If not, what can you do to improve your business's identity and image?

Counting on the outside for help, too

Although everyone knows you can't tell a book by its cover, people still make judgments about you and your business based on what they see on the outside. Whether their ultimate judgments are right or wrong, these judgments can mean the difference between getting new customers or clients and losing them.

Here are some ways to make sure what's outside (and easily seen) reflects what's inside (and not so easily seen):

- **Create a top-notch Web presence.** The days of being able to get away with an amateurish-looking, clunky Web site are gone. Invest some money in building a top-notch Web site that absolutely exudes quality and experience. The good news is that many Web-hosting services offer inexpensive and easy-to-use templates that instantly give your business a professional look. And don't forget to leverage social media to your advantage. Twitter, Facebook, MySpace, and, of course, your own blog can be very powerful promotional tools for your home-based business (check out Chapter 13 for more on using social media to help promote your business).
- **Create a custom logo and design for your stationery, business cards, and promotional materials.** If your logo's good enough for a multibillion-dollar corporation, it's good enough for you. The money you invest in making your business look more professional will pay off many times over in the number and quality of clients that you attract. (Check out the "Creating an identity" sidebar for more info.)

  The quality of the paper and other materials you deliver to your client says a lot about the quality of your work and the importance you place on delivering a quality product. What does the paper you use say about you and your business?
- **Incorporate.** Those three little letters — *Inc.* — say something about your business. They say that you're established, that you're serious, and that you're in it for the long haul. Not a bad impression to leave with your potential customers. (See Chapter 10 for more information on incorporating your business.)
- **Dress for success.** As a general rule, always dress one level higher than the client you're meeting with. If your client is dressed casually, you should have a jacket and tie (for men) or a dress, skirt and blouse, or pants suit (for women). If your client goes for jacket and tie, wear a suit. Of course, if you're at home — and there's no chance a client will be popping by unannounced — you can wear whatever makes you comfortable.
- **Get a dedicated phone line.** Nothing screams "unprofessional!" more loudly than a 5-year-old answering a client's call. You'll make a much better impression by having a dedicated phone line for your business, hooked up to a dedicated answering machine or voice mail system.

  You can dedicate either a land line or a cellphone for your business. Although either option is fine, you may find it more convenient (as Peter does) to assign your business phone number to a cellphone. That way, when you're out of town on business — or on vacation far away from your office — your customers and clients can still directly contact you. If you want to take calls on your land line when you're back in your home office, simply forward your cellphone to your home phone line.

Just be sure to avoid answering business calls when you're in a decidedly nonbusiness environment, such as in your car driving your child's victorious soccer team to the ice cream shop. Make sure the message you project on the outside reflects the high level of quality and commitment to your customers that you hold so dear inside.

Serious doesn't mean you can't do it your way

One of the most liberating things about having your own business is that you get to decide when and where you're going to work, what work you're going to do, and for whom you're going to do it. According to surveys by *Home Office Computing* magazine, home-based businesspeople have different approaches for doing things their own way. For example:

- Fewer than 10 percent work a traditional, 9-to-5 schedule.
- Eighty-one percent dress casually (6.5 percent don't wear anything at all!).
- Fifty percent don't wear shoes while they work.
- Eleven percent wear formal business attire.
- Sixty percent listen to music while working.

Separating Your Work from Your Personal Life

Although being closer to your loved ones (even if it's just your goldfish) is one of the big attractions to working at home, you'll definitely have times when you have to draw a line between your home life and your work life. By taking the time to anticipate this requirement upfront, you can make the transition to your home-based business smoother — not just for you, but for your clients, customers, family, and friends, as well.

You can use a number of barriers to separate the business and personal sides of your life. Here are some of the most important ones to consider:

- **Use a separate room.** Having a room apart from the hustle and bustle of your regular home life — one that is dedicated *exclusively* to your business — is the first step in making your home office a real office.
- **Set a work schedule.** When you own your own business, you can work whenever you like. You may find it easier (and more productive), however, to establish a regular work schedule. That way, your housemates know when it's okay to interrupt you and when it's clearly not okay.

- **Have a separate entrance.** A separate entrance (or at least an entrance to your office close to the front door) helps keep your work life separate from your home life. After all, you don't want your clients to have to pass through a gauntlet of toys, cereal bowls, and cranky children (or spouses!) to get to your office. Many home-based businesspeople may not currently have the luxury of a separate entrance, but it's something to think about if you have the opportunity to build, buy, or rent a new house in the future. If not, you always have the option of meeting your clients at a convenient off-site location, such as your local coffee shop or favorite lunch spot.
- **Get help.** Instead of trying to juggle your obligations at home while trying to keep up with your work obligations, consider getting the help you need to allow you to focus exclusively on your work when you need to do so. For example, you can hire a housekeeper to clean your home and relieve you of that burden. Or you can hire a babysitter to watch your young children while you work. Or you may be able to get your spouse or a relative or friend to help cover for you. The main thing to remember is that you do have alternatives available to you if you feel overwhelmed.

REMEMBER

Keep in mind that the degree to which you separate your work and personal lives is totally up to you. The good news is that you can be far more flexible than you ever could be working for someone else. You can strengthen the separation when you're under the gun at work and loosen up when things are a bit more relaxed. In this way, you really can enjoy the best of both worlds, where you're able to do the work you love in the place you most want to be — your own home.

ASK PAUL & SARAH

Getting off the preschool bus route

Q: Once when my neighbor was in a jam, I offered to pick up her son from preschool. She has since asked me to repeat this favor several times. How can I explain to her, without damaging our friendly relationship, that just because I'm working at home doesn't mean I'm not working as hard as her corporate acquaintances?

A: You don't need to explain. The way to let her know that you're working as hard as her corporate acquaintances is to tell her that even though you'd like to help, you can't pick up her son because you're working. Be warm. Be sincere. But be clear and definite that your business is such now that you can no longer take time off during working hours. She will probably be disappointed, as she has come to rely on you. But if you want her to take you off her emergency help list, you may need to reinforce your message several times, repeating that you're sorry and wish you could help, but because of your work, you simply can't. She may call you several more times, just to be sure. But if you continue to be clear that you'd like to help but can't, she'll eventually get the idea and find new resources.

Avoiding Interruptions and Distractions

Every job has its interruptions and distractions. When you're in a regular office, you may have a co-worker who drops in on you regularly to unload his or her latest thoughts about your company's management team. Or you may have a boss who is so busy assigning you new tasks that you never seem to be able to get around to the old ones.

Without a doubt, however, working at home offers its own unique set of interruptions and distractions. From television soap operas to your neighbor's ear-splitting leaf blower to that refrigerator calling your name, almost an unlimited number of interruptions and distractions are waiting to take you away from your work. Your job is to find ways to ignore them or to avoid them altogether, which is where the following sections come in.

Dealing with interruptions

You can't always prevent interruptions, but you can take some steps to remove them after they occur and then get back on track and back to work. Here are some ways to deal with interruptions:

- **Focus on your goals and priorities.** Although you may not be able to keep from being thrown off track when an interruption occurs, you should be able to quickly return your focus to the goals and priorities at hand. How? By resolving the interruption as quickly as possible and then refocusing your full attention on your work.
- **Be kind but firm.** The wrong way to deal with interruptions is to get mad at the person who's interrupting you. The right way is to firmly explain, in a loving and supportive way, that the interruptions will have to stop while you're working. Kids especially need this kind of caring treatment. They probably aren't aware that they're interrupting your work; they simply want a chance to spend some time with you.
- **Take action.** Don't try to ignore interruptions — chances are they won't go away, no matter how little attention you pay them. In fact, by not taking action, you send the person doing the interrupting the message that it's okay to interrupt you — or even that you welcome it — all the while building resentment within yourself.
- **Stay loose.** No matter what you do, someone somewhere will interrupt you. The key is to stay loose and not let the interruption totally destroy your ability to jump right back on task. Figure out how to be flexible, and find ways to get back on task quickly.

With a bit of practice, you'll soon be able to deal with your interruptions like a pro, and you'll find that you can take charge of them instead of letting them take charge of you.

Is TV the problem or the symptom?

Q: I'm often tempted to watch TV during work hours. At first, I set a rule that I would watch TV for only one hour during my lunch break; however, I sometimes get sucked into a show and watch longer than I should. Then I rationalize by saying I'll work longer hours. Sometimes I even have the TV on in the background and then press the mute button when I get an outside call. Do you have any suggestions on how I can break this bad habit?

A: Take the TV out of your office. Watching TV is one of the top five home-office bad habits. Get a VCR (or, even better, a digital video recorder, such as TiVo) if you don't have one, and tape your favorite daytime shows. If you don't like a show well enough to watch it after work hours, something must be missing from your workday. Find out what that something is, and replace your bad habit with new, more appealing habits that serve you better. For example:

- **Are you bored with your work?** What has made watching daytime TV more interesting to you than the work you do? There will always be a few tasks in any business that are so mindless, you may as well be watching TV while you do them, but you're in the wrong business if that's how you feel about most of your workday. Has your business lost its magic — or never had it? How can you make what you do more exciting and challenging? What attracted you to go out on your own in the first place? What do you like best about your work? What can you do more of in your work that will make you forget all about watching TV? Find answers to these questions and put them to action.
- **Do you miss the social interaction of an office setting?** Arrange to have more contact with people you enjoy. Call up a colleague. Get active in a local business or professional organization. Join an Internet newsgroup. Sign up for a class or ongoing social activity you enjoy.
- **Are you stressed out and working too hard?** Give yourself something else to look forward to, such as planning an exciting evening for when you've finished working. Or replace your bad habit with a better one. Many home-business owners, for example, enjoy listening to talk radio or music while they work. Others walk outside over the lunch hour or take an exercise break like running, biking, or participating in an aerobics class. What do you enjoy doing most?

Dealing with distractions

Interruptions generally occur when people take you away from your work — by walking into your office and demanding your immediate attention or by calling you on the phone and talking your ear off for half an hour. Distractions are often more subtle. For home-based businesspeople, common distractions include the Internet, a favorite daily soap opera, or a refrigerator full of goodies.

TIP

Here are some ways to deal with distractions:

- **Remove the sources of distraction.** Is that television on your file cabinet begging you to turn it on? Is there a long list of blogs you have to read each morning before you can start to work? Are you spending more time looking through your magazines than producing billable work? One of the best ways to avoid distractions is to remove their sources. Turn them off, throw them out, or move them to another room. If the Internet or e-mail is the problem, set definite times — perhaps during lunch or maybe no more than five minutes every hour — during which you allow yourself to spend time on those activities.
- **Avoid procrastination.** Putting work off until later, sometimes much later, is a powerful enemy of the home-based businessperson. And it's an enemy that you must defeat in the short run if you hope to be successful in the long run.
- **Reward yourself for achieving your goals.** Don't forget to give yourself some sort of reward for accomplishing a significant task or achieving an important milestone. Take a day off. Meet your significant other for a long lunch. Go shopping. Go for a bike ride with your kids. Whatever makes you feel good. Not only will these rewards make you feel better, but they'll also motivate you to stay focused on your work and tune out distractions.
- **Schedule (and take!) regular breaks.** Do you find yourself fidgeting or unable to stay focused on your work? Take a short break from your work. Forward your calls to voice mail, and get out of your office. You can relax and take your mind on a brief vacation by going for a brisk walk outside or enjoying a cup of coffee or tea on your back porch. Don't leave taking breaks to chance; schedule regular breaks into your daily work plan.

You can control the effect of distractions on you and your business by taking action to remove their sources and by providing sufficient structure and motivation in your work. Don't let distractions get in the way of your doing the best job you can do — and building the best business you can build.

TRUE STORIES

Sometimes, despite all your efforts to deal with interruptions and distractions, they may get the best of you. Peter, for example, is usually able to keep his work separate from his very active kids, but, occasionally, the thin line that divides them breaks. More than once, Peter has thought about how nice it would be to rent an office in a small building in the village — a guaranteed refuge from the demands of three busy kids. But that thought passes quickly (when he remembers just how much he'd have to pay each month in rent), and Peter again remembers all the advantages of having an office in his home. What Peter does when he absolutely needs to focus on his work without any distractions is send his family on vacation for a few days. Past vacations include Disneyland, Palm Springs, and Pismo Beach, California. Peter gets his work done while his family has a good time — it's a win-win for everyone.

Resisting the call of the fridge

Q: I'm embarrassed to say that I've gained some weight since I began working at home. I think part of the problem is that I eat out of stress, and, of course, the refrigerator is now just a few steps away from my desk. Do you have any suggestions for how I can moderate my eating habits?

A: You're not the only one to gain weight in the comforts of working from home. But although you have more access to excess at home, you also have more control over what you do and how you do it.

The best way to beat this problem is to find new ways to de-stress: Take a walk, call a friend, or lean back and listen quietly to some of your favorite music. Thinking of something — anything but food — will help you relax. It may take a while to find what satisfies you more than food, but, on the way to the kitchen, take a deep breath and think of what else you may enjoy at that particular moment.

Also, stock your refrigerator and kitchen cabinets with lots of low-calorie, low-fat, healthy-but-filling foods that don't make you want to eat until the bag is empty, the way that chips and cookies do. Apples or rice cakes are good examples. We find that eating small, balanced snacks can help keep snacking within bounds. For example, you may have half an apple with an ounce of cheese and a couple of almonds or a teaspoon of almond butter. Alternatively, you can remove the incentive to visit the kitchen between meals by keeping the beverages of your choice in your office. Consider picking up one of those mini shelf-top refrigerators if you like cold drinks.

Be aware, too, that evidence is beginning to show that one's body type makes some foods fattening for one person that are not fattening for someone else. If you'd like to check this out, see the book *The GenoType Diet,* by Dr. Peter J. D'Adamo (Random House), or check out D'Adamo's Web site at `www.dadamo.com`. Following his guidelines, if you do snack, you shouldn't put on pounds.

When interruptions and distractions get the best of you, you certainly do whatever you can to resolve them. But what happens when you can't resolve your interruptions and distractions and they actually begin to threaten your ability to get your work done?

It may be time to take drastic action. Here are just a few ways you can really shake things up and get back on track:

- **Change your schedule.** Work when your chances of being interrupted or distracted are minimized. If you can't seem to avoid being distracted by your noisy roommates who party late into the night, do your work in the morning and afternoon — well before the partying begins.
- **Learn to live with the distractions.** Of course, doing so is easier said than done, but perhaps you can learn to live with the distractions — accepting them but tuning them out and ultimately ignoring them.

- **Move your work.** Sometimes a temporary change of scenery can do wonders for your concentration, especially when the source of distraction or interruption is a short-term one. Try out an outside deck or even a local café, library, or park. With a cellphone and a laptop computer, you can take your work wherever you want whenever you want.
- **Move your office.** If you have a long-term, ongoing problem with distractions and interruptions, and it doesn't appear that you can solve the problem with a temporary change of scenery, consider moving your office altogether. At a minimum, choose a different room or other location within your home. In a worst-case scenario, you may need to move your office out of your home and into a regular, leased office space.

REMEMBER

Don't let interruptions and distractions get in the way of your success. If you're serious about your home-based business and about the potential for succeeding at it (and we're sure you are!), take action before things get so bad that your business suffers irreparable harm.

Managing Your Time

When you work at home, getting off track is easy to do. What starts out as a day full of promise for getting things done can easily turn into a day full of wasted time, personal detours, and lost opportunities. Good time management doesn't happen by accident. You have to work on managing your time each and every day. In this section, we consider some of the best ways to manage your time.

Letting routines rule

Routines are a part of life. They help you stay focused on the things that are most important. They provide the structure and continuity that you — and your clients and customers — rely on to do business efficiently and effectively. Routines are a good thing.

TIP

When it comes to running your home-based business, some routines are better than others. Here are some tips for establishing the right kinds of routines — the kinds that can bring you success rather than failure:

- **Establish a regular work schedule.** Maintain regular business hours just as you would if you worked for a regular business. It doesn't matter if you decide to work from 9:00 to 5:00 or from 5:00 to 9:00, so long as your schedule meets your needs and the needs of your clients and customers. As the owner of your own business, you get to decide!

- **Take plenty of short breaks.** When you work in a regular business, you have lots of opportunities to take breaks from your routine. A phone call from a friend, a visit from a vendor, a lunch break with your associates, or a quick walk to a nearby deli all offer a break from the routine. When you work at home, such breaks are much fewer and farther between, but you have to make a point of taking them.
- **Schedule appointments for you, your friends, and your family.** The everyday events that take place in a typical business — home-based or not — can quickly fill up your schedule. While you may have planned to get out for a relaxing lunch with friends, go to the gym to work out, or attend your daughter's awards ceremony, you may find yourself glued to the phone or computer instead. Instead of "trying" to do the things you want to do, schedule firm appointments to do these things. Just as you would schedule an appointment to meet with a client, schedule an appointment to meet with your spouse over lunch or to go for a walk.
- **Start your workday the same way every day.** Create a routine around starting your workday. For example, you may make a pot of coffee, check your e-mail and voice mail, read *The Wall Street Journal,* and then begin making sales calls. You decide what to do in your routine; the point is to have a routine and to follow it.
- **End your workday the same way every day.** So many businesspeople complain about not having enough time to sit down and really think ahead and plan, but few do anything about it. Here's your chance to do just that. At the end of your workday, take 15 minutes to go over what happened that day and then review your priorities and schedules for the next day. File away any papers that need filing, and straighten up your desk so that you come back to an organized workspace on your next day of work.

If you feel that your work life — and maybe even your personal life — is chaotic and out of control, perhaps you should step back for a moment and take a close look at how you run your life. Using the preceding list, create routines in your life that you can rely on day after day, week after week.

What's a priority, and what isn't?

Priorities can — and should — have a significant impact on what work you decide to do and when you decide to do it. Most people think they know what's most important in their businesses, but many don't follow through on this knowledge and, instead, let trivial events and distractions rule their schedules.

Missing the hustle and bustle

Q: I know home-based business owners often complain about noise distracting them, but my problem is the opposite: Sometimes it gets so quiet in my home office that it unsettles me. Do you have any suggestions for creating a little bit of good old-fashioned office noise?

A: You're not the only one who doesn't work well in silence, which is undoubtedly why home-based business owners avidly listen to talk radio. Of course, background music helps many people stay productive, and, rather than being a distraction, it can energize your brain and your work. We sometimes like to have Steven Halpern's album *Enhancing Creativity* playing in the background while we work. (Visit his Web site at `www.innerpeacemusic.com` to order this album or choose from many others.) Alternatively, you can listen to radio stations, music or talk, over the Internet. Pandora Internet Radio (`www.pandora.com`) lets you customize your own music program choosing only the music you like.

We've also met people who spend part of their day working over lunch at a restaurant or coffeehouse. Others prefer to work on their corporate client's premises several days a week. When graphic designer Nancy Rabbit couldn't stand the sound of silence, she decided to expand her business by bringing several coworkers into her home.

We also like the sound of water, so we keep a small fountain gurgling throughout the workday. You can find a reasonably priced tabletop fountain in many retail stores.

As for office noise, if that's what you miss, you can ask a client or colleague to let you tape 10 or 15 minutes of office sounds on an endless-loop tape that you can then play in the background while you work.

To separate your real priorities from the wannabes, start by asking yourself these questions when you're trying to decide whether a particular action is a real priority:

- **What's the action's impact on your firm's bottom line?** Everyone has reasons for being in a particular business, but one of the main reasons for creating a business is to make money, pure and simple. Sure, you want to do fulfilling work that taps your creativity, but if it doesn't pay the bills, you won't be doing it for long. What kind of impact will the action have on your bottom line — will it reduce your expenses or increase your revenues? The greater the impact an action has on improving your bottom line — your profitability — the higher it rates on your list of priorities. If an action has little or no impact on your bottom line, give higher priority to other actions that do have such an impact.

- **Is the action in response to a client emergency?** Another reason why many people start their own businesses is to solve their client's problems and to provide them with solutions. Because clients in many ways are the heart and soul of any business, solving their problems is clearly a priority. So when your clients have emergencies, the actions you need to take to solve them should be top priorities for you.

It all comes down to consciously identifying a business's highest-priority actions and then taking a single-minded approach to tackling them. This single-minded approach may mean ignoring the calls of a salesperson, forwarding your phone to voice mail for a day, or even throwing your priority list into a drawer and working only on your number-one priority until it's done. The good news is that prioritizing gets easier with experience.

REMEMBER

Don't forget, you hold the key. It's up to *you* to decide what's most important to your business and then to act on it. You're the boss now; no one else is going to decide for you.

Teaming Up with a Spouse or Other Loved One

You can find countless examples of husbands, wives, siblings, parents, and kids who have pulled together to build successful enterprises: the Wright Brothers of Dayton, Ohio, who owned and operated their own bicycle shop (and later became famed pilots); brothers Walt and Roy Disney, who founded the Walt Disney Company and built it into a global entertainment powerhouse; and Barry Allen and Pauline Field, who created International Fieldworks, Inc., a multimillion-dollar company that provides work for hundreds of others through project-management contracts. The list goes on and on.

For many people, teaming up with a spouse, boyfriend, girlfriend, sibling, parent, son, or daughter may seem like the ultimate dream. And for many home-based business owners, this dream is a reality. After all, if working at home is right for you, why not see whether it's right for the people you really care about, too? Unfortunately, though, for others, teaming up can turn into the very worst kind of nightmare — scary beyond all belief. The secret is knowing when to team up and when not to — and what to do when a good team goes bad.

In the sections that follow, we take a look at when to team up with people you care about, how to team up with them, and how to build a successful, long-term relationship — both at work and away from the job.

Knowing when to team up

As in the rest of life, some times are better than others to team up with a friend or family member. For instance, you definitely want to team up when doing so will create a positive experience for you, your partner, and your customers. In contrast, you definitely don't want to team up when doing so will create a negative experience for any of you.

Here are some times when teaming up with a friend or family member is a good idea:

- **When a friend or family member has relevant skills and interests:** If you decide to start a plumbing business in your home and your close friend or relative has solid bookkeeping skills that will help you better keep track of the financial end of your business, teaming up makes perfect sense.
- **When a friend or family member purchases a business opportunity or franchise:** You won't find a better time to team up than when a close friend or relative buys into a business opportunity or franchise — assuming, of course, that the business opportunity or franchise is something you want to do, too.
- **When a friend or family member can make a positive contribution to your business:** It's definitely time to team up when a friend or family member is at the exact right place in his or her life to make a positive and substantial contribution to your business and to your customers and clients.
- **When a friend or family member has a resource you need:** What if you need a large amount of cash to get your business off the ground and your close friend or relative wants to help by providing you with a loan? Or what if he or she has a network of contacts that would be very beneficial for you to approach? Such resource synergies can make teaming up a very smart move.
- **When a friend or family member has more work than he or she can handle:** Teaming up can be a win-win situation when a friend or family member is so successful in his or her business that he or she needs help and needs it fast.

Not every business team or partnership is going to work. Working closely together — day after day — may bring out the worst in your partner (or you), and you should always be ready to break up your team if necessary. *Do not* — we repeat, *do not* — allow a bad situation to become worse because you're afraid to tell a friend or relative that your partnership isn't working out. Always be honest — with yourself and with your partner. And never team up out of weakness or pity for a friend or family member who just can't seem to get his or her act together. Finding the right time to team up is a must if you want your business relationship to be successful over the long run.

Figuring out how to team up

How you team up with a friend or family member is just as important as — if not more important than — *when* you team up. Doing it the right way can help reinforce your relationship and increase the likelihood of your success. Doing it the wrong way, on the other hand, can be a recipe for disaster — not only for your business, but also for your relationship.

As you begin to team up with your friend or family member, consider taking the following actions:

- **Define clear goals and assign clear responsibilities.** Although you may have different approaches to achieving your goals, you and your partner should agree on definite and clear goals and on who will be responsible for different jobs and tasks within the business. Confusion isn't a good thing in business or in relationships, so define each of your responsibilities from the very beginning.
- **Get important agreements in writing.** Of course, you should be able to trust your friend or family member without question, but it's always best to get your important agreements in writing. You may choose to incorporate these agreements into a legally binding contract. After all, people forget; misunderstandings arise; relationships are broken. Why not prevent these misfortunes by laying everything out on paper from the start?
- **Encourage each other to communicate openly.** Communication is incredibly important to the success of any business; thus, it's equally important that you and your partner communicate openly and honestly with each other about all aspects of your relationship and your business. Always be upfront and open with your business partners, no matter who they are or how closely you're related.
- **Treat each other with respect.** You treat your clients and customers with respect, and you should treat your partner with respect, too. If you don't respect your partners enough to treat them with the utmost respect, don't team up with them in the first place — you may want to reconsider your relationships, too.
- **Take a break from each other whenever necessary.** People get on each other's nerves from time to time, no matter how good the relationship is. Rather than getting mad or stewing on it, take a break from each other for a while. Doing so gives you both time to get over whatever issue is bugging you and to remember why you got together in the first place.

If you do it right, teaming up with a friend or family member can strengthen and deepen your personal relationship. Work hard on bringing out the best in both of you instead of the worst. For more information on collaborating with others, see Paul and Sarah's eBook (co-authored with Rick Benzel) *On Your Own But Not Alone* (Pine Mountain Institute).

Building a healthy, long-term relationship

If all goes well, working with a friend or family member in your home-based business can go a long way in helping you build a deeper and even more profound personal relationship. And if you decide to team up with someone you love, nurturing your personal relationship is just as important as developing a healthy business relationship. If one suffers, the other is sure to suffer, as well.

The following tips can help you build healthy, long-term relationships — both personal and business — with your friends or family members:

- **Do be clear about who's in charge.** In most businesses, one person is ultimately in charge and has the right to veto the suggestions or actions of others, including partners. Make it clear at the outset who's in charge, but be sure to ask for the input of your partner and to seriously consider that input. If your business is a true, legal partnership — with ownership shared in equal amounts — be sure that you establish a system for making decisions when you're in disagreement with your partner. If making decisions is problematic for you and your partner, you probably shouldn't be in a business partnership in the first place.
- **Don't interfere with how your partner achieves his or her goals.** Focus on agreeing on what your goals are, and then let your partner decide how he or she will reach them. Avoid the temptation to micromanage your partner's efforts or to interfere with or second-guess them. You'll only build resentment and erode your long-term relationships.
- **Don't forget to nurture your private lives.** All friends or family members who work together need to take time away from the demands of their business to focus on themselves and their relationship. You can find a number of ways to be fun and spontaneous in your relationship. Close the office for a day, and enjoy a long weekend at a resort, at the beach, or in the mountains. Take a long lunch together, or treat yourselves to an afternoon of pampering at a spa or health club. Or simply turn off the phone and sleep in late one morning.
- **Do seek the help of a professional counselor if needed.** Sometimes relationships break, and you need the help of a professional to put them back together. Don't hesitate to seek counseling if your relationship is broken — the sooner you do, the easier it'll be to get things back on track.

Long-term relationships can be the most meaningful relationships in your life, and there's no reason why you can't share a meaningful and productive business relationship with someone with whom you share a close personal relationship. It has worked for Paul and Sarah, and it has worked for Peter and his wife, Jan. Don't be afraid to explore the possibilities!

Working at home with a baby

Q: Though I've just had a baby, I obviously can't take maternity leave from my home-based business. How do I balance the needs of my business and my clients with the needs of a demanding newborn, each of which take an incredible amount of time?

A: Get help. Most female home-based business owners *do* take some type of maternity leave. They stagger contracts or clients so they have a one- or two-month break, hire temporary or part-time personnel, or subcontract work to colleagues for a period of time. Get help caring for your baby, get help running the business, or arrange for some combination of the two. Begin by deciding what kind of assistance will be most helpful. Ask yourself the following:

- How much time during each day do you want to devote entirely to your baby?
- What aspects of your baby's care can you get help with? What do you want to do yourself?
- Which business tasks are the most burdensome right now? Which ones demand your full attention without interruption?
- Which tasks must you do? Which ones can others do?

By working from home, you have many more options for tailoring child-care arrangements to your particular needs. For help with your newborn, for example, you can hire a nanny to come to your home for a few hours each day while you work. We hired an elderly woman to help us when our son was an infant. Alternatively, you may be able to line up help from family or friends, or exchange babysitting hours with other new mothers. When you feel comfortable taking the baby out, you can place him or her in a nearby family day-care home for several hours a day.

Sometimes new fathers can take paternity leave. Having Dad at home, even part-time, can be a big help. Mom and Dad can care for the baby in shifts, and Dad can help answer the business phone and do other business-related tasks. Taking simple steps, such as getting a voice mail service or hiring an answering service to take your calls, can free you to better concentrate on both family and business matters. Hooking up a baby monitor between your baby's room and your office may also help.

Set up a schedule that suits both your needs as a new mother and your work habits. For some people, doing so means working only mornings, afternoons, or evenings. For others, it involves fitting work around the baby's sleep times. To keep your sanity, remember that this is a special time. It can be exhausting, but it will pass all too soon, so arrange your schedule to enjoy it while you can.

Chapter 15

Growing Your Business in Good Times and Bad

In This Chapter

- Understanding success and how to achieve it
- Deciding whether or not to grow
- Partnering with others smoothly and effectively
- Choosing an exit strategy when you need one

A time comes in the life of every business owner when he or she has to decide whether or not to grow the business. Some home-based businesspeople may find a few clients they like working with and decide they're comfortable with keeping things just the way they are. But if you're good at what you do and your customers love the products and services you sell them, don't be surprised if, after you start your business, they tell their friends and colleagues about you — bringing more business your way. If enough prospective customers show up at your door, you may be faced with more business than you can handle in your present state.

When your business increases to a point where you can't accommodate it in the normal course of your day, you have to make a conscious choice: Reject this extra work and maintain the status quo (or perhaps even cut back the time and effort you devote to your business to allow yourself to spend more time with loved ones, volunteer in your community, or just relax) or take on the extra work and grow.

For many home-based business owners, this question never even crosses their minds. For them, being in business means growing the business, pure and simple. When you grow your business, you have the opportunity to make more money, and making more money is a powerful motivator for many people. For many others, however, the prospect of growth is something they prefer not to embrace. They're comfortable with things the way they are, have made a decision to spend less time working and more time with family and friends, or have any of a thousand different reasons why growth doesn't hold any attraction for them.

In the case of growth, the right answer is the one that's best for you. And what's best for you may or may not be what's best for your clients and customers, your family and friends, and any employees or contractors you may have.

In this chapter, we consider what makes a business a success and examine the good and the bad news about owning a growing company. We take a close look at expanding your operations and bringing partners into your business. Finally, we explore strategies for selling your business and moving on to other opportunities.

Becoming a Success

Success is a relative thing. For example, while one home-based business owner considers himself a smashing success as he pulls down a $25,000-a-year, part-time salary, enjoys lots of time with family and friends, and makes a nice contribution to the family finances, another may consider that minimal level of income to indicate failure.

As the owner of your home-based business, *you* get to decide how to define what success means *to you;* no one else can or should define it for you. You may decide to measure your own success in terms of money or in terms of how many clients you can help. Or you may define it by the high quality of the products and services you deliver. You may also measure success in terms of your ability to achieve an equal balance in your work and personal lives. When you're the one who decides what success means to you, there really is no wrong answer.

After defining what success means to you, though, you have to have a strategy or plan for achieving the goals you've set for yourself — like anything else you want to achieve in life. Although anyone who puts his or her mind to it will find some measure of success, starting up a successful enterprise involves more than just working hard.

William Bygrave, former director of the Center for Entrepreneurial Studies at Babson College and one of the nation's top experts on entrepreneurship, described nine keys to success for an entrepreneurial business in his book (co-edited with Andrew Zacharakis) *The Portable MBA in Entrepreneurship,* 3rd Edition (Wiley). Bygrave called these keys the *Nine Fs:*

- **Founders:** Every startup must have a first-class entrepreneur. (That's you.)
- **Focused:** Entrepreneurial companies focus on niche markets. They specialize. (Fuzzy companies lead to fuzzy customers; people are willing to pay top dollar for products and services that clearly appeal to their wants and needs, not ones that may or may not work out.)

- **Fast:** Entrepreneurial companies make decisions quickly and implement them swiftly (but never so quickly that they don't take time to understand and consider the alternatives before they implement their decisions).
- **Flexible:** Entrepreneurial companies keep an open mind. They respond to change. (Small, home-based businesses can often respond much more quickly to change than larger businesses — a key advantage in today's fast-changing, information-driven marketplace.)
- **Forever innovating:** Entrepreneurial companies are tireless innovators (at least until 2 or 3 in the morning, when most of them make sure they go to bed to get some sleep).
- **Flat:** Entrepreneurial organizations have as few layers of management as possible. (Quite an easy feat when you're a sole proprietorship and have no employees.)
- **Frugal:** By keeping overhead low and productivity high, entrepreneurial organizations keep costs down (which makes them more profitable).
- **Friendly:** Entrepreneurial companies are friendly to their customers, suppliers, and workers. (And because of that quality, their customers, suppliers, and workers are friendly right back, demonstrating their friendliness with orders for products and services.)
- **Fun:** Being associated with a successful entrepreneurial company is fun. (Owning your own home-based business doesn't mean you can't have fun — indeed, if you're not having fun, why bother?)

Compare the way you do business with the Nine Fs Bygrave describes. Do the two have any similarities, or are they miles apart? The more Fs you find in your own home-based business, the greater your chances of finding success at the end of your rainbow.

Identifying the Upside and Downside of Growth

Business growth has ramifications that extend far beyond the simple day-to-day running of an organization, including the following:

- Growth means new work, new clients, and new opportunities, but it also means more time, more effort, and more energy from you.
- Growth means more money coming into your business, but it also means more money going out.
- Running a growing business can make your life incredibly busy and hectic, but it can also be incredibly rewarding — both financially and personally.

What are your long-term goals for yourself and for your business? Do you want to make a certain amount of money every year — enough to allow you to support yourself and your family? Do you want to make a certain level of profit or service a certain number of customers or clients? Do you want to work for a certain number of years or save enough money to travel the world — or buy a new car or boat or retire early?

Whatever your long-term goals are, if you decide that growth is indeed in the cards for your business, you can't leave it to chance — you have to have a plan to achieve that growth. But don't forget: Your business will change, as will your feelings about it. Be flexible and prepared to change your plans as your goals change.

Growth has both good and bad aspects. In the following sections, we explore growth in detail so you can decide what growth means to you and whether you'd rather grow, maintain the status quo, or perhaps even shrink your business operations.

Understanding why you may want to grow

Whenever a business provides quality products or services that people need at a fair price, that business tends to grow as new customers seek it out. Although the pressure to grow seems inevitable for many businesses — especially ones that do a good job for their customers and clients — growth is something that's almost completely within your power to control.

Too many clients? Trim back your client list by removing the marginal ones that cost you more to service than they earn you in profit. Too much work? Turn down new work until you reach a level you're comfortable with. Not enough time for yourself or your family? Do less work and focus more on the things in your life that are most important to you. You're in charge; you're the boss. The decision is yours.

So given the possible attraction of maintaining the status quo (having less work-related stress, spending more time with loved ones, and so on), why grow? Here are a number of good reasons:

- **To increase revenue and profits:** The immediate impact of growing your business is an increase in revenue and — as long as your costs of doing business don't grow out of proportion — an increase in profit. And if we're not mistaken, increasing your profit is probably one of the reasons you're in business for yourself in the first place.
- **To build equity:** *Equity* is the amount of money you have left over after you subtract all your company's liabilities from its assets (see Chapter 6). If your business is profitable over a long period of time, or if your business

catches on with the public and undergoes rapid and substantial growth, this number can be quite large. Growing your business is likely to grow your equity, as well.

- **To take advantage of economies of scale:** The larger your business, the more you can take advantage of *economies of scale* — that is, paying lower prices for items you buy in larger quantities. You can, for example, purchase a case of laser printer paper at your local Costco warehouse store and pay far less per ream than you would if you bought each ream individually at FedEx Office.

In the absence of any compelling reasons not to grow, why not grow your business? Growth can be exciting and fun, and who knows — it may lead you to new and more exciting adventures down the road.

Of course, it's okay not to grow, if that's the way you decide to run your business and your life. As any successful entrepreneur can tell you, growth brings with it its own set of headaches and problems. Many people have become home-based business owners for just that reason — to leave the rat race and get off the never-ending treadmill of business that devours their personal lives. *Propreneurs* — business owners who make a conscious choice not to grow — are active and vital players in the U.S. economy, and they tend to be just as happy as their entrepreneurial (and more growth-oriented) counterparts.

Recognizing the many different ways to grow

When you make the decision to grow your business by increasing your sales and enlarging your customer base, realize that you have a number of ways to do so. The exact approach you take depends on your growth goals and plans and on the nature of your business. The following are some of the most common approaches for growing a home-based business:

- **Expand beyond your locale.** Do you do work only for people who live within a few miles of your home or only for close personal acquaintances? If you do, one of the quickest ways to grow your business is to expand the area in which you do business. What if you did business citywide or countywide? Or perhaps even beyond the boundaries of your state? Expanding beyond your immediate locale dramatically increases the number of potential clients and customers available to you — potentially resulting in increased sales and profits.
- **Get on the Web.** With the right Internet presence, the number of people who view your product catalog or see your work can mushroom (be sure to check out Chapter 13 to find out exactly how to establish the

right Internet presence). Many home-based businesses have seen tremendous growth after capturing the imaginations of their customers on the Internet.

- **Go international.** It's a great big world out there, and depending on the products and services you sell, a huge, underserved international market may be waiting for you to tap in to. Web sites such as eBay.com and Alibaba.com can turn you into an entrepreneur with nationwide and even global reach quite literally overnight. For many growing businesses, a plan for expanding into international markets is a key success strategy.
- **Expand your product line.** If you currently carry ten different products and you want to double your business, what's the quickest way to achieve your goal? Carry 20 different products. Although the exact impact your decision to carry more products will ultimately have on sales depends on the products, their pricing, and the extent to which you promote them, expanding your product line is a quick and easy way to grow your business.
- **Add employees.** Adding employees to your business by definition means that you're growing it. Just be sure that you don't hire new employees before you have sufficient business to support them. If your revenues are flat or decreasing as you add employees, you have what's commonly known as a *going-out-of-business plan,* and, as you may have guessed, it's not a plan for home-based business success. Although hiring employees can provide your business with the capacity it needs to increase sales, it can also dramatically increase your expenses. For lots of information on the right way to interview and hire employees, check out *Managing For Dummies,* 2nd Edition, by Peter Economy and Bob Nelson (Wiley).

REMEMBER

You know your business better than anyone else, so think about what you can do to grow your business. One of the benefits of being your own boss is that you can do whatever you want with your business, whenever you want. Think you have a good idea? Give it a try. Tired of providing a particular product or service? Get rid of it. Want to enter a new market or exit an old one? Just do it. The more things you try, the higher the probability you'll find something that works.

Begging the question: To grow or not to grow?

If you've anguished over the decision of whether or not to grow your business, you know that the decision isn't just a business decision — it's a personal one, as well. Because you're the one who has to live with the consequences of your decision to grow or not, it's in your best interest to thoroughly examine yourself, your business, and the marketplace to make sure that whatever decision you make is the best one for you and your business.

As you consider whether or not to grow your business, we recommend that you look in these four places to find the answer:

- **Your heart:** The first place to look when you're thinking about growing your business is deep inside your heart. Take some time to get away from the hustle and bustle of your business and really listen to what your heart tells you. Are you looking forward to the excitement that business growth will bring with it, or are you secretly dreading the possible consequences of such a choice? What does your heart say? If you haven't been in touch with your heart lately, we highly recommend that you read the book *The Alchemist* by Paulo Coelho (HarperCollins).
- **Your lifestyle:** Will your preferred lifestyle support or be in conflict with the growth of your business? If, for example, the growth of your business will take you away from your family — and spending more time with your family is one of the key reasons why you started your home-based business in the first place — you'll likely resent the extra time you have to devote to your business, as will your family, who will have less of your time. You can be sure that growing your company will change your life. Be sure that the changes are consistent with the lifestyle you want for yourself.
- **The numbers:** Of course, your heart and lifestyle may say "go," while your business (more specifically, your business's financials) says "no." If your company's sales are too low or costs too high, growing your business probably isn't the best thing to do. Can you somehow increase sales or decrease costs enough for growth to make sense? If not, either figure out some way to put your financials on the right track or put your growth plans on the back burner until the numbers do make sense.
- **The market:** You may think it's time to grow, but the market in which your business operates may not be ready for you. Before you invest lots of time, money, and effort in growing your business, be sure that enough potential customers and clients are interested in buying your products and services. If they aren't, you're wasting your time and your hard-earned money — two things that are especially precious for every home-based business owner. Remember that your business will thrive only when you provide quality products or services that people actually want to buy.

All these factors play a role in the growth decision; the weight that you place on each depends on your own personal desires and goals. Many businesses have succeeded, for example, when the numbers didn't make sense or when the market didn't seem to offer broad support for a business's new initiatives. But behind businesses that succeeded in these kinds of conditions are incredibly motivated and hard-working business owners.

ASK PAUL & SARAH

Diversifying your client list

Q: I've been in business for three years, and about 80 percent of my work comes from one client. How can I find the time to diversify while still keeping my client satisfied?

A: As great as the steady cash flow is, getting the bulk of your income from just one client puts you at great risk should that client suddenly decide to work with someone else. You sound as though you not only get 80 percent of your income from this one client, but also spend most of your time serving him or her. To free your time to market and serve new clients, you need to get some additional help. Evaluate what portions of your work can be done by an assistant, associate, or outside contractor. Arrange to free up at least two hours a week for marketing, and begin breaking in someone to work with you so that when you generate new business, you have dependable help to meet the demand.

Although you don't mention the nature of your business, in many fields, self-employed individuals can't or prefer not to market themselves, preferring instead to subcontract their services to someone else. Such individuals like to work with people like you. Be certain, however, that all the billing and all funds come through you. Be sure you get clear, written agreements preventing associates or subcontractors from contracting directly with your clients. Also, you need to line up individuals you can depend on to do high-quality work within necessary deadlines.

To find associates you can count on, get referrals from sources you trust. Be sure to review their work, and talk with them about how they approach their work and what their priorities are. Ask for — and check — references. Most importantly, start with one small, low-risk assignment. Set a clear goal and a specific deadline. If the deadline is more than a week away, check progress intermittently and, if possible, ask the associate to turn in portions of the work as he or she completes them. Doing so can help you identify possible problems before they develop.

Keep in mind that working with someone else will, in and of itself, take some additional time — especially at first. But by building a network of others you can subcontract work to, you can expand without taking on debt or adding to your employee or other operating expenses until you have sufficient business to cover them and hire one or more employees.

Bringing In Partners

A *partnership* is when two or more people team up in the ownership and operation of a business. Many well-known businesses started out as successful partnerships (and home-based businesses at that), including the following:

- **Microsoft founders Bill Gates and Paul Allen:** They developed and sold their first software product out of Bill's dorm room at Harvard.
- **Apple Computer founders Steve Jobs and Steve Wozniak:** They started their company in the garage of Jobs's parents.

- **Google founders Larry Page and Sergey Brin:** They started their business in a friend's garage and then promptly raised $1 million from friends, family, and other investors to fund their startup.

Although these businesses quickly outgrew their original partnership structures — eventually becoming large, multinational (and publicly owned) corporations — the combination of the original partners provided the spark of creativity and energy that led to great success.

When a partnership works, the business runs like a well-played symphony. When it doesn't, it runs more like a scene from the film *Titanic* (specifically, the part when the ship sinks). Unfortunately, you can't really know how things will turn out until you actually create a partnership and you begin to work together with your partner — or not. A partnership is sort of like a marriage; you really don't know how things are going to work — or even if they will work — until the honeymoon is over.

More than a few friendships, families, and personal relationships have been destroyed by partnerships gone bad. Partners can clash in a variety of ways, and these clashes may only occur in a business environment under the pressures of deadlines and busy schedules, which is why you should always apply the same standards of care when you decide to partner with family or friends that you would when hiring a stranger.

The following are some tips for ensuring that your partnerships operate smoothly. (For more specific information on the partnership form of business — including its advantages and disadvantages — take a look at Chapter 10.)

- **Date first.** Before getting married, you probably want to date your prospective mate for a while first — a few months or even a few years are ideal. Not only does doing so allow you to develop trust and find out how to communicate with each other, but it also allows you to see both the good and the bad sides of your partner. Business partnerships work the same way: Get to know your prospective partner very well before you tie the knot. Consider doing shared marketing or a specific project together first.
- **Partner only with someone you trust.** Trust is the glue that holds a partnership together and allows you to achieve great things. Don't even consider — not for a single second! — partnering with someone you don't trust or respect. The road to business success is littered with broken partnerships that fell apart as soon as the trust that kept the partners together vanished.
- **Don't partner until you can stand on your own.** Partner from a position of strength, not weakness. Otherwise, your business will become a codependency and, thus, dysfunctional. And a dysfunctional company will have problems serving its customers well and making money.

- **Enlist partners who add to the business.** Ideally, your partner will complement you and bring positive personal value to the company. Short on cash? Then find a partner who will provide the cash you need. Need help marketing? Then find a partner who's a strong salesperson. Don't like managing the business? Then find a partner who's a strong leader and administrator. Just as you hire employees who shore up your weaknesses, choose partners to cover the skills or connections you lack.
- **Share the equity (and the burden of risk).** Sharing equity means sharing ownership of the company with your partners. If you don't share ownership with your partners, they won't act like they're owners — they won't value the business the same way you do, and they won't be willing to make the same sacrifices as you to keep the business alive and healthy. They may even come to resent you because you hold all the cards. But if you agree to share ownership of your company, be sure to require your partner to share equally in the risks associated with the business, too.
- **Create a written partnership agreement.** Formalize your partnership in a written agreement that spells out — clearly and unambiguously — the ownership stake of each partner, rights to business proceeds, and his or her responsibilities to the business. Our advice is to spend the relatively small amount of money necessary to have an attorney draw up a proper partnership agreement for you and your prospective partner to sign. Many business partnerships eventually fail; when they do, a well-written partnership agreement can help protect the huge investment of time and money that you've made in your business.

Follow these tips, and your partnerships should be happy ones. Of course, there are no guarantees. If your partnership turns out not to be one made in heaven, you can always split up the partnership and try again, but you'll have a much easier (and more profitable) time if you do your homework and get it right the first time. Keep in mind, too, that as Paul and Sarah and Rick Benzel describe in their book *Teaming Up* (Tarcher), partnership is only one of many ways to collaborate with others; many of the other methods for collaboration carry less risk than partnership.

Cashing Out and Other Exit Strategies

Although most entrepreneurs with young businesses focus on starting and growing their businesses, eventually their thoughts turn to other goals — specifically, the goal of selling their businesses and cashing out their stake and retiring or moving on to something new. For some people, this phenomenon occurs at an early age (Peter still dreams of retiring before he hits 55; however, the reality of his currently advanced years, along with three kids rapidly approaching college age, may have its own say in the matter). On the other hand, some business owners plan to work literally until they take their last breaths.

Partnering with a spouse or significant other

Turning your life partnership with a spouse or significant other into a business partnership can be great for your home-based business. Or it can be living hell. Because you both live under the same roof, this new relationship can turn into a never-ending tunnel with no easy or apparent exit. Entrepreneur.com (`www.entrepreneur.com`) offers the following five steps for creating a home-based business with your spouse or significant other that's more heaven and less hell:

1. **Divide your roles and responsibilities.** Each of you has your own unique strengths and weaknesses. Take time to assess who is best at what. You, for example, may be great with numbers and organizing your business, while your spouse may be the salesperson of the year. Have clear divisions of responsibilities so each of you knows who's supposed to do what.

2. **Develop an effective way to air differences and resolve disputes.** Don't let differences of opinion or disputes with your significant other business partner fester, unaddressed and unresolved. Deal with them as they occur, and put them behind you as quickly as you can. Doing so not only makes for a better and more effective business, but it also helps ensure that your relationship is built to last.

3. **Put a child-care plan in place.** If you have kids, you need to find a way to do business while making sure you also meet their needs. Consider bringing in a part- or full-time sitter — students at local colleges are often a great source — or split your duties so that one partner takes care of the kids in the morning, and the other is in charge of the kids in the afternoon. If you have relatives in town who can help (and they want to help), use them.

4. **Make sure both of you have enough room to work.** Although you and your significant other may enjoy getting cozy every once in a while, working full-time jammed into the same small closet of a room can eventually drive even the most lovey-dovey couples temporarily insane. If you share an office or workspace with your business partner, make sure it offers plenty of elbow room for both of you — and for your computers, files, cabinets, desks, tables, chairs, and other office equipment.

5. **Agree on an exit strategy before you begin.** What happens if one or both of you decide you want out of the business? Or if you and your partner have irreconcilable differences and decide that splitting up your business partnership is the only way to save your life partnership? In the same way a prenuptial agreement can make a divorce easier for both parties, taking time to decide the terms and conditions of the dissolution of your business partnership in advance of the event is the smart thing to do. Doing so may also save your personal relationship.

If and when you decide to exit your business, you'll be faced with even more decisions — in particular, when and how to gracefully sever your ties to the business so that you don't damage its value in the process. You can find all kinds of strategies for exiting your business, from mild to extreme. Here are some of the most common ones:

- **Sell it.** Businesses are bought and sold all the time (take a look at sites like `www.businessesforsale.com` or your local newspaper classified advertisements for a plethora of examples). If you've built a strong customer base or have a valuable inventory, or if your operations are particularly profitable or otherwise attractive to a potential buyer, you may be able to make some significant money in the process of selling your business. And that's not a bad thing!
- **Merge it.** Merging your operation with another business can create a new business that's more powerful and profitable than the two businesses were separately. In a merger, you have the option of stepping aside in favor of having the owner of the other company run and operate the combined companies while you maintain an ownership stake, or you can accept some form of one-time or ongoing payment or royalty while acting as a part-time consultant or adviser to the business. Either option can make a lot of sense, depending on your personal preferences.
- **Pass it to a family member, friend, or employee.** If you have a son, daughter, close friend, or employee who's particularly interested in keeping the business going, you always have the option of passing it on to him or her. You can choose to pass it on for free, sell it, or set up some sort of compensation arrangement, such as an ongoing royalty or payment based on a percentage of sales.
- **Close it.** Of course, you can simply close the business, unplug your answering machine, and move on with your life. For many home-based business owners interested in exiting their businesses, this option is by far the simplest. If you decide on this option, don't just leave your customers hanging out to dry, wondering where their orders are — make sure you take care of them before you call it quits. See the "Shutting down your business" sidebar for ideas on how to make sure your loyal customers are taken care of.

Whatever you decide, be sure to carefully match it with your long-term goals. If you merge the business with another or pass it to a family member, friend, or employee, you may have the opportunity to keep your finger in the business's operations if you so desire. If you sell or close it, however, chances are slim (very, *very* slim, in the case of a closed business) that you'll be able to have anything further to do with it. Is that what you really want? Are you really ready to call it quits? Only you know the answers to these questions, and only you can make the ultimate decision.

Shutting down your business

Unfortunately, not every home-based business is destined to last forever, which means that, at some point, you may have to close yours — whether by choice or because of circumstances out of your control. According to a study released by Discover Small Business Watch in 2009, 36 percent of small business owners reported that they would close their companies if they could find a better paying job working for someone else. This figure is up from 30 percent in 2008. According to the study, the reasons for this increase are because of the difficulty of finding new business during the recession and the hassle of dealing with government regulations.

If you decide to close your business for whatever reason, here are a few tips to ensure that your customers aren't left out in the cold:

- Give your customers plenty of notice. A month isn't too much time.
- Refer your customers to companies like yours, including former competitors. (After all, you don't need to worry about them anymore, right?) The idea is to give your customers as many options and alternatives as possible.
- Offer to train your customers to do what you do. You may have a customer or two who'd like to start a business like yours or add your business to their own. You may even decide to become a consultant — training others to do what you've been doing for so long.
- Subcontract the work to another company or individual in your field.
- If you have a contract that's legally assignable, sell or transfer it to another company capable of satisfying your client's needs. Whether required by your contract or not, preparing your client for a change in who'll be providing his or her goods or services is always a good policy to follow.
- Sell your client list to another company or individual in your field, letting your customers know you're doing so and introducing them to the person or company who'll be filling their needs in your place.

Putting a value on your business

If you decide to sell your business, the first question your potential buyer is likely to ask is "How much do you want for it?" So, do you have any idea how much your business is worth? If you do, are you sure the price is right?

You can establish a price for a business using a number of different methods. If you're thinking about selling your home-based business, consider the following:

- **The firm's earning capacity:** How much money does your business rake in every month or year? Are your sales high enough to offset expenses and leave a reasonable profit behind? The higher the earning capacity of a business, the more it's worth to a potential buyer and the more he or she is willing to pay you for it.

- **The value of its assets:** If you have a lot of money tied up in physical assets, such as *inventory* (the products you keep on the shelf to sell to customers), *machinery* (medical transcription equipment or mechanic's tools, for example), or *intellectual property* (trademarks, patents, trade secrets, and so forth), the worth of your business will surely be influenced — or perhaps even determined — by the value of your assets. The higher the value of your assets — and the ease with which they can be converted to immediate use by a buyer or into liquid assets such as cash — the more money you can demand for your business.
- **The market value of similar firms:** The value of firms similar to yours inevitably has a significant influence on the value of your firm. You can get a rough idea of your firm's value by finding out what similar businesses are selling for. Try listings of businesses for sale in your local newspaper classified ads or check out `www.businessesforsale.com`.
- **The value of the company's stock:** If your business is organized as a corporation and you have issued stock, that stock has value. Because buying stock in a company is the same as buying the company itself, the value of that stock can often determine the value of the business.

Now what?

So you've sold your business or handed it over to your daughter, and you've done your best to keep your nose out of how she's running it. But for years, you've spent the better part of your waking hours working and, lately, running your own business. Now what?

Many people dream about retirement their whole working lives, but, after they get there, they find that they miss the action, the demands, and the responsibilities of a busy business environment. Of course, others adjust to their retirement just fine and spend their days traveling the world, fishing, or enjoying a good book. If you're ready to take the next step, but you're not exactly sure what that step is, be sure to read Paul and Sarah's eBook *The Practical Dreamer's Handbook: Finding the Time, Money, & Energy to Live the Life You Want to Live* (Elm Street Library).

REMEMBER

Whatever you decide, don't forget that you always have one option open to you: starting another business. As this book describes, starting your own home-based business can be amazingly simple, and the rewards can be many.

Part V
The Part of Tens

The 5th Wave By Rich Tennant

"I have read your resume, Ms. Cothman. Now please, come ... sit ... speak..."

In this part . . .

These short chapters are packed with a plethora of quick and powerful ideas to help make your home-based business the kind of success you've always dreamed of. We cover how to succeed in your home-based business and what to do when times are tough. We also discuss some enduring home-business opportunities. Read them when you have an extra minute or two.

Chapter 16

Ten Tips for How to Succeed in Your Home-Based Business

In This Chapter

- Doing what you love
- Being businesslike in your dealings
- Charging what you're worth
- Building a solid customer base
- Asking for referrals

Although no one can guarantee that your home-based business will be a success, if you work hard, price your products and services right, and keep your customers satisfied, you stand a good chance of building a successful company. The results you get out of your business are a direct result of the work you put into it. As you probably already know, that relationship between work and results is one of the real joys of having a home-based business. If you do a good job, you will be rewarded. Plus, you get the satisfaction of having happy clients and customers tell you how much they enjoy doing business with you — and buying more of your products and services.

The most successful home-based business owners — those who get the results they hoped for — share a variety of traits. We discuss ten of these traits in this chapter.

Do What You Love

All jobholders dream about the jobs they'd love to do if only they had the opportunity. Unfortunately, many people work their current jobs mostly because they have to pay the bills, not because they've always dreamed of doing their particular work. But what if you could do what you really loved to do? Wouldn't that be great? Well, it is, and it's exactly the opportunity you get by starting your own business. But to do what you love, you first have to know what kind of work you really want to do. This discovery requires deep introspection and an understanding of which kinds of work get your creative juices flowing and which kinds dry them up.

Doing what you love also sometimes requires that you ignore what other people want you to do for a living. You may decide, for example, that you'd really like to start a photography studio in your home, but your spouse or best friend may think something more practical, such as buying a successful pet store in the local mall, makes more sense. Ultimately, you must decide what you really want to do for a living — even if it means you can't work at home.

REMEMBER

It's *your* dream — you're the one who gets to choose it (and live it!). No one else has the right to tell you what kind of work you should love — and do.

Treat Your Business like a Business

If you want your business to be a *real* business — an organization that generates the kind of money that will allow you to become financially independent — you have to treat it like one, not like a hobby or a momentary fling. Here are some ideas to help you treat your business as what it is — a business:

- Set aside an entire room in your home — not just a closet or a shelf — exclusively for your business (see Chapter 14).
- Make a serious investment in business equipment and supplies: a decent computer, a dedicated phone line, and whatever else is required to effectively and efficiently run your operation.
- Create a marketing plan and follow through with it (see Chapter 4).
- Publicize your company's products and services to a wide audience of potential customers and clients.
- Build a strong customer base and make plans for future growth (see Chapter 15).

REMEMBER

Being serious about your business doesn't mean that you can't have fun, though, or that you can't make up your own rules along the way. Indeed, being your own boss means that *you* get to decide how you're going to run your business. If you want to work only on weekday afternoons, for example — setting aside mornings for exercise or spending time with your kids — you can do so and still have a serious business.

Become an Expert

People naturally respect those who know more than they do. By specializing in a particular area of expertise — whether it's where to dig a new water well, how to scrapbook, or what to do in a financial crisis — you assume the role of a presumed expert, even if you've just started your business. It makes good business sense for your clients to hire an expert instead of someone less experienced. By avoiding the mistakes and dead ends that someone with less experience may make, you can help your clients spend less money by hiring you — even if your hourly rates are higher.

The interesting thing about becoming an expert is that the passage of time makes you increasingly more experienced in your field. As time goes on, potential clients and customers will seek you out just to get the benefit of the expertise you've developed through experience and education.

Don't Be Shy

Companies don't spend millions of dollars advertising their products in the media for no reason; they do so because media advertising is a particularly effective way to get the attention (and, ideally, the business) of potential customers. Unfortunately, far too many people believe that a good idea is all a successful business needs. In the real world, however, it takes far more than that; the world is chock-full of good ideas that have gone nowhere fast. Even the best ideas have to be packaged, presented, and sold, and the key is to identify and use marketing methods best suited to both your personality and your business.

Although you may never have had to sell yourself or your products before, you can't avoid doing so when you own your own business. After you generate momentum and build a strong customer base, you can rely more on referrals from your happy clients to do the marketing for you. (Peter, for example, rarely seeks new business — most of his new clients come to him via referrals from satisfied customers.) But when you're getting your business off the ground, consider and attempt every possible method for selling your products and services.

For a complete discussion of the hows and whys of marketing your products and services, check out Chapter 4.

Charge What You're Worth

No matter how hard you work, if you charge your customers less than you're worth, you won't be able to stay in business for long. Why would you charge less than you're worth? Well, some people do so because they don't realize exactly how much they *are* worth. Others charge less than they're worth because they're embarrassed or afraid to ask for an amount that reflects their true worth. Whatever the reason, if you don't get paid what you're worth, you may very well drive yourself out of business.

TIP

If you don't know what you're worth, find out what other companies charge for similar products or services by researching catalogs, price lists, stores, and e-commerce and auction Web sites. If you can't find written prices or listings on the Web, call or e-mail the companies for information. From there, develop a pricing or fee structure that will help you attain your personal goals. (Check out Chapter 7 for more info on setting the right prices.)

TIP

After you figure out what you should charge, use the following tips to get the price you want:

- **Become a master at selling the value that your products and services offer to your customers and clients.** They won't know why your products and services are better than others if you don't tell them, so tell them often and in a variety of ways.
- **Be creative in how you're paid.** Many successful home-based business owners take cash out of the equation by bartering their products or services with others. For example, Valerie Whitlock — owner of Fancy Pants Jewelry — has received microdermabrasion treatments, a used Apple G4 iBook computer, and Marc Jacobs jeans in exchange for her hand-crafted jewelry.
- **Get past any hang-ups you have about charging your customers and clients what you're worth.** Practice asking your price in front of a mirror or with someone you trust to give you constructive criticism just as you would practice a request for a raise or a speech. Believe us, after you go through the process a few times with prospective clients — and discover that they still want to hire you — you'll find it easier to demand a price that reflects what you're really worth.

Avoid Unnecessary Expenses

Shopping for the latest and greatest business gadgets and equipment is fun — a *lot* of fun. And treating clients to expensive lunches and dinners and driving that snazzy new company car are also fun. The bad news about all this fun is that it can be expensive (and some of it may not be tax-deductible) and detrimental to your company's financial health and welfare.

Spend your company's hard-earned money only when you have to. A good example of this is your personal computer. Every other week, computer technology makes another great leap forward, which may constantly tempt you to upgrade to the latest and greatest and fastest computer with all the latest bells and whistles. Unless your older, slower, and less flashy computer — and the software within it — is actually getting in the way of your ability to do business efficently, stick with it for as long as you possibly can. Think about adding a bigger hard drive, more RAM, or other upgrades that improve performance at a cost far less than buying a new computer. Eventually, you'll need to replace that old slug of a computer, but the longer you can defer the expense, the better for your company's bottom line.

Do your best to hold the line on all the other expenses that simply drain your financial reserves while bringing in little or no additional revenue. If you're going to eat out, for example, go to less expensive places. Save the expensive meals for your highest-paying customers. Or consider inviting your best customers over as dinner guests in your home.

Manage Your Cash Flow

Cash, or the lack of it, is one of the key indicators of a company's success over the long run. If you have cash, you can buy and stock new products for your customers, develop innovative new services for your clients, pay for your day-to-day operations, and expand your business. If you don't have cash, your business will certainly suffer, and so will your customers and clients. You may even jeopardize your own personal or family financial situation.

Simply watching your cash flow — the money going in and out of your business — isn't enough; you also have to actively *manage* it. Managing your cash flow means looking to the future, planning and scheduling your projected cash inflows and outflows, billing quickly, staying on top of money owed you, and paying attention to the money that goes in and out of your business. Peter's most important business tool after his computer is the rolling cash-flow projection he uses to project how much cash he will receive from customers each month for a year into the future. See Chapter 6 for more ideas.

Keep Your Day Job

The best way to work into your own successful home-based business is to start out while retaining your full-time conventional job. Not only does maintaining your day job keep your income safe and sound while your home business's revenues ramp up — a process that can take months or even years — but it also allows you to keep your healthcare and other benefits in place (not to mention it allows your employer to continue making contributions to the cost of these benefits, if applicable in your case). A rule of thumb for when to transition to your business full time is when your business income will sustain your minimal living expenses and you feel confident that by putting in more time, you'll increase your business's earnings. (Check out Chapter 3 for more details.)

When Peter embarked on his new writing career a number of years ago, he did so within the safety of his full-time job. While he established his business on his own time — during lunch hours and after work — Peter drew a regular salary, health benefits, and a retirement plan from his day job. Finally, when the time was right, Peter left his day job and moved into his home-based writing career full time.

By approaching the transition to self-employment this way, you can discover whether you've picked the right business — and whether you're right for the business — without risking unemployment if it doesn't work out.

Build a Solid Customer Base

One of the most important ways to establish a successful business is to build a solid base of customers who stick with you through thick and thin. This solid customer base becomes the foundation on which you grow your business.

Of course, building a solid customer base is much easier said than done. At the heart of the process is creating an organization that values its current customers and goes out of its way to ensure their satisfaction and happiness. Customers are smart — they can tell whether they're high or low on a company's priority list. If they sense that you don't care much about whether or not they do business with you, they'll likely jump ship as soon as another company that really does care about them comes along.

Always remember the feeling you get when you land your first customer and receive your first payment for your products; then treat all your customers as though they were your first. Value them every day, and, in turn, they'll value you.

Ask for Referrals

The word-of-mouth referral is probably the least expensive and the most effective way of getting new business — for any business — which makes referrals the most important way for home-based businesses to market themselves. Here are some of the best ways to earn great referrals from customers:

- **Do great work.** When you do great work, your clients are happy to give you great referrals. When you do less-than-great work, you'll be lucky to get a kick in the pants, much less a referral.
- **Do your work on time and within budget.** Do you want to know the quickest way to your customer's heart? Do your work on time and within budget. If you consistently deliver on your promises, you'll soon have more business than you ever thought possible. And you'll earn your clients' referrals at the same time.
- **Keep your clients well informed.** When clients spend their money on you, they want to be kept apprised of your progress, not only to stay in touch with the project, but also to keep a watchful eye out for problems before they get out of hand. Do your clients a favor, and keep them informed about your project's progress. Whether the news is good or bad, your clients and customers will appreciate your forthrightness and candor.
- **Be dependable.** If anything, you should always keep your word — even when it hurts. If you promise to do something, do everything in your power to keep your promise, no matter what it takes to follow through on it. Who would impress you more (and earn your referral) — a business owner who consistently delivers a week or even a month later than promised, or an owner who delivers on time, every time?
- **Be flexible.** Customers and clients appreciate vendors who are flexible and willing to meet their needs, no matter what those needs may be. Not only do they appreciate that flexibility, but they also pay more for it. Think about what you can do in your business to better meet your customers' needs, and then do it.
- **Thank your clients for their referrals.** Everyone likes to be appreciated for what they do. Your customers are no different. Be sure to thank them for their referrals with a hand-signed card or small gift.

Many small businesses get the vast majority of their new business through referrals. They really are worth their weight in gold! Take a look at Chapter 4 for more on referrals.

Chapter 17

Ten Enduring Home Business Opportunities

In This Chapter

- Providing recycling and cleaning services
- Looking at modern-day repair work
- Helping out with human services

Some home-business opportunities are here today, gone tomorrow. In this chapter, we present ten home business opportunities that are built to last. Get started with one of these, and you're likely to have a business you can grow old with.

Architectural Salvage

Whether you're motivated by the fact that you can make money from reusing what would otherwise be waste, saving something from the past, or keeping landfills from filling up, architectural salvage may be just the right business for you. Architectural salvage as a business field will continue to grow in the future as the economies of China, India, and other nations continue to expand rapidly, gobbling up building supplies and materials in the process. These economies have to get their materials from some place — why not get them from you?

When you tear down a 2,000-square-foot home, for example, you can reuse (and thus sell) 125,000 pounds of mined metals and other minerals in the form of bathroom fixtures, bricks, ceramic tiles, mantles, piping, and so on. The same is true for remodeled homes and buildings, which leaves you with ample material for salvage (and thus ample material to sell).

Obtaining these materials requires deconstructing a home or building, which is a slower process than just tearing it down, which is where you as an entrepreneur come in. You do the deconstruction in exchange for what is salvaged. Before you can sell what you salvage, you may need to refurbish it. Then you can sell the salvage to one of the many architectural salvage stores opening in cities across the country, on `www.craigslist.com`, which has the advantage of charging no listing fees, or through architectural galleries like `www.architecturals.net`.

TIP

You can get accredited in deconstruction, thus making yourself more credible and marketable, by taking a one-day course offered by the Building Materials Reuse Association (check out `www.bmra.org` for more info).

Cleaning Services

Although many people deem having a maid or cleaning service a luxury — and something that may be cut when budgets are tight — this business won't go away until the supply of dust and mold runs out. In fact, new opportunities arise in a down economy as building and store owners decide to contract out cleaning services instead of paying salaries and benefits for full-time employees.

Cleaning services take many forms, ranging from home and office cleaning services that do routine cleaning to more specialized services that require either specific equipment, such as pressure cleaning and rug cleaning, or the willingness to do particularly challenging or unpleasant work, such as window washing, crime scene and disaster clean-up, and rubbish removal.

A growing number of people who associate allergies and respiratory illnesses with air pollutants are seeking green cleaning services for their homes and offices. Green cleaning services use special cleaning methods, nontoxic products, and equipment and supplies like HEPA-filter vacuum cleaners and microfiber cloths that clean surfaces without chemical cleaners.

Another significant market for cleaning services is elderly people living independently who no longer have the physical ability to do their own cleaning. Sometimes their children pay someone else — who could be you — to keep their parents' homes clean.

TIP

To find out more about the basics of cleaning, check out Home Depot, Lowes, and janitorial supply stores for free training classes.

Collections Work

Bill collectors keep busy because companies, service providers, and government agencies have to collect money owed to them. Today the need is particularly high among doctors, hospitals, and other healthcare providers because 62 percent of bankruptcies are caused by health expenses. This reality and the fact that people fall behind in all kinds of bills translate into a home business for anyone who can be part parent, part counselor, part teacher, and part coach in helping debtors organize their finances to repay what they owe. Most people want to pay their bills but are under economic distress and need coaxing and coaching to do so.

Home-based bill collectors with low overhead expenses have an advantage over high-pressure, results-driven staffs of large collection companies because they can take the time to be more successful in working with debtors. Having second-language skills can also give you an edge over your competition. Be aware that some states require licenses of collection agencies and some require posting a bond.

TIP

The Debt Collectors Collection Training System (available at `www.MichelleDunn.com`) and sites such as `www.startingacollectionagency.com` can help you get your own collections business underway. These resources can provide key information you need to know, such as the Fair Credit Reporting Act, the Fair Debt Collection Practices Act, and postal regulations.

Community Management

Community management isn't a new concept, but it is growing in new ways in today's society, which is where you and your home-based business come in. The most established form of community management is managing one of 300,000 homeowner association–governed communities, many of which are large enough to hire their own manager or to contract with a management company (which could be you) that provides virtual management, in which case you don't have to live in the community you manage.

The number of management opportunities continues to grow as four out of five new homes are built in association-governed communities. Community associations that enable seniors to live independently in their own homes also have a need for professional community management. The model for this type of association is Beacon Hill Village in Boston (`www.beaconhillvillage.org`). Cooperative housing developments that are too large for their resident owners to manage on their own are another example of a community in need of the increasingly popular community management services that you can offer from the comfort of your own home.

Community associations are a combination of a de facto government, a business organization, and a social entity composed of many (sometimes conflicting) human needs. Thus, to be a successful community manager, you need to be a leader with a wide range of disparate skills. The largest association of community managers is the Community Associations Institute (`www.caionline.org`), which provides training and certification.

Elder Services and Home Care

While people may need elder services at an earlier age today (thanks to the geographic scattering of families and the physical damage caused by stress and unhealthy lifestyles), the fastest growing segment of the population is people older than 85. From just more than 4 million in 2000, the number of people older than 85 will quintuple to 21 million by midcentury. Improvements in medical care enable people to live longer — and to live independently longer, although *independent* living is somewhat of a misnomer because the elderly who live in their own homes often require support services of one kind or another. This need for support means potential customers for many home-based home-care businesses.

Geriatric care managers who assess the needs of seniors are very much in demand; however, you can't receive certification to be a geriatric care manager unless you have a recognized credential in gerontology, nursing, social work, or psychology. Luckily, you can find some home-based opportunities for people without a background in the health field.

Nonmedical caregivers help elderly clients manage their daily activities. Responsibilities range from cleaning homes and doing laundry to paying bills to helping with personal grooming to driving seniors to appointments. Tricia Lee, who operates TimeSavers of Pensacola, Inc., a home-based business that provides transportation services to seniors and others so they can go to the doctor, the grocery store, and other places, said, "This is satisfying work. I look forward to seeing my customers. We love each other. We hug when we meet and when we part."

Seniors also may need to move, and, when they do, they need help. Companies like Gentle Transitions (`www.gentletransitions.com`) and Smooth Mooove Senior Relocation Services (`www.wemoveseniors.com`) provide moving services tailored to the special needs of seniors, and you can, too.

When seniors can't afford to pay you, often their adult children — who may live far away or who just can't provide these services themselves — are willing to pick up the tab.

TIP: The AARP Guide to Internet Resources Related to Aging (`www.aarp.org/internetresources`) provides quite a few links related to senior services that can help you start researching this business field.

Investigative and Security Services

The challenges of protecting yourself and your assets from thieves, terrorists, crooks, and computer crime is spurring a growing security industry. The result is a flood of new investigative specializations, such as data recovery and electronic theft investigation — each of which requires special training. Other businesses are adapting their existing experience and know-how to create new niches in the security field. Specialization is particularly important in this field because it enables the home-based businessperson to more easily identify, reach, and gain the respect of clients.

Surveillance work and background checking are staples of the investigation field. Here are some additional specialties:

- **Security consulting:** Some security consultants sell products from which they earn a commission; others provide expertise and are paid by the hour or on a per-project basis. They write security plans and design and install systems. Areas of specialization include customer theft, product piracy, electronic theft, electronic security systems, employee theft, protection of intangibles like client lists and proprietary technology, and real estate or other tangible property protection.
- **Site consulting:** Security is an issue for virtually every building and office, from high-tech industrial complexes to distribution centers, retail stores, self-storage facilities, housing developments, hotels, resorts, casinos, parking lots, and hospitals. Site consultants help businesses and institutions address security concerns about their facilities. They evaluate the physical design of buildings and spaces. They determine what security risks a site poses and recommend countermeasures, from hiring guards to installing electronic security systems with cameras and electric lights, or a combination of such methods and policies.
- **Systems design:** Security system designers prevent security problems by developing specifications and providing architectural or engineering support during the design phase of a security consulting project. Systems designers may also develop new electronic security tools to be used at specific locations.
- **Forensic consulting:** Forensic security consultants step in after security problems have already occurred. They serve as expert witnesses in trials where security breaches are at issue, such as those involving fires, thefts, break-ins, and so on. Forensic consultants may focus on any of the security specialties.

TIP

You can find dozens of links (sorted by location) related to security specialties on the *PI Magazine* Web site at `www.pimagazine.com/links`.

Microfarming

Microfarming, or farming on small acreages, feeds a growing public appetite for locally grown food, which makes it a great business to get into. Whether or not it's grown to meet organic standards for certification, microfarmed food most often comes to harvest with no or few chemical pesticides or fertilizers and no or little irradiation. Small growers produce many of the locally grown produce, fresh herbs, spa products, and edible flowers you find at farmer's markets, roadside stands, and gourmet restaurants. People who microfarm say it provides a deep sense of physical well-being and a spiritual connection to the land, whether they do so to feed people in nearby households or to produce an unusual crop for export.

You can locate a microfarm in a basement, a backyard, or on a few acres. And plants aren't the only crops being produced on small farms; people are microfarming fish and livestock, too. New technologies are increasingly available to make microfarming in a city easier. For example, the Topsy Turvy Upside Down Tomato Planter (`www.topsygardening.com`) eliminates the problem of weeding and ground insects. As you may expect, people living in warmer climates have the advantage of being able to grow several crops a year.

Among the many available microfarming resources are the ATTRA National Sustainable Agriculture Information Service Web site (`www.attra.org`) and New Farm, an online newsletter and Web site from the Rodale Institute (`www.rodaleinstitute.org/new_farm`).

Repair and Restoration Services

Repair and restoration businesses do particularly well during economic downturns, but survey after survey shows that people plan to remain cost conscious even when the economy picks up. This attitude bodes well for repair and restoration businesses because fixing or restoring something often costs less than tossing out the old and buying something new, particularly when what's new isn't affordable.

Repair businesses mend things to sound or working condition; *restoration* businesses return damaged or worn things to their original, normal, or unimpaired conditions.

The kinds of repair businesses you can operate at home or out of your truck or van include fixing toys, bikes, lawnmowers, lamps, jewelry, watches, clocks, and anything else people would rather fix than replace, along with sharpening knives and scissors.

Restoration work can transform one person's junk into another person's valuable antique — turning a $50 craigslist purchase into a $1,000 collector's item. Restoration can take many forms: stripping, caning, staining, varnishing, repairing porcelain and enameled iron work, and more. You can restore smaller items from your garage, or you can restore other people's homes and offices on site.

TIP

Find out more information about the restoration business at the Association of Restorers' Web site (www.assoc-restorers.com).

Robot Repair

You can find robots in hospitals, homes, schools, factories, and soon even on farms. People today are just beginning to see the many ways robots can become a part of their home and work lives. In fact, according to Glenn Dantes, partner in Industrial Control Repair, Inc. (www.industrialcontrolrepair.com), which has created several niches in the expanding robotics field, "Anywhere a person is doing a physical task, a robot can do that task."

One day soon service robots like "Nursebot" and "Carebot" may "live" in the homes of elderly people, helping them to live independently. Prototypes for robotics-assisted exoskeletons that will give people who are disabled, elderly, or injured the ability to walk, run, and climb stairs, are already being created. Such dependency on robotic assistance means that robot repairs will have to be immediate whenever a robot breaks down. Robots also require ongoing maintenance, and their growing pervasiveness opens opportunities for home businesses — self-employed technicians and specialists — to participate in this field.

To find out more about industrial robots, check out the Robotics Industry Association's Web site at www.roboticsonline.com; for consumer robots, check out Robotics Daily at www.roboticsdaily.com.

Tutoring and Adult Education

Since the last edition of this book, tutoring has grown from being exclusively a local face-to-face business to also being a popular online business. As a tutor, you can both develop a local clientele and offer what you know at sites like www.teachstreet.com, www.eprep.com, and half a dozen others.

Because learning has become a lifelong activity for many people, both by choice and by necessity, tutoring possibilities extend far beyond just academic subjects to life skills, such as finance and accounting, boat building, and search engine optimization. Here are a few examples of both academic and adult education tutoring:

- **Academic tutoring:** Most public education doesn't prepare students for the demands of entering college or beginning a career in the 21st century. As a result, all age levels need tutors. Beyond the success parents seek for their children, the No Child Left Behind program creates an extensive demand for tutoring. To get into college, students need tutoring to pass tests like the SAT and ACT, along with the PSAT if they seek National Merit scholarships. After enrolling in college, 28 percent of freshmen are enrolled in remedial math or English, and many of these students turn to tutors for help. To get into graduate schools, college seniors need tutoring to prepare for tests such as the GRE and LSAT. Check out the National Tutoring Association's Web site (`www.ntatutor.org`) for more info on academic tutoring.
- **Adult education:** With the rapid changes in the economy brought about by global competition and advances in technology, many adults continually need new skills. Others seek to develop skills or hobbies they didn't get a chance to learn when they were younger, whether it's voice, piano, golf, or guitar. Thus, adult education is becoming more and more prominent in today's society. Check out the American Society for Training and Development's Web site at `www.astd.org`.

Chapter 18

Ten Things to Do When Times Are Tough

In This Chapter

- Maintaining good relations with customers and getting them to pay their bills
- Finding ways to cut expenses
- Offering special promotions

Make no mistake about it: Starting and operating a home-based business — and making a profit — isn't easy. In fact, it's a real job. Although failure rates for home-based businesses aren't nearly as high as many people have been led to believe (see Chapter 3 for details), more than a few give up every year. Why? Because even the best of plans sometimes go awry, if only for a short time. Because of your business's inherent smallness, you may not have enough clients to manage the financial roller coaster that can result when a customer goes bankrupt, puts you on a slow-pay plan, or switches vendors.

Good planning can help you see far enough out on the horizon to anticipate the most serious financial shortfalls — and then take steps to avoid them — but it's impossible to anticipate each and every bump in the road and miss them when they arrive. Use the ten tips in this chapter to help you weather the unpredictable storms and emerge stronger than ever.

Save for a Rainy Day

Even if you find yourself making a lot of money for some period of time — for weeks, or even months — every business owner knows that there are no guarantees, and tough times can be right around the corner. One of the best things you can do is put aside money when times are good. Although it's tempting (and fun!) to run out and purchase the latest computer, the most recent software update, or a new furniture setup when the money's rolling in, first be sure that you set aside cash in your business savings account or money-market fund to help you through a rough patch of business.

Here's a goal that will help you weather a storm when it arrives: Build a cash reserve sufficient to run your business for a minimum of three months, preferably six to twelve months. After you have your cash reserve established and funded, you can go out and buy all that fun stuff you've had your eyes on.

Manage Your Cash Flow

Cash flow — more specifically, maintaining a *positive* cash flow — is by far the number-one financial issue facing every small business owner. And if you rely 100 percent on the proceeds of your home-based business to support you and your family or significant other and to pay for healthcare and other essential benefits, without the kind of steady income that a regular job brings, a shortfall in cash can quickly bring financial disaster.

TIP

The solution is to manage your cash flow (see Chapter 6), which means making a habit of doing the following:

- **Keep an eye on your net cash flow.** List all the cash you expect to receive (cash inflows) during a specific period of time, and compare that amount with the cash you expect to pay out (cash outflows) during the same period of time. Study this information religiously, at least once a week. You can put together a simple handwritten or computerized spreadsheet, or many popular business accounting programs, such as QuickBooks, have built-in functions for monitoring cash flow. Use them!
- **Be proactive in bringing cash into your business as quickly as possible.** Don't sit around waiting for customers to pay you when they get around to it; get your money as soon as you can. Try to get paid when you deliver your products or services instead of invoicing your customers after the fact. You can do so by requiring customers to pay by credit card or by negotiating advance payments with them. Or simply require payment by cash or check upon delivery. If you sell over the Internet or through an online-store host (such as Yahoo! Store), most customers already expect to pay by credit card or a payment service such as PayPal.
- **Pay your bills only when they're due, but do so in time to avoid interest and penalties.** There's no advantage for you to pay your bills before they're due. In fact, after you pay a bill, you lose the advantage of having the cash in your own bank account. If payment on a vendor invoice isn't due for 30 days from today, don't pay it tomorrow. Pay it when it's due. If you make your payment online, pay your bill a day or two before it's due to ensure your payment is credited electronically by the due date. If you mail in your payment, put the envelope in the mailbox a week before the due date. The idea is to be paid by your clients before you have to turn around and make payments to your vendors. By paying as late as you possibly can — while still paying on time — you can optimize your cash flow.

Keep in Touch with Your Customers

Business is all about relationships: More than just a few businesses have found incredible success because of the close relationships their owners have established with their clients and customers. After all, given the option, wouldn't you rather work with someone you like than someone you don't like?

When times get tough, your first priority should be to ensure that your current customer relationships are *solid.* Drop in for a visit, schedule a lunch, send an e-mail message, send some flowers, do whatever you can to keep your relationship on the front burner. And while you're busy keeping your relationship active, let your customers know that you're actively seeking more work. This gentle reminder that you're out there often leads customers to send more work your way — exactly what you need when times are tough!

Push Your Clients to Pay Their Bills

On the long list of things that home-based businesspeople enjoy least about their jobs is having to call clients to encourage them to pay their bills. But no matter how great your customers are, there are going to be times when you have to do just that.

So how do you know when payments due to your business are running behind? You can find out by monitoring *receivables* — the money owed to your company by your clients and customers. QuickBooks and other business accounting programs have built-in receivables *aging reports* that make the task easy by showing you who owes you money, how much they owe, when it's due to be paid, and how late the payment is if you haven't yet received it. And when you discover that one of your client's payments is overdue, act immediately — especially when the amount owed is substantial.

TIP

Here are some tried-and-true ways for collecting your money:

- **Call or visit your customer, and ask for payment.** The direct approach is often the best when it comes to getting customers to pay overdue invoices. Don't simply rubber-stamp a copy of the invoice with a note that says "We value your business — we hope you'll pay soon" or "Second notice — we would really like to be paid now." Chances are these halfhearted efforts will be ignored. It's much harder to ignore you if you make a personal appeal for payment.
- **Offer to help.** More times than most companies like to admit, a payment gets held up because the accounting department loses an invoice, doesn't have proof of delivery, or can't find the purchase order that

authorized the item in the first place. Find out what's holding up payment, and offer to assist in getting what the customer needs.

- **As a last resort — and only if you aren't concerned about getting any future business from your client — turn the matter over to a collections agency.** If your client is taking no action to pay you and is ignoring your phone calls, take action quickly. Sometimes all the client needs is a gentle nudge by a good agency to free up your payment right away. When Paul and Sarah received a bad check for a speaking engagement years ago, they made numerous calls to try to get paid — even contacting a U.S. senator for help — to no avail. Today they still regret not turning the client over to a collections agency to begin with.

Whatever you do, when a payment is late, get on it immediately — don't wait for days or weeks (or months!), hoping it'll come in. Keeping the money coming in on time should be one of your key concerns, and this task needs your immediate attention. Check out Chapter 6 for more details.

Minimize Expenses

When times are tough, you essentially have two ways to hunker down: increase the amount of money that comes into your business or decrease the amount of money that goes out (or both). Minimizing expenses is one of the quickest ways to help weather the storm, and you need to act immediately when you go into survival mode.

Before you buy anything, ask yourself whether you can survive without it for a while. Can the expense be deferred for a few days, a few weeks, or even a few months? Can you borrow or rent equipment instead of purchasing it? Can you barter your services or products in exchange for the products and services of other businesses?

Be careful, however, about exactly what expenses you cut. Do *not* cut expenses that will bring significantly more money into your business; instead, you may actually need to increase them.

Offer a Special Promotion

By far the best way to turn things around when times are tough financially is to bring in more business. Cutting expenses certainly helps, but it isn't the best long-term solution. The best long-term solution is selling more of your products and services.

To quickly generate more business, offer your customers a special offer on your products or services — perhaps 10 percent off all orders during July or a two-for-the-price-of-one offer. The exact form of your promotion varies, depending on the nature of your business, but you should be clear to your customers that they need to act quickly to take advantage of the special offer.

Alternatively, offer your clients and customers a premium — a value-added product or service — for placing an order during a specific period of time. For example, every customer who places an order of at least $100 during February receives a gift certificate for $10 worth of merchandise or a free video. You can also offer a special price to customers who are willing to commit to a contract. Be creative!

Subcontract for Others

Many home-based businesses — especially those with only one employee (you!) — are subject to extreme swings in business. One month, the business may be overwhelmed with orders; the next month, the phone may never ring.

To help offset these extreme business swings, you should develop a network of business contacts — perhaps other home-based businesses — to subcontract your work *to* in times of feast and to subcontract work *from* in times of famine. Sure, it may sound a bit strange to turn work over to a competitor, but it actually makes good business sense. The key is for you to remain the primary contact with the client and to ensure that the work from the contractor is of the same high quality that you would insist on if you did it yourself.

Volunteer

Every business has times when business is down. Down times are perfect for developing new contacts who may eventually turn into customers or who may refer you to future customers. If you still have time left after servicing your current customers, you may consider doing volunteer work in your community as a way to meet new people.

Not only can volunteering be a terrific way to put your skills to work for your community, but it's also a good way to increase your network of potential clients. And as that network expands, so will your future business. Believe us, you never know whom you'll meet when you volunteer in your community.

That woman next to you doing volunteer work at a children's hospital may be the president of a local bank or the purchasing manager of a large manufacturer.

Moonlight

When starting your business, it's a good idea to keep your day job — at least until your home-based business is generating enough income to allow you to pay all your bills. But even after your business is established, you may find that *moonlighting* — in the form of a part-time job — offers a number of benefits, including the following:

- Creating a steady source of income that you can rely on, independent of the ups and downs of your home-based business's income
- Providing a range of benefits that your own business doesn't, including health and dental insurance, life insurance, 401(k), stock options, and more
- Being a potential source of work for your home-based business

If you do decide to moonlight, make sure you're not taking too much time away from your own business — time that you could devote to building higher levels of sales or expanding your business.

Refuse to Give Up!

When times are tough, you may be tempted to throw in the towel and give up. But what's much more challenging — and ultimately much more rewarding — is to fight for your business and refuse to give up, *no matter what.* When interviewed and surveyed, successful entrepreneurs most consistently attribute their good fortune to *persistence.*

You can fail only if you allow yourself to do so. By not considering giving up an option, you force yourself to focus on doing the things that help pull you through your tough times — things like the other nine items in this chapter.

Index

• Numerics •

• A •

• B •

• C •

• F •

• G •

• H •

• I •

• J •

• K •

• L •

• M •

• O •

• P •

• U •

• V •

• W •

• Y •

• Z •

Business/Accounting & Bookkeeping

Bookkeeping For Dummies
978-0-7645-9848-7

eBay Business All-in-One For Dummies, 2nd Edition
978-0-470-38536-4

Job Interviews For Dummies, 3rd Edition
978-0-470-17748-8

Resumes For Dummies, 5th Edition
978-0-470-08037-5

Stock Investing For Dummies, 3rd Edition
978-0-470-40114-9

Successful Time Management For Dummies
978-0-470-29034-7

Computer Hardware

BlackBerry For Dummies, 3rd Edition
978-0-470-45762-7

Computers For Seniors For Dummies
978-0-470-24055-7

iPhone For Dummies, 2nd Edition
978-0-470-42342-4

Laptops For Dummies, 3rd Edition
978-0-470-27759-1

Macs For Dummies, 10th Edition
978-0-470-27817-8

Cooking & Entertaining

Cooking Basics For Dummies, 3rd Edition
978-0-7645-7206-7

Wine For Dummies, 4th Edition
978-0-470-04579-4

Diet & Nutrition

Dieting For Dummies, 2nd Edition
978-0-7645-4149-0

Nutrition For Dummies, 4th Edition
978-0-471-79868-2

Weight Training For Dummies, 3rd Edition
978-0-471-76845-6

Digital Photography

Digital Photography For Dummies, 6th Edition
978-0-470-25074-7

Photoshop Elements 7 For Dummies
978-0-470-39700-8

Gardening

Gardening Basics For Dummies
978-0-470-03749-2

Organic Gardening For Dummies, 2nd Edition
978-0-470-43067-5

Green/Sustainable

Green Building & Remodeling For Dummies
978-0-470-17559-0

Green Cleaning For Dummies
978-0-470-39106-8

Green IT For Dummies
978-0-470-38688-0

Health

Diabetes For Dummies, 3rd Edition
978-0-470-27086-8

Food Allergies For Dummies
978-0-470-09584-3

Living Gluten-Free For Dummies
978-0-471-77383-2

Hobbies/General

Chess For Dummies, 2nd Edition
978-0-7645-8404-6

Drawing For Dummies
978-0-7645-5476-6

Knitting For Dummies, 2nd Edition
978-0-470-28747-7

Organizing For Dummies
978-0-7645-5300-4

SuDoku For Dummies
978-0-470-01892-7

Home Improvement

Energy Efficient Homes For Dummies
978-0-470-37602-7

Home Theater For Dummies, 3rd Edition
978-0-470-41189-6

Living the Country Lifestyle All-in-One For Dummies
978-0-470-43061-3

Solar Power Your Home For Dummies
978-0-470-17569-9

Available wherever books are sold. For more information or to order direct: U.S. customers visit www.dummies.com or call 1-877-762-2974. U.K. customers visit www.wileyeurope.com or call (0) 1243 843291. Canadian customers visit www.wiley.ca or call 1-800-567-4797.

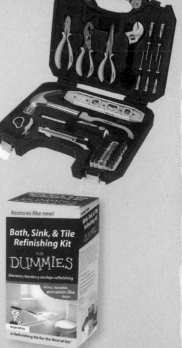

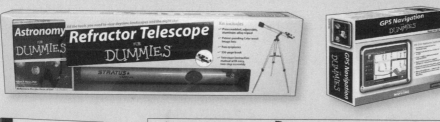

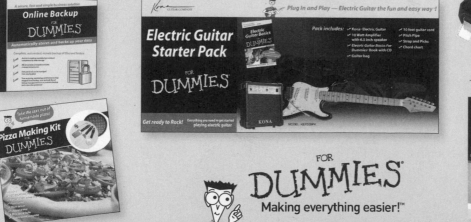